THE RHETORIC OF
ENGLISH INDIA

The Sodhees have in general an evil reputation for immorality, intoxication, and infanticide, the latter being justified by them on the ground that it is impossible to marry their female children into ordinary Sikh families. . . . The subject of the photograph resides at Lahore. He has lost an eye, which is covered by an ornament pendant from his turban; and it is a strange peculiarity of this person, that he dresses himself on all occasions in female apparel.

From *The people of India* (1868–75)

THE RHETORIC OF
ENGLISH INDIA

Sara Suleri

THE UNIVERSITY OF CHICAGO PRESS
Chicago and London

Sara Suleri was educated at Kinnaird College in Lahore (Pakistan), Punjab University, and Indiana University. She is associate professor of English at Yale University and the author of *Meatless Days* (University of Chicago Press, 1989).

The University of Chicago Press, Chicago 60637
The University of Chicago Press, Ltd., London
© 1992 by The University of Chicago
All rights reserved. Published 1992
Printed in the United States of America
00 99 98 97 96 95 94 93 92   5 4 3 2 1
ISBN (cloth): 0-226-77982-3

Published with the assistance of the Frederick W. Hilles Publications Fund of Yale University.

Library of Congress Cataloging-in-Publication Data

Suleri, Sara.
    The rhetoric of English India / Sara Suleri.
        p.   cm.
    Includes bibliographical references and index.
    1. Indic literature (English)—History and criticism.   2. Anglo-Indian literature—History and criticism.   3. English literature—Indic influences.   4. English language—India—Rhetoric.
5. Imperialism in literature.   6. British—India—History.
7. Colonies in literature.   8. India in literature.   I. Title.
PR9484.3.S85   1992
820.9'3254—dc20   91-13014
                                                                          CIP

Frontispiece courtesy Field Museum of Natural History,
Neg. # A111654, Chicago.

For my father

جس سے جگر لالہ میں ٹھنڈک ہو وہ شبنم!
دریاؤں کے دل جس سے دہل جائیں وہ طوفان!

Contents

Acknowledgments

THIS BOOK HAS RECEIVED MORE SUPPORT THAN I FEAR IT MAY DESERVE. MY FIRST thanks I must proffer to my students, whose energies have kept me buoyant through many a long hour of writing. While it would be impossible to list the friends and colleagues at Yale who have wittingly or unwittingly come to my intellectual rescue, I owe particular gratitude to timely comments on my writing by Michael Holquist, Patricia Meyer Spacks, Christopher Miller, David Bromwich, Akeel Bilgrami, and Peter Brooks. The editorial collective of the *Yale Journal of Criticism* deserves equal thanks for its enabling interest in the work of each of its editors. Furthermore, this work was both impelled and impeded by the constant encouragement of such friends as Dale Lasden, Nuzhat Ahmad, Jamie MacGuire, and Anita Sokolsky. My thanks to them.

I am grateful to Yale University for providing me with a Morse Fellowship to conduct research on this project, and to the Griswold grant that allowed me to travel to India and Pakistan. My research in both countries was greatly aided by Kum Kum Sangari, Sheherezade Alam, and Zarene Shafi.

Earlier segments of the chapters on V. S. Naipaul and Salman Rushdie have appeared in the *Yale Journal of Criticism* and the *Yale Review:* both journals must be thanked for their permission to reprint. The brief afterword to chapter 8 (p. 218, note 19) first appeared in *Transition* 51 (1991).

Finally, I am happy to acknowledge the imaginative patience of my editor, Alan Thomas, and his remarkable capacity to justify to me the expansive possibility of deadlines. His professional commitment to my writing has been nicely tempered by my siblings' somewhat impatient refrain, "Get it done." My one regret is that I did not "get it done" before Nuzhat Suleri could have taken pleasure in the text's reality. If on this earth, however, she would be the first to agree that my ultimate thanks should go to Fawzia Mustafa, whose astonishing friendship provides the periods for each sentence I may write.

1

The Rhetoric of English India

"THIS WAS HOW IT HAPPENED; AND THE TRUTH IS ALSO AN ALLEGORY OF Empire," claims Kipling's narrator, as he opens with grim brevity the quasi tale of 1886, "Naboth."[1] Like much of the early writing that Kipling published in the *Civil and Military Gazette* of Lahore, the story itself represents a dangerously simple moment of cultural collision: situated on the cusp between the languages of journalism and fiction, its three pages record an occasion of colonial complicity that bears testimony to the dynamic of powerlessness underlying the telling of colonial stories. The colonialist as narrator carelessly throws a coin to the "native beggar" in his garden, "as kings of the East have helped alien adventurers to the loss of their Kingdoms" (p. 71). Naboth to the narrator's Ahab, the beggar initiates an act of counter-colonialism, setting up a confectionery stall in the colonizer's garden that profits with a surreal speed, growing from a trading post to a set of shops, and finally, into a brothel. When the narrator puts a violent end to this invasion of his role as invader, he offers the following commentary on colonialism's ambivalent relation to the anxiety of empire: "Naboth is gone now, and his hut is ploughed into its native mud with sweetmeats instead of salt for a sign that the place is accursed. I have built a summer-house to overlook the end of the garden, and it is as a fort on my frontier from whence I guard my Empire. I know exactly how Ahab felt. He has been shamefully misrepresented in the Scriptures" (p. 75).

Kipling's tale functions as a cautionary preamble to my present work, which both seeks location within the discourse of colonial cultural studies and attempts to question some of the governing assumptions of that discursive field. While the representation of otherness has long been acknowledged as one of the must culturally vexing idioms to read, contemporary interpretations of alterity are increasingly victims of their own apprehension of such vexation. Even as the other is privileged in all its pluralities, in all its alternative histories, its concept-function remains too embedded in a theoretical duality of margin to center ultimately to allow the cultural decentering that such critical attention surely desires. As the allegory of "Naboth" suggests, the story of colonial encounter is in itself a radically decentering narrative that is impelled to realign with violence any static binarism between colonizer and colonized. It calls to be read as an enactment of a cultural unrecognizability as to what may constitute the marginal or the central: rather than reify the differences between Ahab and Naboth, Kipling illustrates both the pitiless congruence in their economy of desire and the ensuing terror that must serve as the narrative's interpretive model.

Such terror suggests the precarious vulnerability of cultural boundaries in the context of colonial exchange. In historical terms, colonialism precludes the concept of "exchange" by granting to the idea of power a greater literalism than it deserves. The telling of colonial and postcolonial stories, however, demands a more naked relation to the ambivalence represented by the greater mobility of disempowerment. To tell the history of another is to be pressed against the limits of one's own—thus culture learns that terror has a local habitation and a name. While Ahab may need to identify a Naboth as a discrete cultural entity, finally he knows that his encounter with the other of culture is only self-reflexive: in the articulation of Naboth's secular story, Ahab is caught up against a more overwhelming narrative that forces him to know he has been "shamefully misrepresented" by the sacred tales of his own culture. The allegorization of empire, in other words, can only take shape in an act of narration that is profoundly suspicious of the epistemological and ethical validity of allegory, suggesting that the term "culture"—more particularly, "other cultures"—is possessed of an intransigence that belies exemplification. Instead, the story of culture eschews the formal category of allegory to become a painstaking study of how the idioms of ignorance and terror construct a mutual narrative of complicities. While the "allegory of empire" will always have recourse to the supreme fiction of Conrad's Marlow, or the belief that what redeems it is "the idea alone," its heart of darkness must incessantly acknowledge the horror attendant on each act of cultural articulation that demonstrates how Ahab tells Naboth's story in order to know himself.

IF THE LIMITS OF CULTURAL KNOWLEDGE DICTATE THE CURIOUS GENEALOGY OF English India, then its chronology is intimately linked with a failure of ignorance to comprehend itself, or to articulate why the boundary of culture must generate such intransigent fears. The term "English India" demands an explication that would render it both literal and figurative at the same time: English India is not synonymous with the history of British rule in the subcontinent, even while it is suborned to the strictures of such a history. At the same time, English India is not solely a linguistic concept, a spillage from history into language, one that made difficult oppositions between the rhetorical and the actual. The idiom of English India expresses a disinterest in the continuity of tense, so that the distinction between colonial and postcolonial histories becomes less radical, less historically "new." In the context of colonialism, English India represents an ambivalence that addresses the turning point of such necessary imbrications as those between the languages of history and culture; of difference and fear. As a consequence, its trajectory is extensive enough to include both imperial and subaltern materials and in the process demonstrates their radical inseparability.

From the vast body of eighteenth-century historical documentation of British rule in India to the proliferation of Anglo-Indian fiction in the nineteenth and twentieth centuries, the narratives of English India are fraught with the idiom of dubiety, or a mode of cultural tale-telling that is neurotically conscious of its own self-censoring apparatus. While such narratives appear to claim a new preeminence of historical facticity over cultural allegory, they nonetheless illustrate that the functioning of language in a colonial universe is preternaturally dependent on the instability of its own facts. For colonial facts are vertiginous: they lack a recognizable cultural plot; they frequently fail to cohere around the master-myth that proclaims static lines of demarcation between imperial power and disempowered culture, between colonizer and colonized. Instead, they move with a ghostly mobility to suggest how highly unsettling an economy of complicity and guilt is in operation between each actor on the colonial stage. If such an economy is the impelling force of the stories of English India, it demands to be read against the grain of the rhetoric of binarism that informs, either explicitly or implicitly, contemporary critiques of alterity in colonial discourse.[2] The necessary intimacies that obtain between ruler and ruled create a counterculture not always explicable in terms of an allegory of otherness: the narrative of English India questions the validity of both categories to its secret economy, which is the dynamic of powerlessness at the heart of the imperial configuration.

If English India represents a discursive field that includes both colonial and postcolonial narratives, it further represents an alternative to the troubled chronology of nationalism in the Indian subcontinent. As long as the concept of nation is interpreted as the colonizer's gift to its erstwhile colony, the unimaginable community produced by colonial encounter can never be sufficiently read.[3] Again, the theoretical paradigm of margin against center is unhelpful in this context, for it serves to hierarchize the emergence of nation in "first" and "third" worlds. The colonial experience renders such numerology illegitimate, perhaps by literalizing how archaic as opposed to modern the will to nation may be. For colonialism ultimately supplies the answer to the crucial question raised by Benedict Anderson, when he ponders the paradoxical elective affinities that the idea of nation poses to contemporary thinking: "In an age when it is so common for progressive, cosmopolitan intellectuals . . . to insist on the near-pathological character of nationalism, its roots in fear and hatred of the Other, and its affinities with racism, it is useful to remind ourselves that nations inspire love, and often profoundly self-sacrificing love. The cultural products of nationalism . . . show this love very clearly in thousands of different forms and styles. On the other hand, how truly rare it is to find *analogous* nationalist products expressing fear and loathing."[4] In colonial encounter, a disembodied nation of cultural exchange merges "love" with "fear and loathing," thus creating a historical context where nationalism is synonymous with terror. As a logical correlative, the narrative of English India poses the following question to the concept of nation: what rhetoric is required to embody, and then to disembody, the communities of faithlessness that colonialism implies?

In other words, if colonial cultural studies is to avoid a binarism that could cause it to atrophy in its own apprehension of difference, it needs to locate an idiom for alterity that can circumnavigate the more monolithic interpretations of cultural empowerment that tend to dominate current discourse. To study the rhetoric of the British Raj in both its colonial and postcolonial manifestations is therefore to attempt to break down the incipient schizophrenia of a critical discourse that seeks to represent domination and subordination as though the two were mutually exclusive terms. Rather than examine a binary rigidity between those terms—which is an inherently Eurocentric strategy—this critical field would be better served if it sought to break down the fixity of the dividing lines between domination and subordination, and if it further questioned the psychic disempowerment signified by colonial encounter. For to interpret the configurations of colonialism in the idiom of such ineluctable divisions is to deny the impact of narrative on a productive disordering of binary dichotomies. To state the case at its most naked, the Indian subcontinent is not merely a geographic space upon which colonial rapacities have been enacted, but is furthermore that imaginative construction through which rapaciousness can worship its own misdeeds, thus making the subcontinent a tropological repository from which colonial and postcolonial imaginations have drawn—and continue to draw—their most basic figures for the anxiety of empire.

This anxiety is most readily identified in a continually dislocated idiom of migrancy. A study that opens with Edmund Burke and closes with Salman Rushdie, as does mine, obviously seeks to make an issue of cultural migrancy in order to situate the language of the colonizer within the precarious discourse of the immigrant. Certainly Burke's great terror of the adolescence of colonial rule has genealogical congruities with Rushdie's comical horror of postcolonial infantilism: English India suggests a family tree that is less chronological than it is perpetually at odds with the geographic location of cultures. The nomadic possibility of vast cultural as well as continental drifts provides an anxious edge to the method through which the colonial project presents itself as an act of cultural interpretation. As a consequence, culture as "order" translates into a principle of misreading that barely knows its own failure in the apprehension of the fluidity of culture. Instead, terror must dictate its discourse. While anthropological self-examination has learned to acknowledge its uneasy relation to the telling of others' stories, colonial cultural studies has yet to articulate a strategy that would allow for a productive reading of terror.[5] We thus confront a discursive field that must take up what are best described as dead-end terms—"terror" and "disempowerment," as well as Benedict Anderson's "self-sacrificing love"—in order to open their various possibilities as tropes of productive loss, which would render their dead-endedness culturally available to a theoretical "immigration."

To deploy migrancy as an interpretive figure is not at all to repress the crucial situatedness of cultures, or to suggest that colonial encounter can be reread only as an abstraction so slender as to be effete. Instead, it implies that the stories of colonialism—in which heterogeneous cultures are yoked by violence—offer nuances of trauma that cannot be neatly partitioned between colonizer and colonized. If both are identifiable as victims of traumatic change, then the idiom of trauma itself requires a reformulation that can provide a language for the slippage of trauma from apocalypse into narrative. The situation of postcolonialism, in other words, informs each inception of colonial encounter, in which the migrant moment of dislocation is far more formative, far more emplotting, than the subsequent acquisition of either postcolonial nation or colonial territory. In historiographic terms, colonial trauma can be read only in the context of an apocalyptic "end" or "beginning" of empire, even though a merely cursory knowledge of the trials of English India makes evident the obsession of that idiom's, and that era's, engagement with the transfer of power. This transference constitutes an immigrant idiom alternative to an apocalypse that cannot see beyond its own vision of localized terror. Such revision, however, is the task of colonial studies today, which must pause to make an obvious point: in the context of Anglo-India, the key term of transaction imposed by the language of colonialism is *transfer* rather than *power*. There are too many Naboths with which Ahab must deal; each moment of appropriation is, as Kipling suggests, a bitter reminder of how precarious is the imperial system of control.

The narratives of anxiety that emerge from such a system are consequently colonial testimonials in which aggression functions as a symptom of terror rather than of possession. Most typically, such terror translates into the ostensible unreadability of the colonized subcontinent: from the early travelogues in the seventeenth century to the proliferation of Anglo-Indian fiction in the nineteenth, the dominant Western metaphor for India suggests a spatial intransigence, or a geography so figural that—like the Marabar Caves—it can be read by Western eyes only after its transmutation into a threadbare and dangerous literalism. This unreadability is of course simply one instance of a discursive transfer of power, which fetishizes a colonial fear of its own cultural ignorance into the potential threats posed by an Indian alterity. Thus, writing in the twilight of the Raj, Edward Thompson offers a summation of a long-standing colonial tradition of discursive fear when he articulates a crucial figure for his reading of "Indian intransigence": "Many Englishmen in India must have had my experience. They have been puzzling over the problem, honestly anxious to find out where the point of exasperation—no, more than exasperation, of severance—came, and to see if anything could be done. Then they have thought that they have found it— yes, it was here, see! *They have pushed hard, only to find that they have gone through a curtain painted like a wall, to find the real wall, granite and immovable, behind* (emphasis added)."[6]

Thompson's figure supplies a useful encapsulation of the discursive equation between "Indian intransigence" and colonial terror, in that his claim depends curiously on the structure of tautology. His conflation of the wall and the veil suggests less a discovery of the unreadable granite at the heart of Indian intransigence than a replication of interpretive terms that implicates both the colonizer and its other in the construction of a novel narrative. In this new story, the unreadability of India functions as a rhetorical device to stave off those peculiarities of cultural reformulations that render both self and other into immigrant configurations. Where empire takes, it equally must lose, causing its migration to generate the culturally tautological idiom of English India. Unlike territory, stories cannot be so easily stolen: their guilt is too declarative of itself to be subsumed into easy categories of imperial binarism. To deploy Gayatri Spivak's casual aphorism in the service of such muddied narration, the genealogy of English India provides a resonant exemplification of her claim that imperialism requires rereading "not because Empire, like Capital, is abstract, but because Empire messes with identity."[7] The narratives of empire do not merely "mess" with the colonial subject, but are in themselves encoded with a dubiety that requires the fiction of intransigence to protect the myth of colonial authority.

This absence of authority is most readily discernible in the colonial will to cultural description, which demonstrates an anxious impulse to insist that colonized peoples can indeed be rendered interpretable within the language of the colonizer. On such descriptive terrain, the cultural landscape of the subcontinent inevitably represents all that the colonizing subject does not wish to see about itself: Thompson's "curtain" does not give way to the "granite" of unreadability but instead opens onto what Edmund Burke terms as colonialism's "great theatre of abuse," or a historical space upon which, with great visibility, the drama of colonial complicity is enacted. On such a stage, vested interests are too great to allow for any unambiguous ethical or political judgments, raising instead the issue of the audience's implication in the successive scenes of disempowerment that it must witness. Here the narratives of colonialism proleptically provide space for the implicatedness that will later supply postcolonial discourse with its most productive complication. For if English India can serve as a discursive model of any interpretive resonance, then it must illustrate a disbanding of the most enduring binarism that perplexes colonial cultural studies: it must provide an alternative to the assignation of "cultures" to colonialism; of "nation" to postcolonialism. It is only in the sorry contiguities of the two terms that the idiom of English India can be located.

IN CLAIMING THAT THE HISTORY OF THE COLONIZATION AND THE DECOLONIZAtion of the Indian subcontinent can function as the guilty territory upon which culture and nation confront their imbrication, I attempt to argue that the event of colonial encounter completely dispenses with chronology. The chronology at hand could also be called a plot, such as the highly suggestive quest for national origins that orders Benedict Anderson's reading in *Imagined Communities*. His plot is obsessed with the modernity of nationhood, so that the concept remains bound to structures of temporal interpretation. Anderson arrives at discursive coherence by positing a familiar hierarchy: "Nationalism has to be understood by aligning it, not with self-consciously held political ideologies, but with the large cultural systems that preceded it, out of which—as well as against which—it came into being."[8] Culture is thus an originary term out of which a sequence can be developed, which furthermore declares that the story of nation can find artic- ulation only after the fact of cultural description. A more intellectually vexing perspective, however, suggests that in the case of the Indian subconti- nent the very occurrence of British colonization was sufficient to transmute the disparate empires of India into disparate nations. Colonialism, in other words, signifies an advent of such disruptive modernity that culture itself acquires the attributes of nation.

The assertion of this modernity, however, is not to participate in a search for "origins" of either culture or nation, but instead is an attempted reading of the dynamic that causes the terms to coalesce in a colonial context. In the radical novelty engendered by colonial encounter, cultural chronology gives way to a temporal condition of such social and political perplexity that it can no longer serve as a preeminence out of which nationality may then emerge. If the location of a colonial plot can be described as a substitute for the more traditional evolutionary model from culture to nation, then the field that defines itself as "colonial cultural studies" is forced to reexamine what the rhetorical thrust of such an emplotment may be. In his introduction to the collection of essays *Nation and Narration*, Homi K. Bhabha argues for a somewhat similarly syncopated narrative of cultural dynamics: "To en- counter the nation *as it is written* displays a temporality of culture and social consciousness more in tune with the partial, overdetermined process by which textual meaning is produced through the articulation of difference in language . . . . Such an approach contests the traditional authority of those national objects of knowledge—Tradition, People, the Reason of the State, High Culture, for instance—whose pedagogical value often relies on their representation as holistic concepts located within an evolutionary narrative of historical continuity . . . . To study nation through its narrative address does not merely draw attention to its language and its rhetoric: it also at- tempts to alter the conceptual object itself."[9] While Bhabha's ensuing conclusions occasionally fall victim to the cultural binarism that he wishes to critique, his apprehension of the process of nation—of its stories and their hesitancies, of its disalignment from evolution—can help to complicate what the "modern" may signify to a reading of the inception of empire today.

To claim that colonialism initiates nation would merely be to replicate in inverse order an enduring imperial stereotype, which suggests that empire confers the rationality of nationhood on its prerational subjects. The colonial condition certainly produces a proleptic understanding of the inevitability of nation, but it cannot be read as the originary encounter that constitutes the site of nation-making. Such discursive strategies of claiming territory or of staking the first claims, however, pose a considerable danger to contemporary interpretations of the relations between colonialism and nationalities. As Edward Said warns in his essay "Orientalism Reconsidered," the proliferation of critiques on the permutations of imperialism both has opened cultural studies to a productive alienation effect in the context of its potential Eurocentrism, and has further led to a danger of developing a critical colonialism within the field itself: "A double kind of exclusivism could set in: the sense of being an excluding insider by virtue of experience (only women can write for and about women, and only literature that treats women or Orientals well is good literature), and second, being an excluding insider by virtue of method (only Marxists, anti-Orientalists, feminists, can write about economics, Orientalism, women's literature)."[10] This warning bears repetition, since it is an implicit caution against the misreadings of alterity to which current reformulations of the relation between empire and nation are continually liable. If we are to read this vexed historical relation with the attentiveness that it demands, then our discourse must necessarily address how the encounter of colonialism and the emergence of nationalism are secret sharers in an act of cultural transcription so overdetermined as to dissipate the logic of origins, or the rational framework of chronologies.

Here, the intimacy of the colonial setting requires reiteration. For the reader of postcolonial discourse provides scant service to its conceptualization when she posits the issue of an intransigent otherness as both the first and the final solution to the political and aesthetic problems raised by the mutual transcriptions that colonialism has engendered in the Indian subcontinent. Diverse ironies of empire are too compelling to be explained away by the simple pieties that the idiom of alterity frequently cloaks. If cultural criticism is to address the uses to which it puts the agency of alterity, then it must further face the theoretical question that S. P. Mohanty succinctly formulates: "Just how other, we need to force ourselves to indicate, is the Other?"[11] Since recourse neither to representation nor to cultural relativism can supply an answer, postcolonial discourse is forced into alternative questions: how can the dynamic of imperial intimacy produce an idea of nation that belongs neither to the colonizer nor to the colonized? Is nation in itself the alterity to which both subjugating and subjugated cultures must in coordination defer? In what ways does the idiom of otherness simply rehearse the colonial fallacy through which India could be interpreted only as the unreadability of romance?

The romance of nation—both in context of the "self-sacrificing love" to which Benedict Anderson refers and that of its stories' perpetual reference to the absence of their own belonging—is a topic of considerable cultural thickness, and cannot be explained away in easy theoretical aphorisms. If, as Anderson suggests, the inception of nation occurs predominantly in creole cultures, then it becomes all the more necessary to study the creole engendered by imperialism in order to determine its own dislocation from the production of nation. In the abstracted admixture of community that the British colonization violently drew out of the Indian subcontinent, the idea of nation registers as an indigenous inevitability: the concept requires no importation other than the presence of the British on Indian territory. The colony's arrival at the idea of nation can thus be seen as coterminous with a cultural recognition that the colonizer was not simply an itinerant, but an excrescence that planned to stay. As a consequence, not only does subcontinental nation-ness claim an autonomy of its own, but British nationalism too is vexed by its formulation in other worlds. Gauri Viswanathan cogently suggests the political ramifications of romance when she argues for the muddied chronology between British empire and British nation: "The importance of the colonies for diffusing, maintaining, and redefining [British class conflicts] makes it all the more urgent to consider English culture first and foremost in its imperial aspect and then to examine that aspect as itself constitutive of 'national' culture. Such a project challenges the assumption that what makes an imperial culture possible is a fully formed national culture shaped by internal social developments; it also provokes one to search for ways to reinsert 'imperial' into 'national' without reducing the two terms to a single category."[12]

The colonial and postcolonial narrative takes shape on precisely such a critical terrain. In negotiating between the idioms of empire and of nation, the fiction of nineteenth-century Anglo-India seeks to decode the colonized territory through the conventions of romance, reorganizing the materiality of colonialism into a narrative of perpetual longing and perpetual loss. Viswanathan makes a claim for the antecedent of imperialism in the construction of British national identity; I make a parallel claim for the autonomy of a similar Indian establishment of nation, but further wish to suggest that both modes of cultural arrival are implicated in the structure of romance, causing their stories to achieve an idea of nation only after dislocation and disbandment have demanded a requisite cost. Such a precarious economy allows Robert Sencourt to conclude his study *India in English Literature* with the paradigmatic claim that "without [a] hunger for the rich and strange, it is impossible for the West to assimilate India. She reserves her value and her fascinations to those who never weary in their attentive study of her subtle lineaments, because their love for her is that restless adventure of imagination, that active longing for what is rare and intangible in its rich hint of life, which has made deeds, and made the most absorbing prose. Its very name echoes the name, as it suggests the power, of Earth's Eternal City. We know it as Romance."[13] We know, in other words, in order that we may not; the structure of national difference is transcribed into a literary genre most attuned to the necessities of absence. "India" becomes the absent point toward which nineteenth-century Anglo-Indian narrative may lean but which it may never possess, causing both national and cultural identities to disappear in the emptiness of a representational mirage.

If the conventions of romance control the literatures of Anglo-Indian colonization, allowing them to posit the fiction that the national realities of the subcontinent lie beyond the pale of representation, then colonial cultural studies are prone to an equally dangerous corollary. While the decentering of colonial discourse and an attendant attempt to redefine the parameters of the colonial subject have been essential to the field, there are limits beyond which an articulation of otherness could cause the discourse merely to ventriloquize the fact of cultural difference. Once the disturbing centrality of alterity has been established as a key area of interpretative concern, a rehearsal of its protean manifestations leads to a theoretical repetitiveness that finally entrenches rather than displaces the rigidity of the self/other binarism governing traditional discourse on colonialism. On a more crucial rhetorical level, however, the language of alterity can be read as a postmodern variant of the obsolescent idiom of romance: the very insistence on the centrality of difference as an unreadable entity can serve to obfuscate and indeed to sensationalize that which still remains to be read.

While the work of such critics as the Subaltern Studies collective attempts to rectify this compulsion toward romanticism, its anguish over its own theoretical elitism comes perilously close to a political allegorization of romance. An awareness of this danger is clearly at work when Gayatri Spivak claims that "the position that only the subaltern can know the subaltern, only woman can know women . . . cannot be held as a theoretical presupposition . . . for it predicates the possibility of knowledge on identity. Whatever the political necessity for holding the position, and whatever the advisability of attempting to 'identify' with the other in order to know her,

knowledge is made possible and sustained by irreducible difference, not identity. What is known is always in excess of knowledge."[14] Spivak's assertion
that identity is beside the conceptual point is certainly a critical commonplace in colonial cultural studies; her emphasis on the irreducibility of
an abstract difference threatens a formalism all too reminiscent of the pervasiveness of romance in the structure of imperialist narratives. Here, we
must recognize the rhetorical echoes at play between a title such as "Can the
Subaltern Speak?" and the cultural question that obsesses Kipling's marvelous boy, "Who is Kim?"

The danger of such conceptual irreducibility is that it can replay the
idea of Indian intransigence into what I have called an alteritist reading of
colonial cultural studies. While alteritism begins as a critical and theoretical
revision of a Eurocentric or Orientalist study of the literatures of colonialism,
its indiscriminate reliance on the centrality of otherness tends to replicate
what in the context of imperialist discourse was the familiar category of the
exotic. When the nineteenth-century Anglo-Indian writer transmuted the
convention of romance in order to make desire take on the lineaments of an
unreadable exoticism, he or she produced an unreadable text psychically dependent on an estranged intimacy through which the metaphor of adultery
could be raised to the power of culture. When, on the other hand, a
twentieth-century Anglo-American critic turns exclusively to the question
of alterity in its colonial context, he or she runs the risk of rendering otherness indistinguishable from exoticism, and of representing "difference" with
no attention to the cultural nuances that differentiation implies. Instead, alteritism reads to reify questions of cultural misapprehension until "otherness" becomes a conceptual blockage that signifies a repetitive monumentalization of the academy's continuing fear of its own cultural ignorance.

An alteritist reading attempts to apprehend the structure of colonial
power by returning the repressed term of the other to the scene of colonialism, thereby seeming to split open the monolith of domination by giving
space to the hitherto unheard perspective of the dominated subject. Such
gestures of intellectual generosity, however, can simultaneously—if unwittingly—represent a conceptual impoverishment, since the subordinated
subject "as other" frequently serves as a site for the breakdown of interpretation: otherness as an intransigence thus further serves as an excuse for the
failure of reading. An alteritist perspective champions the illegitimate only
insofar as it functions as a confirmation of all that legitimacy wishes to deny
about the inherent instability of power. As such, contemporary rereadings of

colonial alterity too frequently wrest the rhetoric of otherness into a postmodern substitute for the very Orientalism that they seek to dismantle, thereby replicating on an interpretive level the cultural and critical fallacies that such revisionism is designed to critique. The fiction of complete empowerment both claimed by and accorded to colonial domination is repeated by the fallacy of the totality of otherness, which too frequently serves the function of a discursive icon, invoked only to distance critical reading from its proper function. In contravention of the astounding specificity of each colonial encounter, alteritism enters the interpretive scene to insist on the conceptual centrality of an untouchable intransigence. Much like the category of the exotic in the colonial narratives of the prior century, contemporary critical theory names the other in order that it need not be further known; more crucially, alteritism represses the detail of cultural facticity by citing otherness as a universal trope, thereby suggesting that the discursive site of alterity is nothing other than the familiar and unresolved confrontation between the historical and the allegorical.

This confrontation is still more starkly represented in the paradigmatic exchange between Fredric Jameson and Aijaz Ahmad, in which Jameson seeks to read postcolonial nationalism as a historical allegory, drawing from Ahmad an eloquent defence of the specific historicity of such nationalities: "All third-world texts," claims Jameson, "are to be read . . . as *national allegories. . . . The story of the private individual destiny is always an allegory of the embattled situation of the public third-world culture and society.*"[15] Jameson's intuitive apprehension of the blurred lines of cultural demarcation between the idioms of postcolonial public and private discourse notwithstanding, his recourse to a rhetoric of "third-worldism" bespeaks a theoretical fear that has still to reconcile the uneasy distance between alterity and the problematic of national specificities. Aijaz Ahmad's very considered response to Jameson's reliance on a first- and third-world binarism, on the other hand, is perhaps too heavily invested in a reading of the "real" to provide an adequate theoretical alternative to the potentially alteritist allegory of Jameson's argument. According to Ahmad, "If one believes in the Three Worlds Theory, hence in a 'third world' defined exclusively in terms of 'the experience of colonialism and imperialism,' then the primary ideological formation . . . shall be that of nationalism; it will then be possible to assert . . . that 'all third world tests are necessarily . . . *national allegories.*'" Such an eventuality Ahmad deplores as a mere rehearsal of the Prospero paradigm: "Politically, we are Calibans, all. Formally, we are fated to be in the poststructuralist world of repetition with difference: the same allegory, the nationalist one, re-written, over and over again, until the end of time."[16]

These two propositions remain necessary misreadings of both each other's claims and of the situatedness of nationalism in the colonial encounter, and thus are important articulations of the critical caveats that colonial cultural studies must address. While Jameson's tendency to subsume historiography into "national allegory" is perhaps too unilateral in its compass, his appreciation of the dissipation of postcolonial identity cannot be dismissed out of hand. Similarly, Ahmad's critique tends to suggest that a recourse to the nostalgia of specificity is the only available alternative to alteritist generalization, and thus fails to consider "nation" as an indigenous as opposed to Western construct. If, however, cultural criticism is to come to terms with the unimaginable community of colonialism's relation to nationalities, then perhaps neither position could be allowed such an easy association of "nation" with "the West" or the "first world." A provisional recourse would be to call for a collapsing of the idea of nation into the structure of allegory, and to read the narratives at hand for their revision of the more precarious question of the complicities of memory between a colonial and a postcolonial world.

If nation is to be wrested from the context of easy allegorization and of an alteritism in which otherness is simply a conceptual vessel for the anxiety that overtakes quests for origins, what forms of rereading would more comprehensively address its psychosocial dimensions in the story of colonialism? Does it demand a meticulous attention to the self-censoring dynamic that the narratives of nationalism accord to the representation of its histories, so that to reiterate the crucial context of historical specificity to colonial cultural criticism is simultaneously to address the seductive overdetermination of fact? Is contemporary discourse in this field capable of a Conradian apprehension of such vertiginous complicity that it can conduct a reading of national narratives structured on the perpetual reconfigurations of the intimacies created by the circuit of colonial guilt? That such questions have to be both formulated and reformulated in colonial discourse implies that in seeking to look beyond the pitfalls of alteritism its language has no recourse but to suggest the obsolescence of a monolithic other.

"How do we negotiate," S. P. Mohanty eloquently queries, "between my history and yours? How would it be possible for us to recover our commonality, not the ambiguous imperial-humanist myth of our shared human attributes which are supposed to distinguish us from animals, but, more significantly, the imbrication of our various pasts and presents, the ineluctable

relationships of shared and contested meanings, values, material resources?"[17] This negotiation may never recover a posthumanist commonality between the diverse histories that compromise colonial encounter, but it
must nevertheless be conducted. Ahab will not see in literal terms his replication in Naboth, but much like the latter, will fail to recognize any mimicry
between strategies of the colonizer and those of the colonized. Ahab's story,
however, remains to be reread, allowing colonial discourse to generate a new
idiom of cultural compassion, as it studies the commonality of loss.

IF THE MATERIALITY OF CULTURAL CRITICISM MUST NOW LOCATE ITS IDIOM IN
the productive absence of alterity, it must similarly realign its relation to the
figure of gender. The figurative status of gender poses a somewhat un-
processed question to such a critical terrain: can gender serve to elucidate a
critical discourse reliant on metaphors of sexuality, or does it merely reify
the sorry biologism that dictates traditional decodings of the colonial encounter? Since the "femininity" of the colonized subcontinent has provided
Orientalist narratives with their most prevailing trope for the exoticism of
the East, contemporary reading of such texts is obliged to exercise considerable cultural tact in the feminization of its own discourse. In other words, a
simple correlation of gender with colonizer and colonized can lead only to
interpretive intransigence of a different order, through which an attempt to
recognize marginality leads to an opposite replication of the uncrossable distance between margin and center. The taut ambivalence of colonial
complicity, however, demands a more nuanced reading of how equally am-
bivalently gender functions in the tropologies of both colonial and postcolonial narratives.

   In *Orientalism*, Edward Said succinctly interprets the Orientalist will
to sexualize as one manifestation of the anxiety of empire: "The relation between Orientalist and Orient was essentially hermeneutical: standing before
a distant, barely intelligible civilization of cultural monument, the Orientalist scholar reduced the obscurity by translating, sympathetically
portraying, inwardly grasping the hard-to-reach object . . . . This cultural,
temporal, and geographical distance was expressed in metaphors of depth,
secrecy, and sexual promise: phrases like 'the veils of an Eastern bride' or
'the inscrutable Orient' passed into common language."[18] The epistemological terror that underlies such an imperial recourse to the language of
sexual promise cannot be repressed from contemporary rereadings of the tropologies of gender that obsess the literatures of imperialism. Despite Said's
insistence on the hermeneutics of this trope, the tendency of subsequent crit-

icism frequently fails to register the implications of his reading: instead, current discourse—in its often unscrupulous conflation of the issues of race, class, and gender—tends to replicate the Orientalist desire to shroud the East in a "female" mystery. The common language of imperialism thus perpetuates itself through what seeks to be an opposing methodology, suggesting that the continued equation between a colonized landscape and the female body represents an alteritist fallacy that causes considerable theoretical damage to both contemporary feminist and postcolonial discourses.

As nineteenth-century anthropological studies have notoriously proven, to ascribe a gender to a culture is to enter highly dangerous territory. Yet the feminization of the colonized subcontinent remains the most sustained metaphor shared by imperialist narratives from ethnographic, historical, and literary fields. In such a history as Robert Orme's, for example, the "strength" of the colonizer is always delineated against the curious attractions of the colonized race's "weakness": "Breathing in the softest climates, having so few wants and receiving even the luxuries of other nations with little labour from their own soil, the Indian must have become *the most effeminate inhabitant of the globe* (emphasis added)."[19] This discourse of effeminacy provides an obvious but nonetheless useful method of ungendering imperial tropologies, since it makes evident that the colonial gaze is not directed to the inscrutability of an Eastern bride but to the greater sexual ambivalence of the effeminate groom. Both the desire and the disempowerment implicit in such a formulation underscore the predominantly homoerotic cast assumed by the narratives of colonialism, and further suggest the manifold complications that gender poses to the cultural location of the imperial tale. While colonized effeminacy ostensibly indicates whatever is rotten in the state of the colony, the hysterical attention that it elicits provides an index for the dynamic of complicity that renders the colonizer a secret sharer of the imputed cultural characteristics of the other race.

The marked homoeroticism of the narratives of colonial encounter could provide a highly productive field of study for the epistemological limits—and their concomitant terror—imposed by an imperial contemplation of the multifariousness of culture. Such a study could furthermore provide cultural criticism with a terrain upon which to complicate and to question the more literal inscriptions of gender-bound metaphors onto the politics of colonialism. For the anxieties of empire are only obscured by a critically unquestioning recuperation of the metaphor of rape, in which colonized territory is rendered dubiously coterminous with the stereotype of a precultural and female geography. The prevalence of this metaphor is evident in the

antiimperialist rhetoric of such Indian nationalists as Nehru, who described
the colonization of the subcontinent in terms of stereotypical sexual aggression: "They seized her body and possessed her, but it was a possession of
violence. They did not know her or try to know her. They never looked into
her eyes, for theirs were averted and hers cast down through shame and humiliation."[20] While it requires a Salman Rushdie to read and to disrupt the
aggression of shame—its traversals between "male" and "female" discourse
in the stories of colonialism—the obsolescence of the figure of rape is too
naked in its figuration to allow for a sustained reading of the valences of trauma that the sexual symbolism of colonialism indubitably implies.

The geography of rape as a dominant trope for the act of imperialism,
however, has been in currency too long for it to remain at all critically liberat-
ing, particularly since it serves as a subterfuge to avoid the striking symbolic
homoeroticism of Anglo-Indian narrative. While the latter only suggests
how closely a reading of colonialism is aligned to a critique of masculine anxiety, no intelligent feminism should be prepared to serve as the landscape
upon which the intimacy of homoerotic invitation and rejection can be enacted. Instead, feminism is implicated in a reading of the homoerotic and what it
theoretically lends to the gendering of colonial cultural criticism. How will
we learn to reread the romance between Kim and his lama in the light of a
colonial erotic, or turn again to the aborted love between Fielding and Aziz?
For the politics of Anglo-India, and the stories which it has generated, are
fraught with a deferred homosexual decorum that lends a retroactive significance to Kipling's infamous claim in "The Ballad of East and West," which
will obliterate the cultural difference of East, West, Border, Breed, and Birth
only when "two strong men stand face to face, though they come from the
ends of the earth." The hysteria and cultural terror embodied by these
"strong men" are amply documented in the histories of the colonization of
India, and suggest a bewildering suspension of power far more complicated
than any conventional interpretation of the confrontation between a dominating and a subordinated culture. Instead, discourses of rationality are
forced to give figurative articulation to the nightmares that the dreams of
colonial rationalism may produce, thus indicating the gender imbrication
implicit in the classification of culture as an anxious provenance partitioned
between the weakness and strength of men.

The outrage of this paradigm is evident. Rather than resort to an ideological indignation, however, it may be more useful to question why such a
gendered weakness—both culturally male but "effeminate" at the same
time—could pose an image of national debility of such seduction to the colo-

nial eye. If nation is to be syncopated into body, then cultural studies must
face a reading of imperialism that is prepared to accommodate the exigencies
of what a racial gaze may signify to a postcolonial reading of gender. At
which point does cultural looking suggest not merely a narcissistic preoc-
cupation with its situation, but the discursive terror that links nation to the
act of recognizing race as the most comprehensive modality by which to examine the dischronologous relation between empire, race, and nation?

"Orientals," Edward Said has claimed, "were rarely seen or looked at;
they were seen through, analysed not as citizens, not even as people, but as
problems to be solved or confined."[21] In the history of the colonization of the
Indian subcontinent, however, such an Orientalist paradigm cannot apply,
for from the eighteenth century on, the imperial power was obsessively looking for ways in which a gendered and a racial fear could be seen. Domination
could comprehend the parameters of its cultural invasion only by looking all
too attentively at Indian races and their concomitant configuration into
"cultures": British imperialism in India is predicated on an act of cultural
looking that then translates into a hysterical overabundance of the documentation of racial vision. The empire looked as though its perspective could be
comprehensive and overarching; the narratives engendered by such a gaze,
however, fearfully locate embodiments of race in culture, of gender in religion. Its compulsive attempt to classify, to categorize, and to construct
racial inventories supplies a postcolonial reader with overwhelming evidence
of the trauma of colonial gendering, which intrudes to illustrate the overdetermination of imperial classification of "cultures."

In the context of the Indian subcontinent, the instructive misreadings
conducted by a colonial racial vision are perhaps most remarkably instanti-
ated by the act of colonial looking that culminated in the multivolumed work
*The people of India: A Series of Photographic Illustrations with Descriptive
Letter Press of the Races and the Tribes of India*, a document serially published between the postmutiny years of 1868 and 1875.[22] This early foray
into ethnographic photography was designed to record a "photographic like-
ness of a few of the more remarkable tribes in India," and became—along
with James Mill's *The History of British India*—a textbook for British administrators training for the Indian civil service.[23] The text is revelatory on
several counts, most crucially in its attempt to represent "caste" as a dominant metaphor through which all the religious subgroups of the subcontinent
can finally be decoded: *The people of India* translates the fears of racial vision
into a figure of "caste" that attempts to interpret cultural systems as both
highly rigid and highly fluid at the same time. Its obsession with classifica-

tions that are dependent on the dissolving grid of caste illustrates a colonial attempt to examine a model of alterity so explosively multifarious that the invading race itself is threatened to be subsumed into such powerlessness. Rather than supply the invader with a key to a system of cultural control, caste represents the symbolic invisibility of the peoples of India, and the disempowering fear that the colonizer cannot function as the other to a colonized civilization that had long since learned to accommodate a multiplicity of alterities into the fabric of its cultures.

While hardly helpful in its claim to be an empirical study, a colonial reading of caste is more informative about the imperial anxiety that forces the act of cultural looking into narratives of profound unlooking. To nineteenth-century ethnographers such as Herbert Risley, this colonial intransigence was necessarily ascribed to the manner in which the structure of caste mirrored the peculiarities of the "Indian intellect": "It is clear that the growth of the caste instinct must have been greatly promoted and stimulated by certain characteristic peculiarities of the Indian intellect—its lax hold of facts, its indifference to action, its absorption in dreams, its exaggerated reverence for tradition, its passion for endless division and sub-division, its acute sense of minute technical distinctions, its pedantic tendency to press a principle to its furthest logical conclusion, and its remarkable capacity for imitating and adapting social ideas and usages of whatever origin."[24] Here, the "femininity" of the "Indian intellect" accounts for its opacity, so that caste functions as a veil behind which lurks a sexual hybridity quite disruptive to conventional genderings of the colonial paradigm. The idea of caste thus becomes an allegory in itself, but an allegory deeply troubling in its own unsettlement: to the colonial imagination, the category of caste signifies the cultural imperative behind the segregation of gender and class as well as the deranged and cross-dressed intimacies licensed by such a principle of division.

It is therefore hardly surprising that a photographic catalog of caste such as *The people of India* received its initial impulse from Lord and Lady Canning's desire to compile an album of picturesque snapshots as a memento of their sojourn in India, and that such a slippage from private desire to public documentation could have occurred without any colonial self-questioning. The ensuing document is fraught with an intimate awareness of its own cultural ignorance, causing the descriptive readings of each photograph to exude a self-punishing hysteria about all that the reading cannot see. The letter press is repetitively ill at ease with its own powers of classification, turning the categories of caste, tribe, and class into metaphors that receive their most

clear figuration through a reading of physiognomy. As opposed to gener-
alizations about caste in relation to Indian "intellect," the physical presence
of the photograph causes the colonial imagination to examine the veil of caste
in relation to face: one such face, for example, can be described as "peculiarly
Mohamadan, of the centralasian type; and while [its features] vouch for the
purity of his descent, [they] exemplify in a strong manner the obstinacy,
sensuality, ignorance, and bigotry of his class. It is hardly possible, perhaps,
to conceive features more essentially repulsive."[25] The face of culture, in
other words, is in excess of the veiled caste that it is purported to represent;
instead, the involutions engendered by its image cause the colonial gaze implicitly to acknowledge a distraught sense that the eye of the beholder is
implicated in the manifold cultural "impurities" that it must observe and record.

   That such an idiom presents the pure and the sensual as mutually interchangeable terms reiterates what the trope of caste signifies to the colonial
imagination, which is an instantiation of the impurity of gender to the cultural readings necessitated by the historical encounter of colonialism. The
conceptual blockage signified by such terms requires attention in its own
right, in order that the psychic predicament of the colonizer can in effect be
disaligned from the monolithic power accorded to him. What face can
Naboth turn to the terrified and terrorizing gaze of an Ahab? Let us turn to a
subcontinental gaze on such a text as *The people of India*, which causes the
nineteenth-century Muslim educationist Sayyid Ahmad Khan to pose an obvious but central question:

> In the India Office is a book in which the races of all India are
> depicted both in pictures and in letterpress, giving the manners
> and customs of each race. Their photographs show that the
> pictures of the different manners and customs were taken on the
> spot, and the sight of them shows how savage they are—the
> equal of animals. The young Englishmen who, after passing the
> preliminary Civil Service examination, have to pass examina-
> tions on special subjects for two years afterwards, come to the
> India Office preparatory to starting for India, and, desirous of
> knowing something of the land to which they are going, also look
> over this book. *What can they think, after perusing this book and
> looking at its pictures, of the power and honour of the natives of
> India?* (emphasis added)[26]

The specificity of Sayyid Ahmad Khan's question "What can they think?"
reformulates the terrors induced by a reading of culture in which both colo-

nizer and colonized are equally implicated. Since it would not be sufficient merely to catalog the mutual fear attendant on acts of colonial self-definition, colonial cultural studies must seek to read more closely the structure of psychic subordination implicit in the history of colonial domination.

WHILE I DO NOT WISH TO SUGGEST THAT COLONIAL AND POSTCOLONIAL NAR-ratives constitute a seamless history of both imperialism and its aftermath, I do posit a dialogic relation between the two. The idiom of postcolonialism is necessarily reactive and, unless it is to be lost in its own novelty, must engage in the multiplicity of histories that are implicated in its emergence. On a similar level, the idiom of colonialism is necessarily proleptic: it must anticipate the transfer of power even in the articulation of the acquisition of power. "English India" accommodates the cultural and political perplexities of both idioms less to provide a chronology of continuity than to superimpose the divergent histories that compromise the Anglo-Indian encounter, illustrating in the process how particular cultures can be emplotted in other peoples' tales. Such a cartography attempts to break down static lines of distinction between the indigenous and the foreign, but at the same time continually questions any synthesizing conflation of this duality. Here, Gayatri Spivak's comments on the "disciplinary predicament" of the postcolonial critic provide a suggestive sketch of the difficulty faced by any act of retrospective colonial cartography: "I cannot understand what indigenous theory there might be," muses Spivak, "that can ignore the reality of nineteenth-century history. As for syntheses: syntheses have more problems than answers to offer. To construct indigenous theories one must ignore the last few centuries of historical involvement. I would rather use what history has written for me."[27]

To use what history has written for us, however, demands a critical strategy that is prepared to acknowledge the implication of interpretive discourse in the object of its study: the readings that follow are as much a part of the rhetoric of English India as are the texts upon which my reading focuses. If this rhetoric is to be comprehended as a dynamic and culturally plangent process, then the reader herself is bound to admit to her participation in its bewildering production of peripheries, or cultural margins that refer to no historical center. Much as the colonizer and colonized can no longer be examined as totally autonomous entities, so must critical discourse recognize its imbrication in the fields of its analyses. The postcolonial condition is neither territorially bound nor more the property of one people than of the other: instead, its inevitably retroactive narrative allows for the inclusion both of its colonial past and of the function of criticism at the present time as necessary corollaries to the telling of its stories.

Such an Arnoldian invocation does not imply a hierarchy in which "English" serves as the subject to which "India" is the predicate, but gestures instead at the cultural curiosity that allows Arnold to exhort his readership to cultivate an "Indian disinterest" in order to discover the best that is known and thought in the world. As Gauri Viswanathan's work has meticulously demonstrated, the issue of the canonicity of English literature was primarily formulated in the laboratory provided by colonial terrain. A historical acknowledgment of this precedence, however, is totally disaligned from any rhetorical establishment of "origins," as Viswanathan succinctly points out. While her study clearly indicates that major canonical and curricular battles of English literary studies took place on the "margin" of the colony rather than at the "center" of colonizing Britain, Viswanathan is at pains to demonstrate the absence of hierarchy that dictates her cultural reading: "Complementarity does not imply that one precedes or causes the other, nor that both are parallel, arbitrarily related developments with few or no points of contact. Its defining characteristic is the necessity for transference . . . of any one or more of these factors—subject, agent, event, intention, purpose—not in the sense of wholesale borrowing, but of readaptation."[28] We reread Macaulay, in other words, less to grieve over the precipitous effect of his infamous "Minute on Indian Education" than to uncover the fallacy of utilitarianism, which, in its rhetorical obsession with the idea of colonial blankness, must banish the undecipherability of an "Oriental" curriculum to the pale of a colonized orality.

How does such an orality reclaim its status as a written language, or a discourse enabled enough to articulate the vexed relation between postcolonial nationhood and prior colonial histories? One possible rhetorical strategy of imploding the oral vernacular into the craft of cultural writing is suggested by the allegory offered by *Midnight's Children*, which concludes in a mocking, self-deflatory apocalypse of the residual effects of English India: "Yes, they will trample me underfoot, the numbers marching one two three . . . reducing me to specks of voiceless dust, just as in all good time, they will trample my son who is not my son, and his son who will not be his, and his who will not be his, until the thousand and first generation, until a thousand and one midnights have bestowed their terrible gifts and a thousand and one children have died, because it is the privilege and curse of midnight's children to be both masters and victims of their times."[29] Rushdie's postcolonial apocalypse suggests that the genealogy of a self-censoring colonial narrative can furthermore be read retroactively, implying that the price of the transference of power is to subsume each collaborator in the rhetoric of English India into "the privilege and curse" of being "both masters and victims of their times."

If the paradigm of master and victim is to be read in terms of its availability to the histories of colonialism and their concomitant narratives, then its rereading as a figure of colonial intimacy—as an interruption in traditional interpretations of imperial power—must necessarily generate a discursive guilt at the heart of the idiom of English India. Its troubled confluence of colony, culture, and nation lends a retroactive migrancy to the fact of imperialism itself, causing a figure like Kipling's Ahab to recognize that narration occurs to confirm the precariousness of power.

2

Edmund Burke and
the Indian Sublime

ON 1 DECEMBER 1783, EDMUND BURKE ROSE IN THE HOUSE OF COMMONS TO deliver the exasperated eloquence of his speech on Fox's East India Bill. The bill in question—one in a series of protracted parliamentary debates on the structure of the East India Company—concerned the Company's accountability to the British government, and proposed specific strategies to limit the Company's capacity to function, in Burke's phrase, as a "state in the disguise of a merchant."[1] The speech theatrically reproduces assumptions which were crucial to the ongoing debate about colonial practice in the latter decades of the eighteenth century, in which neither the entity of state nor that of merchant was seen to be inherently problematic. Difficulty arose, it seemed, only when an entity in action encroached upon the scope or powers of the rival entity; that is, when it failed to remain within the confines of its proper narrative. In the discursive struggle that ensued, the colonization of India functions as a stage upon which—in the context of English India—the colonizing of government by speculative finance is far more at stake than the actual conquest of someone else's land. The latter remains only a frame for the bitter contest between the language of the merchant and the language of the state: territorial expansion becomes less a subject of concern itself than an absorbing occasion upon which the colonial imagination can redefine its encounter with the new imperialism of the eighteenth century.[2] While colonialism's anxiety for immediate material acquisition can never be exaggerated, the encounter described here produces rhetorical convolutions far exceeding the requirements of that motive alone—ambiguities of discourse, some, but not all, of which may be traced to an interest in deception or self-deception. For in attempting to arrive at a dynamic model of economy, both state and merchant were forced to question the principle of personification that delimited their functions in consolidating the colonization of the subcontinent. Until its economy could be wrested away from an established sense of who possessed the gains of that distant empire, both mercantile and state interests in Britain were constrained to come to terms with the obsolescence of the banners under which they fought. Impersonators trapped in their own discourse, how else could they articulate their understanding of the colonial project's scale but through guilty recognitions of the necessity of theft between state and merchant? In this as yet inchoate political discourse, for one interest to expose the other's culpability was simultaneously to apprehend its own.

Two possible conquerors, therefore, approach the territory of India; and in order that it may be completely possessed, each must come to terms with the other's machinery, or powers of usurpation. Their battle encapsulates a discursive issue of some importance in eighteenth-century England's attempt to articulate the consequences of its heady arrival at empire: how could Parliament license the precocity of trade and its powerful will to wealth, and yet contain such overabundance within legislature's need to domesticate, to subordinate the novelty of colonial capital to its own traditions of control? Furthermore, was legislative discourse itself exempt from the mythmaking of that era's cultural imaginings, in which the distant exoticism of India could be conceived and represented only by a metonymic extravagance with descriptions of the miraculous fashion in which money was seen to reproduce itself in the remoteness of that land?[3] Fox's bill, of which Burke wrote the bulk, attempted to warn both state and merchant of the dangers inherent in the desire to perceive India as a land of perpetual surplus; in order to preserve better the potential imperialist interest in India, the bill argued, the British government and the East India Company should coalesce into a governing body that could serve as a prudent conduit between the merchant's desire to act as a state and the state's desire to own the power of the merchant. Such an alliance would not only force both entities into a redefinition of the materiality of colonial power, but would further censor representations of the wanton abundance of Indian wealth, and only in its wake would India truly fall into British control. Fox's bill was defeated on December 13.[4]

By 1783, Burke had been actively engaged in acquiring information about the "Indian question" for eighteen years, an engagement that was to reach a wrenchingly theatrical conclusion in his part in the impeachment trials of Warren Hastings, the legal spectacle of which lasted from 1786 to 1794. Despite the prophetic stance of his parliamentary discourse on India, Burke's immersion in the idea of the subcontinent is not without its delusional aspects, illustrating the terrors encoded within the perspicacity of his historical imagination: P. J. Marshall and Glyndwr Williams argue that "it is doubtful whether more than one or two British political figures found it necessary to acquire anything more than the most superficial knowledge of India; but Burke was one for whom India did become exceptionally vivid. . . . What he had learnt may or may not have accorded with reality, but it had given him a deeply-felt sympathy for a society entirely alien to him."[5]

Even within Burke's lexicon, however, sympathy is a difficult term.[6] To read Burke reading India is of course to acknowledge the tropological cast of his historical view of the subcontinent, and further to assume that such a powerfully influential discourse need not be tested for veracity in order to determine its crucial influence on the rhetoric of English India and how such a language learned to become self-questioning. For during the decades of Burke's Indian engagement, the vocabulary that imperial England had developed in regard to the prospect of an Indian colony underwent some compelling changes: before the 1780s, India had largely functioned in the British imagination as an area beyond the scope of cartography, a space most inviting to European wills to plunder and to the flamboyant entrepreneurship of such a figure as Robert Clive.[7] The course of Burke's association with India subsequently demonstrates how many further complications that colony would pose to the imperial psyche, as it dealt with both the loss of the American colonies and the impending advent of the French Revolution. Burke's discourse is preternaturally aware of how many losses are enfolded within the British acquisition of India, which in this sense, as well as chronologically, serves as a watershed between two other violent ruptures: in North America and in France. His obsession with loss initiates a novel vocabulary, in which the conceptual distance of India is inextricably linked to the proliferating anxieties of empire. As the most eloquent and certainly most widely read member of Parliament to debate the question of India, Burke supplied imperial England with an idiom in which to articulate its emergent suspicion that the health of the colonizing project was dependent on a recognition of the potentially crippling structure of imperial culpability.

The economy of guilt has a central place in Burke's rhetoric, both in his literal indictments of the East India Company's policies, and in his abstracted vision of the actual turf over which merchant and state were battling. A classic text such as his speech on Fox's East India Bill dramatizes this economy less by the eloquence of its moral zeal than by its new insistence on the difficulty of representing India at all in the English language. In place of the popular vision of an exotic India excessively available to traversal and description, Burke offers an alternative reading in which the subject of India breaks each attempt to put it to an inventory. With his characteristic reliance on the locutions of astonishment and horror, Burke's speech insists on the futility of approaching India as though it could be cataloged or would ever be categorizable:

All this vast mass, composed of so many orders and classes of men, is again infinitely diversified by manners, by religion, by hereditary employment, through all their possible combinations. This renders the handling of India a matter in an high degree critical and delicate. But, oh, it has been handled very rudely indeed! Even some of the reformers seem to have forgot that they had anything to do but to regulate the tenants of a manor, or the shopkeepers of the next county town.

It is an empire of this extent, of this complicated nature, of this dignity and importance that I have compared it to Germany and the German government—not for an exact resemblance, but as a sort of middle term, by which India might be approximated to our understandings, and, if possible, to our feelings, in order to awaken something of sympathy for the unfortunate natives, of which I am afraid we are not perfectly susceptible, whilst we look at this very remote object through a very false and cloudy medium.[8]

The "false and cloudy medium" upon which the speech insists allows Burke to illustrate painstakingly how British colonial discourse must come to terms with the central representational unavailability that Indian cultures and histories, even its sheer geography, must pose to the colonizing eye. In the absence of "exact resemblance," Burke makes similes of India in order to imply a more illicit imperial difficulty, or that point where the colonizing imagination is forced to admit that to analogize is to be an idiot.

"Difficulty," however, is itself frequently a peculiar and attractive term in Burke's lexicon, suggesting a discursive circumnavigation at the very point when the orator is casting up his rhetorical hands at the impossibilities of navigation. The speech on Fox's East India Bill equates the functioning of imperial power in India with a discourse of difficulty that is dependent on invocations of magnitude, thickness, resistance—which in turn, artfully allow an urgent clarity to take shape out of the very opacities of the Indian theme. An attentive reader will recall that prior to 1783 Burke had once before located his own rhetorical lucidity in a vision of the obscure, as those members of the House who had read *A Philosophical Enquiry into the Origin of Our Ideas of the Sublime and Beautiful* would surely have recognized. "It is an arduous thing," they heard, "to plead against the abuses of power which originates in your own country, and affects those whom we are used to consider as strangers . . . [We are] so little acquainted with Indian details, the instruments of oppression under which the people suffer are so hard to be understood, and even the names of the sufferers are so uncouth and strange to our ears, that it is very difficult to fix upon these objects" (*CW,* vol. 2, pp. 464–65). When had his listeners last been asked thus to concentrate upon the difficult, upon the license to precision that a contemplation of the remote and the obscure can allow? Whether or not his audience was cognizant, Burke was: India had become the age's leading moral example of the sublime.

It would be facile to read Burke's rhetorical swerves into the sublimity of India as an aestheticizing of political discourse, or as idiosyncratic retreats from the parameters of rationalism into the categorization of irrationality that the sublime signifies. While the implication of sublimity in eighteenth-century political discourse has been the object of compelling critical reading, most notably by Hayden White and Donald E. Pease, its invocation in the context of the colonization of India suggests divergent consequences.[9] Burke's conflation of India as a conceptual possibility with the operation of the sublime works less to defamiliarize that idea than to render it canny through the very depictions of its difficulty. Consequently, such a rhetorical reconfiguration implies a fictive simultaneity of historical event and the act of historiography that Burke undertook. This was, in short, an occasion in which not only would parliamentary law be passed on colonized India, but all figures of speech pertaining to that colony would similarly receive spontaneous legitimation. "Despite all *revolutionary* rhetoric invested in the term," claims Donald Pease, "the sublime has, in what we would call the politics of historical formation, always served conservative purposes."[10] In the context of Burke's desire to conserve the imperial project in India, this claim is irrefutable, although it is less applicable to his startling rhetorical strategy of turning the sublime on its head in order to represent India as a catalog of the uncategorizable. The speech on Fox's East India Bill is replete with categories and comparisons that will not work, that Burke wills not to work, in his effort to create a narrative of difficulty through which the Indian sublime becomes indistinguishable from the intimacy of colonial terror.

When Burke invokes the sublimity of India, therefore, he seeks less to contain the irrational within a rational structure than to construct inventories of obscurity through which the potential empowerment of the sublime is equally on the verge of emptying into negation. The paradigm that he establishes can be schematized as follows: India as a historical reality evokes the horror of sublimity, thus suggesting to the colonizing mind the intimate dynamic it already shares with aesthetic horror; such intimacy provokes the desire to itemize and to list all the properties of the desired object; the list's inherent failure to be anything other than a list causes the operation of sublimity to open into vacuity, displacing desire into the greater longevity of disappointment. While Burke's speech ostensibly shapes this paradigm into a passionate warning against the abuse of colonial power, his method of exemplification clearly reveals that the catalog itself carries more weight than its abundant moral. The "map" of India that he offers to the voting members on Fox's bill is consequently fraught with a repressed acknowledgment of the futility of such ethical cartography:

> In the northern parts it is a solid mass of land, about eight hundred miles in length, and four or five hundred broad. As you go southward, it becomes narrower for a space. It afterwards dilates; but, narrower or broader, you possess the whole eastern and northeastern coast of that vast country, quite from the borders of Pegu,—Bengal, Bahar, and Orissa, with Benares, (now unfortunately in our immediate possession,) measure 161,978 square English miles: a territory considerably larger than the whole kingdom of France. Oude, with its dependent provinces, is 53,286 square miles: not a great deal less than England. The Carnatic, with Tanjore and the Circars, is 65,948 square miles: very considerably larger than England. And the whole of the Company's dominions, comprehending Bombay and Salsette, amounts to 281,412 square miles: which forms a territory larger than any European dominion, Russia and Turkey excepted. Through all that vast territory there is not a man who eats a mouthful of rice but by permission of the East India Company. (CW, vol. 2, pp. 443–44)

The very repetitiveness of this catalog is designed to dissolve rather than to consolidate the image of India that Burke seemingly wishes to create: in seeking to represent the physical tangibility of the subcontinent, he succeeds only in essentializing size into a numbing sequence of figures, thereby drawing out from the magnitude of the sublime its inherent capacity to disappoint. Even as the numbers function as abstract ciphers of intangibility, Burke's vision of India is shrunk and distorted into the singularly disturbing icon of the subcontinent as a hungry mouth.

Burke's cartography of the Indian sublime is further complicated by his reliance on a sequence of comparisons that work to measure India against the example of the West, so that the priority and recognized reality of European dominions become the only compass by which the geography of the colonized territory may be read. Here, his discourse anticipates the massive nineteenth-century attempt to reconstruct Indian history on a European model, rendering the proliferation of alien events into a shape amenable to the demands of Western narrative. "India was to be provided with a linear history following a nineteenth-century positivist historiography," writes Bernard Cohn; "Ruins could be dated, inscriptions made to reveal king lists, texts could be converted into sources for the study of the past. Each phase of the European effort to unlock the secret of the Indian past called for more and more collecting, more and more systems of classification, more and more building of repositories for the study of the past and the representation of the European history of India to Indians as well as themselves."[11] While Burke's rhetoric shares in such an aim to translate the East into an idiom comprehensible to the West, however, his subterranean understanding of the failures of classification suggests how each of the catalogs that colonialism constructs leads less to conclusion than into another catalog. This representation of India exactly mirrors the methodology that nineteenth-century ethnographers like Herbert Risley brought to the study of the caste system in the subcontinent, where to read even one stratum of the structure of caste was inevitably to discover potentially endless subdivisions of both casted and casteless groups, shifting with a dynamism that defied the stable grid upon which the British sought to read the very category of caste.[12] As Burke's parliamentary speeches turn obsessively to inventories of both the colonized territory and the abuses perpetrated on it by the East India Company, he adds to the rhetoric of English India its most enduring and self-conscious engagement with the sublime failure of lists.

In order to supply a speedy index for the compelling rhetorical significance of such a discovery, I am obliged to digress into a critical list of those colonial list makers whose catalogs are intricately if indirectly bound to Burke's ferocious sense of failure. For Burke's engagement in the futility of lists is by no means limited to the parliamentary idiom of eighteenth-century Anglo-India or to the received ignorance of such an official exercise in ethnographic photography as *The people of India*, but has acute bearing on the shape of Anglo-Indian narrative in the nineteenth and twentieth centuries, which is heavily dependent on the metonymic structure through which the travelogue and the adventure tale are shaped upon the incremental license of a catalog. To reduce experience to a list, or itinerary, becomes the driving desire of a fiction unwilling to decode experience into an act of cultural reading, content instead to remain within the named parameters of a catalog.[13] Such acts of colonial self-protection literalize the Indian sublime and refigure it in the peculiarly oblique mode of the picturesque—as I will show later in discussing Fanny Parks's memoir, *Wanderings of a Pilgrim in Search of the Picturesque*, and Harriet Tytler's mutiny journal.[14] The uncataloged horror of the colonial sublime, however, returns with a Burkean power when E. M. Forster transmutes the impulse to list into an uncanny image of the inefficacy of colonial description:

> The caves are readily described. A tunnel eight feet long, five feet high, three feet wide, leads to a circular chamber about twenty feet in diameter. This arrangement occurs again and again throughout the group of hills, and this is all, this is a Marabar Cave. Having seen one such cave, having seen three, four, fourteen, twenty-four, the visitor returns to Chandrapore uncertain whether he has had an interesting experience or a dull one of any experience at all. He finds it difficult to discuss the caves, or to keep them apart in his mind. . . . Nothing, nothing attaches to them, and their reputation—for they have one—does not depend on human speech.

Here, Forster gives a symbol, both tangible and resistant to cognition, for the fear that complicates the course of Anglo-Indian narrative, calling attention to the disempowerment of description that seizes colonial discourse even as it continues to subscribe to the possibility of imperial inventories. As with Burke's attempt to delineate the geographical boundaries of the subcontinent, or Risley's effort to list the castes of India, Forster's representation of the discursive imperviousness of an "Indian experience" can lead only to the question posed by sublimity's proliferation within its own emptiness: "But elsewhere, deeper in the granite, are there certain chambers that have no entrances? Chambers never unsealed since the arrival of the gods. Local report declares that these exceed in number those that can be visited, as the dead exceed the living—four hundred of them, four thousand or million. Nothing is inside them, they were sealed up before the creation of pestilence or treasure; if mankind grew curious and excavated, nothing, nothing would be added to the sum of good or evil" (p. 118). To the colonizing imagination, the Indian sublime is at its most empty at the very point when it is most replete, dissolving the stability of facts and figures into hieroglyphs that signify only the colonizer's pained confrontation with an object to which his cultural and interpretative tools must be inadequate.

The actual political weight of geographic acquisition, however, can obscure the centrality of a colonial obsession with the burden of inadequacy; it may also conceal from us the impact that such fears made on the policy by which the domains of India were finally brought under British rule. Here the discourse of Edmund Burke remains proleptically crucial, less for its contri-

bution to modern theories of imperialism than for its passionate recognition
of the dubieties inherent in any narrative of colonial possession.

One of the most significant recognitions in his speech on Fox's East India Bill concerns the adolescence of the colonizing mind, when once the
ungovernability of its youth is unleashed as a power on alien territory. In
contrast to the sobriety of the British government in England, the aims of the
officers of the East India Company are depicted as extravagant to the point of
derangement:

> The Tartar invasion was mischievous: but it is our protection
> which destroys India. It was their enmity; but it is our friend-
> ship. . . . Young men (boys almost) govern there, without
> society and without sympathy with the natives. They have no
> more special habits with the people than if they still resided in
> England,—nor, indeed, any species of intercourse, but that
> which is necessary to making a sudden fortune, with a view to a
> remote settlement. Animated with all the avarice of age and all
> the impetuosity of youth, they roll in one after another, wave
> after wave; and there is nothing before the eyes of the natives but
> an endless, hopeless prospect of new flights of birds of prey and
> passage, with appetites continually renewing for a food that is
> continually wasting. (CW, vol. 2, p. 462)

The youthfulness of colonialism, its availability to the mythmaking of adolescent adventure, remains a central figure in the rhetoric of English India,
even when it becomes a method of valorizing the "civic" energy with which
the British claimed to bring modernity to the "feudalism" of the subcontinent.[15] In Burke's early apprehension of this adolescence, however,
indifference rather than energy is the driving impulse, which produces a su-
perflux of power great enough to be perpetually courting its own disinte-
gration:

> It stands as a monument to astonish the imagination, to
> confound the reason of mankind. I confess to you, when I first
> came to know this business in its true nature and extent, my sur-
> prise did a little suspend my indignation. I was in a manner
> stupefied by the desperate boldness of a few obscure young men,
> who, having obtained, by ways which they could not com-
> prehend, a power of which they saw neither the purposes nor the
> limits, tossed about, subverted, and tore to pieces, as if it were in
> the gambols of a boyish unluckiness and malice, the most estab-
> lished rights, and the most ancient and most revered institutions,
> of ages and nations. (CW, vol. 2, pp. 499–500)

When Burke indicts the colonial project as "the desperate boldness of a few obscure young men," he dismantles, a century before its time, the prevailing colonial stereotype of Anglo-Indian narrative, in which a tale-questing and abundant British imagination traverses the ancient and reprehensible lassitude of the Indian subcontinent. The adolescence which registers with Burke as an ethical and epistemological vacuity will be recuperated in the era of the Raj as a source of national pride and self-congratulation.

An astonishing development in the narratives of Anglo-India is the rapidity with which the British understanding of the dynamics of Indian civilization atrophied into a static and mistrustful interpretation of India as a locus of all things ancient, a backdrop against which the colonizing presence could not but be startled by its own novelty. Both Burke and his great antagonist, Warren Hastings, were possessed of an imaginative respect for Indian social structures and institutions, while their highly influential intellectual successors like James Mill and Thomas Babington Macaulay were completely impervious to the possibility of cultural sympathy.[16] In Mill's reading, India's claim on the ancient is represented either as apocryphal or as illustration of the subcontinent's perpetual arrest in prehistory. Thus book 2 of *The History of British India* opens to warn its readership that "rude nations seem to derive a peculiar gratification from pretensions to a remote antiquity. As a boastful and turgid vanity distinguishes remarkably the oriental nations they have in most instances carried their claims extravagantly high."[17] Similarly, Macaulay's "Minute on Indian Education" is infamous for the ease with which it obliterates cultural nuance and consequently fails to see any continued vitality in indigenous Indian languages and modes of learning: "I have no knowledge of either Sanscrit or Arabic.—But I have done what I could to form a correct estimate of their value. . . . I am quite ready to take the Oriental learning at the valuation of the Orientalists themselves. I have never found one of them who could deny that a single shelf of a good European library was worth the whole native literature of India and Arabia."[18] What appeared to Burke as an abundance of tradition and of history too difficult to catalog, in other words, has been contained by a figure as old and as unreadable as a Marabar Cave.

Implicit in such containment is of course not simply cultural aggression but a more overdetermined fearfulness that the colonial imagination must experience in relation to its Indian novelty. Here, the banality of adolescence that Burke deemed to be the disempowering impropriety of colonialism makes an unacknowledged return: even in Macaulay's intransigence there lurks a fear of callow misreadings that the West may impose on the possible sublimity that India could represent to a European imagination. While Macaulay's discourse translates the horror of a Burkean sublime into a depiction of the fundamental "irrationality" of all the productions of Indian culture, it simultaneously evinces psychic impoverishment which suggests that for a colonialist to confront the ancient is to be deeply shocked. The age of India is delusionally exaggerated less to address its potential venerability than to recoil from the alternative civic society that it further represents. Since India is too old to be rational, it follows that the colonial need waste as little time as possible on attempting to read the social structures that are in place on the colonized territory. In the rhetoric of English India, as a consequence, the ancient cannot command respect but instead represents a malevolent entropy, a choric reminder that on the stage of imperialism the British arrival at the possession of India has indeed been premature.

Throughout the popular fiction of the late nineteenth and early twentieth centuries, the nervous cultural blindness of Macaulay's paradigm is continually rehearsed. India is old, and to be old is evil; only the litmus test of British colonialism will usher the subcontinent into rationalism and modernity. On the obverse of this belief, however, lies the hidden fear that the colonizer is young, too young to understand the addictive functioning of a power so phantasmagoric that it may amount to nothing but its own dismantling. Thus Edmund Candler's turn-of-the-century tale *The Mantle of the East* merely repeats a well-worn Anglo-Indian stereotype when it mourns: "We soar the Ganges for them with iron, and the faithful use our road to approach their gods without sparing any of their awe for the new miracle. To the devout we and railways are a passing accident, to be used or ignored as indifferently as stepping stones across a brook. . . . India is too old to resent us. Yet who can doubt that she will survive us? The secret of her permanence lies, I think, in her passivity and power to assimilate. The faith that will not fight cannot yield."[19] Despite the fatalism of Candler's judgment, the colonial storyteller had already muddied the clear cultural demarcations implied in the metaphors of youth and age. In keeping with Burke's horrified vision of the "desperate boldness of a few obscure young men," a masterwork of Anglo-Indian narrative had indeed confronted the cultural complicities that Candler's Macaulayan binarism seeks to avoid. It had put youth and age on the same road and the same railway; it had made them collude across the social and ethnic divide of their desire; it had allowed a colonial conception to the overdetermined adolescence that is the curiosity of *Kim*.

With *Kim*, Anglo-Indian narrative returns to the ethical and aesthetic ambivalence that governs Edmund Burke's construction of an Indian sublime even when his discourse is most vociferous on the abuses of power that determine the course of eighteenth-century colonialism. The adolescence of the colonial imagination is given its most charming personification in the transcultural fetish of Kim, and is further rendered politically problematic by a narrative thrust which increasingly suggests that such a fetish is destined to be a casualty of its own ebullience. When the potentially tragic implications of colonial phantasmagoria turn the terrain of Anglo-India into a narrative space most threatening to those who seem best to possess its adventure, then the genre of the adventure tale collapses into its own potential claustrophobia. Kipling's pitiless mapping of the colonial system reveals how even the most otherworldy of quests can be duped into playing for colonialism's Great Game, converting the illusion of Kim's cultural agility into an increasingly stringent psychic imprisonment. Not only is the colonial myth of energetic adventure subjected to an ironic rereading, but the subcontinent's relation to the sublime is once again measured on a dubiously political grid. In one peculiarly uncanny gesture of colonial disrobing, Kim—playing the Great Game in the high wastes of the Himalayas—is forced to divest himself of the ethnographic tools he has seized on behalf of the British from a group of Russian spies:

> A thousand feet below lay a long, lazy, round-shouldered bank of mist, as yet untouched by the morning sun. A thousand feet below that was an hundred-year-old pine forest. He could see the green tops looking like a bed of moss when a wind-eddy thinned the cloud.
> "No! I don't think anyone will go after you!" The wheeling basket vomited its contents as it dropped. The theodolite hit a jutting cliff-edge and exploded like a shell; the books, inkstand, paint-boxes, compasses, and rulers showed for a few seconds like a swarm of bees. Then they vanished; and, though Kim, hanging half out of the window, strained his young ears, never a sound came up from the gulf.

Read as a post-Burkean imperial paradigm, this scene suggests how much the colonizing imagination is both dependent on and mistrustful of its own implements of cartography. By exploding the instruments of ethnography, *Kim* points toward an alternative reading of what colonization signifies to the subcontinent, one less convinced of the efficacy of a Western need to chart, to map, and to evaluate its psychic and political geography. As a powerful rereading of the temporal divisions between colonizer and colonized, *Kim* is genealogically linked to Burke's prior horror at the adolescence of the colonial enterprise, or the brute usurpation through which a tropological youthfulness could explain away colonial crime as a production of modernity. Even as Kipling dislocates criminality to the point where it can find ready abode in every ethnic household of Anglo-India, he breaks down the persistent stereotype adjudicating imperial age between conquered and conquering civilizations. That Kim's youth is ultimately translated into the terror of his cultural mobility corroborates what Burke had anticipated a century before: on colonial territory, no generational metaphor can obtain; adolescence is already a spoilage in the universe of an Indian sublime.

THE YEAR 1757, IN WHICH *A PHILOSOPHICAL ENQUIRY INTO THE ORIGIN OF OUR Ideas of the Sublime and Beautiful* was first published, is by historical accident a turning point in the narrative of the East India Company's survival in Bengal. Exactly one hundred years before the Indian Mutiny of 1857 and the Company's final dissolution, Robert Clive's victory at the Battle of Plassey not only ensured the Company's control over Bengal but has further been conventionally regarded as the symbolic beginning of British imperialism in the subcontinent. [20] While Burke's treatise on the sublime predates his active involvement in the politics of the colonization of India, it constitutes a figurative repository that would later prove invaluable to the indefatigable eloquence of his parliamentary years. The *Enquiry*, however, is not merely aesthetic fodder for the subsequent intensity with which Burke was compelled to address the Indian question, but provides in itself an incipient map of his developing political consciousness: as a study of the psychic proximity of aesthetic discourse with the concomitant intimacy of cultural terror, Burke's *Enquiry* converts the sublime into that theatrical space upon which he can most closely observe the emergence and disappearance that empowerment signifies to any discourse of control. As such, sublimity becomes the first terrain in which Burke can bury his intuitive understanding of the irrationality that lies at the heart of rationalism, that which insistently shapes the narrative of the latter's will to control.

The figure of the theater is central both to Burke's discourse on the sublime and to what he would later call the "conspicuous stage" of political oratory. [21] It supplies him with a sensationalism to which his rhetoric is inevitably drawn, and further becomes one of the means through which Burke can map out his perception of the fictionality of historical action. While his obsessive reading of the deranged plot of colonialism fuels his later writings on India, even such an early text as the *Enquiry* is impelled to embed aesthetic evaluation in an imperial idiom, so that his readings continually turn to the potential historicity of the sublime. In arguing for the horror of sublimity, Burke's obsessive trope remains the theatrical fall of empires, and the uncanny delights produced thereby: "This noble capital, the pride of England and of Europe, I believe no man is so strangely wicked as to desire to see destroyed by a conflagration or an earthquake, though he should be removed himself to the greatest distance from the danger. But suppose such a fatal accident to have happened, what numbers from all parts would croud to behold the ruins, and amongst them many who would have been content never to have seen London in its glory?" (*CW*, vol. 1, p. 121). In the discursive collapse that such a passage represents, the sublime is robbed of any innate autonomy that it may possess as an aesthetic category and is instead rendered curiously contiguous to a narrative of specific historical action, demonstrating Burke's inchoate desire to assess the demarcated newsworthiness of sublimity. At the same time, however, the *Enquiry* implicitly questions the preeminence of historicity over a system of universal categories such as the beautiful and the sublime: each is placed in uneasy dialogue with the other, in order that Burke may examine the shared phantasmagoria in dialectic exchange between aesthetic and political discourse.

The sublime, therefore, functions as a conduit between the delusional aspects of empire-building or breaking and the very solidity of history, which appears to suggest a continually stable hold on what the proper course of events may be. That such stability is in itself a fictive plot becomes a realization that dictates the somewhat obsessive structure of Burke's *Enquiry*, which, in its will to subdivide and categorize, becomes a catalog of the impossibility of constructing immutable categories. The text is thus fraught with a theatrical exchange between the category of sublimity and the catalog of history, with neither idiom finally achieving control over the other. Section 15 of part 1 on the *Enquiry* is subtitled "Of the effects of TRAGEDY," and points poignantly toward the epistemological confusion of this unfinished debate: "I imagine we shall be much mistaken if we attribute any considerable part of our satisfaction in tragedy to a consideration that tragedy is a deceit, and its representations no realities. The nearer it approaches the reality, and the further it removes us from all idea of fiction, the more perfect is its power. But be its power of what kind it will, it never approaches to what it represents" (*CW*, vol. 1, p. 120). Here, the failure of representation—the inefficacy, in other words, with which the sublime purports to be mimetic—claims a tragic substantiation of event above interpretation. Burke's ensuing analogy, however, dissipates rather than reinforces the greater tangibility of actual "event":

> Choose a day on which to represent the most sublime and affect-
> ing tragedy we have; appoint the most favourite actors; spare no
> costs upon the scenes and decorations; unite the greatest efforts
> of poetry, painting and music; and when you have collected your
> audience, just at the moment when their minds are erect with
> expectation, let it be reported that a state criminal of high rank is
> on the point of being executed in the adjoining square; in a mo-
> ment the emptiness of the theatre would demonstrate the
> comparative weakness of the imitative arts, and proclaim the tri-
> umph of real sympathy. (*CW*, vol. 1, p. 120)

The occurrence of "real sympathy" cannot assert the priority of historical action over aesthetic fact, but instead suggests how both modes are equally implicated in the fraught and partial knowledge granted by political spectatorship.

If the functioning of the sublime is dependent on the spectator's guilty recognition of his or her complicity in the rise and the decline of the process of empowerment, then such an acknowledgment of ethical limitation is only redoubled when the theater upon which sublimity enacts itself is the conquest of other nations. While Burke has no specific act of colonization in mind as he writes the *Enquiry*, the operation of the sublime is continually represented as parallel to the structure of colonialism, until it becomes more the property of the colonizing world than the aesthetic one. Here, Burke's peculiar use of the term "sympathy" requires redoubled attention, since it is emblematic of his unsparing understanding of the dynamic of complicity between the spectator and the event. The section "The effects of SYMPATHY in the distresses of others" clearly maps out the pattern of this exchange: "I am convinced we have a degree of delight, and that no small one, in the real misfortunes and pains of others; for to let the affection be what it will in appearance, if it does not make us shun such objects, if on the contrary it induces us to approach them, if it makes us dwell upon them, in this case I conceive we must have a delight or pleasure of some species or other in contemplating objects of this kind. . . . The prosperity of no empire, nor the grandeur of no king, can so agreeably affect in the reading, as the ruin of the state of Macedon, and the distress of its unhappy prince. Such a catastrophe touches us in history as much as the destruction of Troy does in fable" (*CW*, vol. 1, p. 118). Sympathy, in other words, is a dynamic of alienation rather than of association, in that it constitutes the empowerment of the spectator at the expense of the spectacle, unleashing an economy of gain and loss at the center of aesthetic experience.[22]

This recasting of the sympathies of spectatorship into a mode of evaluating the casualties incurred by either the spectator or the event is exemplary of Burke's obsession with the phantasmagoria of the sublime. The chiasmatic relation that he constructs between audience and event illustrates sublimity's proximity with the terror of precedence, in which to observe is inevitably to have already observed, even at the moment of an act's unfolding. Burke's famous catalog of the horrors of sublimity is thus strongly linked to a sense of temporal disarray, to a conviction that sequential derangement must necessarily attend the spectator's implication in the sublime. If a discourse of difficulty is the only idiom that will suffice to represent such derangement, then it demands to be recognized as clarity on its own territory, and resists a translation into aesthetic luminosity. For in paying such strained attention to the concept of difficulty, the *Enquiry* achieves an astonishing act of colonization in itself: it wrenches the "difficult" from its religious and scriptural associations, and instead bandies it as a political and contemporaneous term that requires a completely different teleology. Prior conceptions of difficulty, as Angus Fletcher has noted, implied "a calculated obscurity which elicits an interpretive response in the reader. The very obscurity is a source of pleasure, especially to the extent that the actual process of deciphering the exegetical content of a passage would be painfully arduous and uncertain. Obscurity stirs curiosity; the reader wants to tear the veil aside. 'The more they seem obscure through their use of figurative expressions,' says Augustine, 'the more they give pleasure when they have been made clear.' "[23] In the Burkean sublime, however, no such unveiling is necessary, for he is all too conscious of the fact that when difficulty strips, it strips into secrecy. His apprehension of the obscure keeps the narrative of obscurity intact, in order that the spectator too can locate the myth of integrity in the possible fiction of his or her invisibility.

In privileging darkness invisible over the ultimate end of translating obscurity into light, Burke adds to the category of the sublime an unreadability that is a proleptic anticipation of the productive difficulty he places at the heart of his representation of the Indian subcontinent. The colonial spectator is as implicated as the audience of sublimity in the structure of event; the former too must learn to read a narrative of obscurity as an unhinged allegory that unfolds beyond the boundaries of conceptual stability. While it takes the years of Burke's Indian obsession to consolidate this reading, the *Enquiry* clearly initiates his understanding of the irrationality of history and further suggests how much of an exception Burke's writing is to what Hayden White astutely describes as "the domestication of history effected by the suppression of the historical sublime."[24] The desublimation that White sees at work in the late eighteenth century may well be applicable to British efforts to contain the idea of the French Revolution, but it is less relevant to the colonization of the subcontinent, which is repeatedly represented as an enactment of the historical sublime. What must be repressed in the domestic imagination, in other words, is at rampant play in the rhetoric of English India, contradicting the genealogy that Hayden White traces:

> While he likened the feeling of the sublime to what the subject must feel in the presence of political majesty, Burke did not explicitly address the question of the sublime and the beautiful with respect to historical and social phenomena. . . . Viewed as a contribution to the aesthetics (or what amounts to the same thing, the psychology) of historical consciousness, Burke's *Reflections on the Revolution in France* can be seen as one of many efforts to exorcise the notion of the sublime from any apprehension of the historical process, so that the "beauty" of its proper development, which for him was given in the example of the "English constitution," could be adequately comprehended.[25]

To move from the *Enquiry* into the *Reflections* is to repeat a short circuit frequently made by readers of Burke, in which his writing on India is somehow deemed to be a detour from the canonical quality of his real thought. In the process, some of his most passionate questioning of the legality of constitutionalization is overlooked. "I must beg leave to observe, that, if we are not able to contrive some method of governing India *well*," writes Burke, "which will not of necessity become the means of governing Great Britain *ill*, a ground is laid for their eternal separation, but none for sacrificing the people of that country to our Constitution. . . . I am certain that every means effectual to preserve India from oppression is a guard to preserve the British Constitution from its worst corruption" (*CW*, vol. 2, p. 436).

Even in the *Enquiry*, Burke holds back from an aestheticizing of history, positing instead the irrationality of both aesthetic and historical event to which the concept of beauty does not hold a plea or offer any resolution. When he moves from his catalog of sublimity into a reading of the beautiful, Burke does not seek to impose a latter-day serenity on his engagement in the sublime, but performs instead a philosophical equivalent to the narrative of *Gulliver's Travels*, in which to contemplate either magnitude or diminution is equally to encounter imprisonment. What rationality is to the sublime, proportion is to the beautiful: both are terms of measurement that Burke casts under implicit or explicit dubiety, connecting his critique instead to an economy of power that links the sublime to the beautiful: "There is a wide difference between admiration and love. The sublime, which is the cause of the former, always dwells on great objects, and terrible; the latter on small ones, and pleasing; *we submit to what we admire, but we love what submits to us*" (*CW*, vol. 1, p. 192; italics added). Such a dynamic of submission is illustrative of the incipient antihumanism that adds color to Burke's reading of what aesthetic categories imply about the structure of human relation. Much as sympathy was seen to be the dominant motive behind the alacrity with which a potential spectatorship would accept an invitation to a beheading, so beauty itself is equated with a mode of imprisonment or a masochistic submission to the idea of submissiveness. The uneasiness with which Burke approaches the category of the beautiful anticipates quite precisely the later enamorment that the rhetoric of English India would evince about the idea of the exotic, in which exoticism translates into a mere power to defer a yielding that it foresees as inevitable and from which it draws its peculiar attraction. To be beautiful, in Burke's grim apprehension of the term, is potentially to be enslaved.

If the *Enquiry* fundamentally describes a dialectic of powerlessness aimed at addressing its inability to identify the locus of empowerment between the spectator and the event, or between the witnessing psyche and the fall of empire, then it rhetorically and structurally replicates such thematic concerns: its division into five parts is further subdivided into exactly one hundred subsections, making the text itself a dizzying example of the mathematical sublime. Furthermore, the *Enquiry* is self-repeating in the curious energy it exudes in relation to the disempowering difficulty and obscurity that it ascribes to the sublime, while the beautiful can evoke in the text only a lackluster description of its potential availability to imprisonment.

Beauty is more troubling to Burke than is the sublime, sending his discourse into vagaries indicative of his own fear, as author, of desiring the subject to yield completely to his control. After having firmly dislodged the category of the beautiful from its association with an Aristotelian proportion, Burke is uncertain of what to do with beauty other than imply the inherent irrationality that underlies the acquisition of its delight. Thus part 3 of the *Enquiry* devotes a catalog of subsections to a deconstruction of the inutility of proportion in an appreciation of beauty, but then can only express dismay at the diminution that it has willed upon this concept. Section 14, titled "Smoothness," opens with a lame inability to address further what beauty may be: "I do not now recall any thing beautiful that is not smooth," muses Burke, in a charming if inadvertent confession of his forgetfulness of the conifer, a tree surely more prone to beauty than to sublimity, particularly in its Himalayan setting. Even more indicative of his uneasiness with the question of how beauty may function within the provenance of power, however, is Burke's catalog of what constitutes the beautiful and the traditional symbol of peace between nations:

> The view of a beautiful bird will illustrate this observation. Here we see the head increasing insensibly to the middle, from whence it lessens gradually until it mixes with the neck; the neck loses itself in a larger swell, which continues to the middle of the body, when the whole decreases again to the tail; the tail takes a new direction; but it soon varies its new course; it blends again with the other parts; and the line is perpetually changing, above, below, upon every side. In this description I have before me the idea of a dove; it agrees very well with most conditions of beauty. (CW, vol. 1, p. 194)

The ebb and swell of this catalog lends such a flux to the condition of beauty that a reader is left somewhat apprehensive about what its ultimate shape may be, for Burke's bird seems perversely drawn to take more directions than even the most appreciative eye could tolerate. More vortex than bird, its various parts struggle against coherence into a nameable object, until the point of stress in this passage becomes less the indescribability of beauty than beauty's will to disembodiment. The centrifugal dread to which the dove moves Burke is further reinforced in the *Enquiry* when its logic moves—inevitably—from bird to beautiful woman: "Observe that part of a beautiful woman where she is perhaps the most beautiful, about the neck and breasts; the smoothness; the softness; the easy and insensible swell; the variety of surface, which is never for the smallest space the same; the deceitful maze, through which the unsteady eye slides giddily, without knowing where to fix, or whither it is carried" (CW, vol. 1, p. 194). Again, rather than proffer any serene coherence of vision, the "condition" of beauty implies an absence of control that infects both the beautiful object and the observer. An aesthetic category that purports to stability is thus transcribed into a vertiginous dynamic through which beauty is imprisoned in the sum of its parts and the spectator in an inability either to add to or subtract from such an aesthetic of uncontrol.

If Burke is, as Hayden White would argue, instrumental in the eighteenth century's aestheticizing of historical discourse, then the peculiarities of his aesthetic must be more closely read in the context of Burke's historical imagination. It would be too simple to read the *Enquiry* as a gendering of aesthetic categories, or to draw further attention to its masculinization of the sublime and concomitant feminization of beauty. What is far more interesting is Burke's rhetorical understanding of the political uses of sexuality, a conceptual moment curiously contiguous to that point at which an aesthetic reading of history recognizes its epistemological limits. The bird that Burke deems beautiful brings no olive branch into his narrative, but vexes it instead into a dilemma of spectatorship, in which to observe and list is furthermore to lose. Similarly, the feminized diminution of beauty cannot lead to the text's control of the concept, since its posture of submission—its "smoothness", its "softness"—suggests a complicated system of imprisonment that forces the text's desiring eye into a recognition of its own limitation. Like the whiteness of the whale, the beauty of the breast is designed to create orphans, forcing Burke into an acknowledgment of the text's unsteady relation to its own authority.

In keeping with the theatricality of the first section of the *Enquiry*, therefore, Burke translates the dialectic between the categories of the sublime and the beautiful into a configuration of spectator and event, granting stability neither to the act of performing nor to that of observing. While some solely aesthetic conclusions may be drawn from such a configuration, it resurfaces in Burke's later work as a crucial instrument of political understanding, or a paradigm whereby he can read the functioning of legislative power. Thomas Weiskel has suggested that "the dissociation or dualism at the core of the eighteenth-century sublime had profoundly ideological implications, and the various forms of alienation reinforced by the sublime—between the familiar and the novel, the human and the natural, the low and the high—could not be shaken until these ideological correlatives were questioned in the ferment of social revolution."[26] In Burke's case, these correlatives were to become the territory for the operation of sublimity, forcing him to read the colonial project as an equally violent clash between aggrandizement and obscurity. The anxious insistence with which the *Enquiry* privileges darkness ("all is dark, uncertain, confused, terrible, and sublime to the last degree"; *CW*, vol. 1, p. 133) is on this score proleptic, for, years before his involvement in the colonization of the subcontinent, it leads Burke into his most startling reading of the pigmentation of the sublime.

In section 15 of the fourth part of the *Enquiry*, Burke offers a telling narrative to exemplify his claims on why darkness is "terrible in its own nature" and thus in frequent attendance on the sublime. "Mr. Cheselden has given us a very curious story of a boy," writes Burke, "who had been born blind, and continued so until he was thirteen or fourteen years old; he was then couched for a cataract, by which operation he received his sight. Among many remarkable particulars that attended his first perceptions, and judgments on visual objects, Cheselden tells us, that the first time the boy saw a black object, it gave him great uneasiness; and that some time after, upon accidentally seeing a negro woman, he was struck with great horror at the sight" (*CW*, vol. 1, pp. 226–27). While the pseudoscientism of the actual tale hardly bears examination, the connection that it established cannot be overlooked: the darkness so crucial to the operation of sublimity is already racially encoded, even at such an early date as Burke's writing of the *Enquiry*. A simple correlation between sublimity and race is, however, not the issue, for what Burke is beginning to envisage is a sublime whose proportions bear a disquieting resemblance to a Conradian heart of darkness, in which aesthetic and epistemological questions are inextricably linked to the economy of historical specificity. It is a darkness, furthermore, that not only functions as a figure for the complicity of spectatorship in the delusional aspects of history, but serves as well—with sublime embarrassment—for the literalism of skin. From such a perspective, the *Enquiry* translates into a text that is politically preparatory for Burke's later writing, providing him with a brooding understanding of the anxieties of empowerment and the difficulty inherent in any attempt to categorize their structures. When Burke turns to the colonization of the Indian subcontinent, he arrives intellectually equipped with a prior reading of the significance of difficulty and a foreknowledge of its ability to construct catalogs or suggest hierarchies that are continually imploding. In assuming the responsibility of a colonial spectator with both astonishment and terror, Burke brings to the theater of Anglo-Indian history a new dynamic of guilt that comes dangerously close to articulating the untouchability of the sublime.

BURKE CONCLUDED HIS SPEECH ON FOX'S INDIA BILL WITH A CLAIM THAT HE would often repeat: his engagement in the affairs of the East India Company, and with the structure of Anglo-Indian legislative practice in general, constituted the most intense labor of his life. This work was "the fruit of much meditation, the result of the observation of near twenty years." Nor, according to Burke, were those years wasted: "For my own part, I am happy that I have lived to see this day; I feel myself overpaid for the labours of eighteen years, when, at this late period, I am able to take my share, by one humble vote, in destroying a tyranny that exists to the disgrace of this nation and the destruction of so large a part of the human species" (CW, vol. 1, p. 536). While such felicity was certainly justified by the brilliant success with which Burke would bring the House of Commons to vote for Hastings's impeachment in 1787, it is rendered ironic by his later acquittal in the House of Lords. The proceedings of the latter trial introduce a further problem, in that the failure they encapsulate is no longer merely public and legislative, but further suggests a rhetorical failure in Burke's discourse as well. As the days of the impeachment trial accumulate into years, Burke evinces an increasing inability to pursue to their horrific end the implications of a rhetoric horrified only at his own insistence. While the hysteria of Burke's indictment of Hastings has been frequently remarked, the overdetermination of such fierce indignation continues to perplex readers of the Hastings trial.[27] What act of colonial allegorizing or de-allegorizing is to be construed from the great scene of misrecognition implicit in the confrontation between Hastings and Burke?

By the time of the opening of the impeachment charges in 1786, Burke had passionately memorized his version of the narrative generated by the colonization of the subcontinent: the East India Company was both profligate and corrupt; it hid its own mismanagement behind a mercilessly extortionist policy toward indigenous populations; it thereby crippled both the dignity of the Indian nations and the potential health of the imperial project. Could his uncanny understanding of the Indian sublime, however, allow him to argue that imperialism could ever be disinfected, or would he in the cause of the latter be forced to censor his reading of the ineluctable logic of horror? It is at this moment of discursive retreat that Burke, unable to admit that his vision of colonial rapacity could never resolve itself into a myth of imperial venerability, hands over to the figure of the political sublime its new untouchability. His reading of India as a locus of sublimity remains intact—indeed, more intact than ever, since it is now untouchable—but the narrative of the horrific power of history has been curtailed, in order that Burke can impute its terror to some instrument of aberration. Such an instrument was Warren Hastings, who, by functioning as a repository of ill-doing, could simultaneously protect the colonial project from being indicted for the larger ill of which Hastings was simply a herald.

The public failure of Burke's political concerns, therefore, only weakly reflects the poignancy of that discursive collapse through which he was forced to represent Hastings as Iago to India's Othello, or the embodiment of guilt on colonialism's "great theatre [of] abuse" (CW, vol. 9, p. 348). It would be dangerous to read this embodiment as too clear-cut a moment of colonial allegorization, since it suggests rather the difficulty of allegory in the narrative of colonialism; it would be equally redundant to condemn Burke for the psychic imperatives that caused him to be disempowered by his own discourse. Encoded in the towering rage with which Burke converts Hastings into the prime mover of colonial reprehensibility is an attendant rage at the powerlessness of that spectator who cannot tolerate to witness until its end an enactment of the shared intimacy of guilt. In a century other than the eighteenth, another spectator of colonial complicity is able to articulate the complications of Burke's implicit helplessness at the sublime he had uncovered: "It would have been too dark," claims Marlow, "too dark altogether." Between the idea of colonialism and its ensuing lie is enacted the anguish of spectatorship, and, however much he was forced to retreat from his heart of darkness, Burke deserves a respectful reading of his engagement in such sublimity.

Despite his vain belief that the system of colonialism could prove self-correcting, however, Burke's representation of India during the impeachment proceedings remains powerfully committed to an understanding of the alternative civil structure of the subcontinent. If, as Bryan S. Turner has argued, the major thrust of Orientalist discourse has been to depict the Orient as though it were "all state and no society," then Burke must be credited for being one of the first voices to articulate the possibility that India comprised cultures and societies as yet unread by the West.[28] In this context, his condemnation of Hastings's exercise of a "geographical morality" is particularly telling: since Hastings's defense depended largely on a concept of Oriental despotism, the rules of which he was forced to follow, Burke's counterreading of India is a sustained critique of such eighteenth-century Orientalism. His speech on the second day of the Hastings trial obsessively questions Oriental governments' reliance on arbitrary power, insisting instead on the written legal codes against which Hastings stood in violation: "I must do justice to the East, I must assert that their morality is equal to ours, in whatever regards the duties of governors, fathers, and superiors; and I challenge the world to show in any modern European book more true morality and wisdom than is to be found in the writings of Asiatic men in high trust, and who have been counsellors to princes. If this be the true morality of Asia, as I affirm and can prove that it is, the plea founded on Mr. Hastings' geographical morality is annihilated" (CW, vol. 9, p. 476). This conflation of legal and ethical terminology causes a contemporary reader to pause, since it appears to confirm Burke's essentially conservative impulse and his concomitant desire to protect the idea of authority rather than to expose the abuses of power. The dialogue that Burke constructs between ethics and the law is, however, more complicated than such a reading would allow, and suggests how persistently problematic the question of precedence remains to the institution of colonial lawmaking.

By representing Hastings as the epitome of an "arbitrary power," Burke draws less on standard configurations of evil and good than he personifies what is indeed at the inception of colonial practice—the absence of precedence from a historical narrative that will never have recourse to the plot dictated by such a law. Instead, it is sequentially dependent on enactments of successive usurpation, with each usurping moment implying a singular and unprecedented logic. Even though Burke collapses the peculiarly disruptive quality of this narrative into the person of Warren Hastings, he still thereby supplies the colonizing imagination with a theatrically grim reading of the arbitrariness of colonial genealogy. Transfers of power, according to this reading, suggest complete ontological loss: "*He* have arbitrary power! My Lords, the East India Company have not arbitrary power to give him; the king has no arbitrary power to give him; your lordships have not; nor the Commons, nor the whole legislature. We have no arbitrary power to give, because arbitrary power is a thing which neither any man can hold nor any man can give. No man can lawfully govern himself according to his own will; much less can one man be governed by the will of another. We are all born in subjection" (*CW*, vol. 9, p. 455). The great law to which Burke continually refers is very frequently synonymous with subjection, with an acknowledgment of limitation as opposed to the invocation of a transcendental political ideal. By conceiving of Hastings as the embodiment of what was and would continue to be the narrative of colonial history in India, Burke's discourse equates the rhetorical figure of personification with acts of historical impersonation, until his very oratory becomes a secret sharer in the forms of usurpation that it wishes to delineate. It too is as sensational and unprecedented as the crimes that it catalogs; its deep nostalgia for a precolonial logic is belied by the uncanny understanding it exudes of the nature of colonialism's relation to arbitrary power. Burke knows the colonial story all too well: his form of subjection is that will which begs him—and the House of Lords—to believe it has a single author.

Eliminate Hastings, argues Burke, and colonial practice will return to the law of accountability. It will recognize the precedence of subcontinental codes of law and constitutionality, thus acting in concert with the cultural and ethical practice of a civilization whose difference is an object of Burke's passionate respect. The tyranny of such a discursive commitment to inno-

cence, however, is not simply the well-willed but misguided contribution
that Burke makes to the rhetoric of English India: its strain is operative in
each linguistic excess to which the Hastings trial moves him. For obscure
workings of sublimity darken the brightness Burke wishes to cast on some
impossibly future colonial stage, and Hastings himself disembodies into an
absent precedent that dictates Burke's vision of what colonialism will be: "It
is the nature of tyranny and rapacity never to learn moderation from the ill-
success of first oppressions; on the contrary, all oppressors, all men thinking
highly of the methods dictated by their nature, attribute the frustration of
their desire to the want of sufficient rigor. Then they redouble the efforts of
their impotent cruelty, which producing, as they ever must produce, new disappointments, they grow irritated against the objects of their rapacity; and
then rage, fury, and malice, implacable because unprovoked, recruiting and
reinforcing their avarice, their vices are no longer human" (*CW*, vol. 10, p.
83). Here, his knowledge exceeds that which Burke overtly allows himself to
know, until the excessive entropy of his catalog implicates the speaker too in
the inevitability of its logic. Despite Burke's will to contain the Indian sublime within a single human body, it proliferates with an antihuman force to
become both the difficulty and the darkness of his discourse, indicting event,
actor, and spectator with an equally disempowering zeal.

"You will be lost," Marlow tells Kurtz, "utterly lost." He then congrat-
ulates himself upon his own veracity: "One gets sometimes such a flash of
inspiration, you know. I did say the right thing, though indeed he could not
have been more irretrievably lost than he was at this very moment, when the
foundations of our intimacy were being laid—to endure—to endure—even
to the end—even beyond." Who here is the greater locus of loss: the colonial
actor, or the spectator who must—in complete understanding of its
futility—continue to tell the imperial tale? When, on the eighteenth-
century stage of colonial self-questioning, Edmund Burke denounces Warren Hastings for being lost, irretrievably lost, he points to his own anguished
intimacy with the object of his denunciation. Impersonation ends, as guilt
becomes as fluid as discourse, and its implications as untouchable as those of
the Indian sublime.

3

Reading the Trial of Warren Hastings

THE EIGHT YEARS OF HASTINGS'S IMPEACHMENT BEFORE THE HOUSE OF LORDS provided eighteenth-century England with a spectacle first of political pageantry and then of boredom. After Burke's theatrical success of bringing the Commons to vote for an impeachment, the trial of 13 February 1788 opened with as much high tension and discursive flair as the most melodramatic pamphleteer of the times could have desired. By the following year, however, the inevitability of Hastings's acquittal was enough in the journalistic air that the trial no longer commanded the intense attention granted to it during the period of 1787 to 1788, even though its proceedings were to continue to accumulate parliamentary time and paper for the next seven years. As a legal narrative, the trial is consequently of little interest in terms of its outcome or its conclusions on the politics of innocence and guilt, implying instead that other colonial questions, more significant than the indictment of one man, were under deliberation. The most fundamental of these issues involved the very nature of the legal discourse in which the trial was to be conducted: by parliamentary process, as sought by the Managers of the Prosecution, or by common law, as was the inclination of the House of Lords? From the Managers' perspective, the peculiarities of the case rendered it a language unto itself that had to be allowed to dictate its own discursive parameters; from the point of view of Lords, however, the precedence of former impeachments was now required to give way to the modernity of the law. Such a clash between political and legal codes suggests the difficulty of finding the appropriate idioms to describe the colonization of India or Hastings's possible violation of the law and, in the impeachment proceedings themselves, lends a curiously two-tiered structure to the discourse of the trial. For despite the new legalism imposed by the House of Lords, Burke adamantly refused to give up the great idiom of excess that he deemed essential to the prosecution: he maintained his indignation over the years, even when it was common knowledge that as one of the century's corpses, the trial had less to do with indicting Hastings than with illustrating the obsolescence of impeachment.

While the rhetorical exaggeration that was the hallmark of Burke's discourse was equally shared by the other Managers of the impeachment charges, the group as a whole took pains to name him author of its idiom: on the seventh day of the trial, Charles James Fox concluded his indictment of Hastings by reminding the House that "the affairs of India had long been hid in a darkness hostile to enquiry, as it was friendly to guilt;—but by the exertions of ONE MAN, these clouds had been dissipated. The ardent virtue, the sublime genius, and that glowing enthusiasm so essential to the operations of both, had, with the application of years, left them with nothing of information at present to desire."[1] The obscurity of the sublime, however, is not so simply dissipated, particularly when the excess to which the subject of India moved Burke is read as an index to his ambivalence on the colonial project. Whether or not Burke's reliance on rhetorical aggrandizement caused the failure of his impeachment effort, it certainly illustrates how his larger goal—of informing both Parliament and England at large about the representational difficulty of colonial India—was too readily subsumed into the person of Warren Hastings. For in the context of his desire to arouse some understanding of the implications of colonialism, Burke's failure was bitter, since the trial itself was regarded not as an indictment of one culture's ability to obliterate the other but as a theatrical exercise in single combat between Hastings and Burke. As P. J. Marshall concludes in his reading of the trial, "It had been a remarkable achievement on Burke's part to persuade the House of Commons and a wider public to concern themselves, even if superficially, with an Indian question on its own merits; but the price of success seems to have been disillusion with the later stages of the impeachment and apathy to India in the future."[2] The questions that the trial raises, therefore, concern the relation between an idiom of excess and concomitant ideological apathy; between legal precedence and an unprecedented subject. When Burke's surplus eloquence was enjoyed, year after year, as rhetoric alone, eighteenth-century England made tacit declaration of its awareness that morality was moribund where colonialism was concerned. There was pleasure, nevertheless, in listening to a voice that could be so loudly obsolete about the possibility of political passion.

In the summer preceding the trial at the House of Lords, Burke had presented to the House of Commons "Articles of Charge of High Crimes and Misdemeanours against Warren Hastings," alleged to have been committed during his tenure as governor-general of Bengal. The twenty-two articles make for astonishing reading, in that the unclassifiability of their discourse indicates how obsessively Burke had worked to encode an Indian obscurity into his legal indictment of Hastings. As a consequence, the charges were

both excessively long and excessively interested in breaking down the constraints of their own legalism, continually spilling over into dialogue and
narrative that muddies rather than clarifies the specificity of each accusation.
For the overwhelming detail with which Burke narrates the enactment of
Hastings's violations is designed to obliterate a belief in the graspability of its
narrative: facticity thus ironically becomes a casualty of an overabundance of
facts. Burke was of course conscious of the originality of such an approach to
the discourse of indictment: in a letter to Philip Francis, Hastings's great enemy, he justified his method by claiming, "You will see my view in the
manner of drawing the articles;—that is, not only to state the fact, but to
assign the criminality; to fix the *species* of that criminality; to mark its consequences; to anticipate the defence, and to select such circumstances as lead
to presumptions of private corrupt views."[3] The charges were to be, in other
words, a trial in themselves, a narrative that not only supplied evidence but
anticipated the counternarrative of the defence, allowing Burke to weave in
and out of legal discourse even as he performed a specifically legal act. After
the Commons had voted for impeachment, it appointed a committee to re-
write the charge, but since Burke was one of its members, few substantive
changes were made. The following February, therefore, the committee of
Managers for the impeachment took to the House of Lords charges of subcontinental proportions, a catalog of crimes so detailed in its exposition that
it came dangerously close to exceeding a criminality recognizable to the law.
Drawing instead on the diffusion of sublimity, Burke's charges defied legal
discourse to attempt to suborn them to the letter of the law.[4]

Whether or not the charges rendered Hastings impeachable, they certainly represent the first exhaustive compilation of colonial guilt to emerge
from the colonization of India. That such a guilt could be apportioned to one
man, however, left the charges dangerously vulnerable to being forgotten
even at the moment of their utterance. Had the impeachment been successful, the punishment of Hastings would have had little effect on the larger
questions of colonial culpability that impel Burke's writing on the subcontinent. Whichever way the verdict fell, Burke was destined to failure, in that
he continued to stand in too inchoate a relation to the enormity of his claims.
The exercise of "arbitrary power" for which he sought to impeach Hastings
could not be so easily expunged from the history of colonization; much of
Burke's rhetorical extravagance suggests a subterranean admission that it
was indeed too facile to assume that Hastings alone could be held responsible
for the exigencies of what it means to colonize. Ironically, both Hastings and
Burke were equally committed to the belief that India should be governed

according to the precedence of indigenous law and custom, a fact not readily evidenced by the impeachment proceedings:

> On one side, your Lordships have the prisoner declaring that the people have no laws, no rights, no usages, no distinctions of rank, no sense of honour, no property—in short, that they are nothing but a herd of slaves, to be governed by the arbitrary will of a master. On the other side, we assert that the direct contrary of this is true. And to prove our assertion . . . we have referred you to the Mahometan law, which is binding upon all, from the crowned head to the meanest subject—a law interwoven with the wisest, the most learned, and most enlightened jurisprudence that perhaps ever existed in the world. (*CW*, vol. XI, p. 219)

Hastings, in his famed preface to Charles Wilkins's 1785 translation of the *Bhagavad Gita*, makes a strikingly similar argument for the autonomy of the Indian aesthetic tradition, but how could Burke stop to acknowledge a congruence that merely confirms the inefficacy of his discourse to locate in its most horrific form the uncontainable nature of guilt?[5]

Of the arcane and multiple charges leveled against Hastings, it is evident that he was guilty of misconduct on several specific counts.[6] Misconduct, however, seems too mild a term to accommodate the human demands imposed by the office of governor-general of Bengal: despite the Regulating Act of 1773, the rapacity of the system that Hastings inherited renders absurd the possibility of a new colonial decorum. His guilt or innocence is therefore an obsolete issue even at the moment of its adjudication, for the transgressions of which Hastings was guilty conform perfectly to the extortionism upon which the East India Company was based. The lie of the impeachment proceedings is thus its failure to admit that Hastings's misdeeds were merely synecdochical of the colonial operation, that to assume that such governorship could take more palatable form was to allow Burke to have his cake of astonishment and to eat it, too. But much as Hastings needs to be released from a representation that casts him as the only begetter of colonial reprehensibility, so too must Burke be exonerated from the charge of moral greed with which his indictment of Hastings has been recently read.[7] His speeches during the impeachment trial indicate an uncanny awareness of the issues at stake that somehow precede and exceed Hastings, so that his focus on the single profile does not preclude comprehension of the more generalized power of that coin upon which such a face could be stamped.

We dread the operation of money. Do we not know that there are many men who wait, and who indeed hardly wait, the event of this prosecution, to let loose all the corrupt wealth of India, acquired by the oppression of that country, for the corruption of all the liberties of this, and to fill the Parliament with men who are now the object of its indignation? To-day the Commons of Great Britain prosecute the delinquents of India: to-morrow the delinquents of India may be the Commons of Great Britain. We know, I say, and feel the force of money; and now we call upon your Lordships for justice in this cause of money. (CW, vol. 10, p. 450)

The returning Indian "nabobs," whose social aggression Samuel Foote's play *The Nabob* was to satirize, are not here under any sustained attack: rather, Burke recognizes that the colonial coin should be held in more ethical dread than the face imprinted on it.

To read the impeachment proceedings is thus to confront less a trial than a documentation of the anxieties of oppression, where both the prisoner and the prosecutors are equally implicated in the inascribability of colonial guilt. For eighteenth-century England, however, the theatricality of the event overshadowed the historical and political questions that it raised, causing the popular imagination to believe that it observed a spectacle with a definite end. Its opening was indeed dramatic: the twenty Managers of the impeachment included Burke, Charles James Fox, Charles Grey, and Richard Brinsley Sheridan, whose speech on the Begums Charge in the House of Commons Byron later described as "the very best Oration (the famous Begum Speech) ever conceived or heard in this country."[8] Oratorical expectations were consequently high, and, as Fanny Burney's vivid account of the opening weeks testifies, the audience was not disappointed.[9] In keeping with the *Enquiry*'s definition of the functioning of "real sympathy," the impeachment at Westminster Hall became the most spectacular stage in London: as one of the Managers, Gilbert Elliot, described it, "[The audience] will have to mob it at the door till nine, when the doors open, and then there will be a rush as there is at the pit of the playhouse when Garrick plays King Lear. . . . The ladies are dressed and mobbing it in the Palace Yard by six or half after six, and they sit from nine till twelve before the business begins. . . . Some people and, I believe, even women—I mean ladies—have slept at the coffeehouses adjoining Westminster Hall, that they may be sure of getting to the door in time."[10] On 3 June 1788, when Sheridan was scheduled to speak on the Begums Charge, tickets for entry were being sold for as

much as fifty guineas: Sheridan spoke for four days, at the conclusion of
which he swooned into Burke's arms. "I believe there were few dry eyes in
the assembly," wrote Gilbert Elliot, "and as for myself, I never remembered
to have cried so heartily and copiously on any public occasion."[11] In the first
year of the trial sympathy was working well, according to Burke's conviction
that "we have a degree of delight, and that no small one, in the real misfortunes and pains of others."

Eloquence and legal discourse, however, are not always identical, and in
many instances the impeachment charges were presented to the House of
Lords in a rhetoric more appealing to the public audience than to the adjudicating body. The new legalism of that body was less sympathetic to the
Managers' theatrical talents, demonstrating its different and perhaps more
realistic assessment of the colonial stakes at hand. For if Burke's rhetoric
were followed to its logical conclusion, the trial would not end with the impeachment of Hastings alone but could further threaten the future of the East
India Company, which was not an eventuality that even the Managers would
have willingly envisaged. When, on the second day of the trial, Burke offers
the following reading of Hastings's abuse of the concept of Oriental despotism, his conclusions are equally applicable to the economic despotism of
the Company itself:

> Despotism does not in the smallest degree abrogate, alter,
> or lessen any one duty of any one relation of life, or weaken the
> force or obligation of any one engagement or conduct what-
> soever. Despotism, if it means anything that is at all defensible,
> means a mode of government bound by no written rules, and co-
> erced by no controlling magistracies or well-settled orders in the
> state. . . . The moment a sovereign removes [such] security and
> protection from his subjects, and declares that he is everything
> and they nothing, when he declares that no contract he makes
> with them can or ought to bind him, he then declares war upon
> them: he is no longer sovereign; they are no longer subjects.
> (CW, vol. 9, p. 458)

That the Company had in effect declared such a war has been exhaustively
demonstrated in contemporary studies of its policies, but even in the absence
of postcolonial hindsight, Burke's discourse is in itself dangerously close to a
similar indictment. His insistence on precedence as the only available logic
for a colonial narrative is scrupulously conscious of the two precedents at war
on the territory of India, and insists with a stubborn ire that British precedence must be subordinated to the prior laws of the subcontinent. On this

score of course Burke draws back from the conclusions implicit in his rhetoric: the battle of two systems of precedence suggests an inevitable collapse into unprecedence, in which laws would remain unwritten to accommodate the modernized despotism represented by the new orality of colonial practice. [12]

The charges of "High Crimes and Misdemeanours" that the Managers brought to the House of Lords are thus fraught with Burke's ambivalence toward the colonial project, which he wishes to read first as a bluff mercantilism not in itself inherently reprehensible and then as a scene of phantasmagoric horror, with Hastings functioning as trope for political ill of every color. In their eight-year litany of such uncontainable evil, the Managers wove together not merely a catalog of the misdeeds of one man, but rather a fabric of colonial anxiety: as such, despite the sentimentality and extravagance of their rhetoric, they remained loyal to Burke's impelling desire to articulate a political sublimity even when it was destined for defeat. Their legal failure to impeach Hastings is thus illustrative of an essential alegality in colonial discourse, in that neither the preexisting law of Britain nor those of the subcontinent could supply a precedence against which to measure the illegality of both Hastings's and the Company's actions. The imperial precedence could no longer apply, for in the Managers' fond imaginations, imperialism was something other than an economic agreement in which the merchants grew hungry for more. In their insistence on maintaining an autonomous discourse of indictment, the Managers of the impeachment metaphorically convey Burke's implicit fear that colonialism was a larger abstraction than he had anticipated, not locatable in either the person of Hastings or the institution of the East India Company. They sought impeachment in a manner that even the last decades of the eighteenth century deemed outdated, but encoded in this desire is no anachronistic attempt to return colonial questions to a precolonial idiom: instead, the Managers were faced with the singular responsibility of articulating charges for which no language was ready.

When the failure of the impeachment charges is assessed, the trial of Warren Hastings is most typically discussed in terms of his acquittal, with its rhetorical achievement being confined to the Managers' most famed flights of eloquence, such as Burke's opening denouncement or Sheridan's delivery of the Begums Charge. As the stage upon which the rhetoric of English India received its first highly public articulation, however, the trial assumes a discursive significance far greater than its literal conclusion. In insisting that impeachment constituted a discourse unto itself, Burke simultaneously dem onstrated that colonialism already exceeded traditional methods through which guilt can be attributed to one man, and further forced the law to confront its own radical obsolescence. "There can be only one reason for regretting the victory of legal orthodoxy in Hastings' trial," concludes P. J. Marshall. "As their own experience in obtaining evidence showed, the Managers had not exaggerated the difficulties in securing convictions for offences committed in India, which had given the Company's servants virtual immunity in the past. A serious attempt to prosecute such offences perhaps deserved some latitude. But the Managers had made no real attempt to overcome the difficulties which faced them, and in their drafting of the articles had in fact added fresh difficulties."[13] On legal grounds, Burke's representation of colonial obscurity must indeed be judged a failure, but his insistence on converting the trial into a reading of colonialism's inherent difficulty requires another order of assessment.

If the eventual acquittal of Warren Hastings was evident from the second year of the impeachment proceedings until the trial's conclusion, then it is equally evident that the Managers were working for something other than simple prosecution: they were dramatizing the limitations of impeachment, thereby exposing how completely the power of the merchant was immune from the law of the state. The intransigence of their claims may well have been a tactical error in the eyes of law, yet it is further evidence of the bravery with which Burke sought to address the widest possible audience to share his increasing horror at the spectacle of colonial guilt. By bringing the British Parliament to conclude that impeachment itself was now outmoded, the Hastings trial performed a symbolic depersonification of responsibility that illustrates the eighteenth-century's growing realization that colonialism required to be judged as a system rather than as a set of misdeeds. Burke overallegorized Hastings to the point where his discourse was forced to become antiallegorical, demonstrating how the subject of colonial difficulty declared itself a sublimity that could not be translated into a less obscure mode. Returning to the dynamic of spectatorship, Burke converted the legal space of the trial into a rhetorical arena that was designed to implicate each member of its audience in its catalog of the Indian sublime. That the impeachment failed on a literal level does not preclude the possibility of its wider symbolic success: it thus becomes necessary to read more closely what the trial signified to the popular imagination of the times.

THE ANONYMOUS *HISTORY OF THE TRIAL OF WARREN HASTINGS* WAS PUBLISHED in 1796, and consists both of a compilation of newspaper reports and of editorial annotations. Its preface clearly indicates complete sympathy with Hastings, of whom a brief memoir is appended: "Such is Mr. HASTINGS; whom neither innocence, nor virtue, nor talents, nor complete and brilliant success in the most arduous as well as important enterprize, was able to save from a Prosecution not more surprizing in its origin than wonderful in its conduct; which, when we reflect on the spirit that dictated, perplexed, and protracted it, may be called, in the emphatic language of the Sacred Scripture, a FIERY TRIAL; and of which it may be remarked, that never was a Trial so long protracted, or so completely triumphant over such a combination of learning, ability and political power." Hastings is humanized in order that Burke may be dehumanized into a vexing "spirit" who keeps the trial in its state of flux, which is in itself an astute reading of Burke's role as the discursive force that set legality in confrontation with the sublime.

Such a disembodiment is further emphasized by the "Plan of the High Court of Parliament" supplied by the text, which maps out in graphic detail the seating arrangements for the trial at Westminster (fig. 1). This floor plan is a less than innocent illustration of the hierarchies of power at work in the impeachment, providing a striking image both of the order of the court and its potential dissolution: directly following the passage into the House of Lords is the seat of the lord chancellor, flanked by the royal and the princes' boxes. The peerage and the judiciary occupy center stage, while the wings of the court construct a choric space for such groups as the ticketed audience and the members of the House of Commons. Facing the lord chancellor and the peers is the prisoner, and in identifying his place, the geometric grid of the *History*'s plan takes recourse to an alternative mode of representation. Breaking down its cartographic decorum, the plan includes a small and be-wigged figure in the space where the prisoner is to stand. This sudden intrusion of realism throws askew the plan's intention of appearing to be an ordinary visual aid to the structure of the trial: instead, the reader is de-manded to confront the conflict of representational codes generated by the impeachment, where the violence of the prosecuting body and its adjudicat-ing audience is given a symbolic emptiness, most fitly imaged by a taut series of lines. The object of impeachment, however, must appear on the page as an actual body, suggesting to the popular reader that the strain of colonial re-sponsibility both resides in and eludes such a depiction of Hastings's humanity.

The *History* is thus a more symbolically complicated document than it first appears, mapping out not merely the course of the Hastings trial but more crucially the problem of its political and rhetorical ambivalence. By

Figure 1. Plan of the High Court of Parliament. Courtesy of the Department of Special Collections, University of Chicago Libraries.

supplying both a narrative of the proceedings and a commentary on it, the work is an index of the dialogue engendered by the impeachment in the popular imagination. While such an exchange may be read as a sentimentalization of the sublime in its focus on the exoneration of Warren Hastings, the narrative itself is more self-questioning than its own ostensible resolution will admit. As justification for its obsession with the impeachment, the preface claims that "it is not either as a gratification of Curiosity, a directory to lawyers, a source of information to Historians, and of instruction to Politicians and the Executive Government in all its branches, that this TRIAL is chiefly interesting—it possesses an interest of a kind still more noble and affecting. In a moral view, it is interesting to all men, and all ages, to whom a good man struggling with adversity can never be an object of indifference." Despite the morality play effect that the preface ascribes to the trial, however, its reading of the actual proceedings offers a more sophisticated understanding of the structure of political narrative. Working to conceal the irrationality of "unaccountable power" with an essentially social discourse, the *History* demonstrates its affinity with the brooding questions Burke continued to raise about the parameters of political guilt. It consequently exemplifies a generic flexibility similar to that most dramatically manipulated by Burke when he first chose to address the issue of colonization in the idiom of the sublime: the *History* is simultaneously an attempt to make a story of the law, to stage a theatrical engagement in the process of legal dialogue, and to offer a choric commentary on the workings of colonial power.

The choric quality of the text is supplied by the footnoted annotations to each day of the trial's proceedings, with the notes occasionally attempting to gossip in popular fashion about the attendant details of the trial, and more frequently evincing attitudes of astonishment on some powerful moment of conflict or exchange. In the opening note, a chorus of female characters is ushered in to establish the high theater of the trial: "Previous to their Lordships approach to the Hall, about eleven o'clock, her Majesty, with the Princesses Elizabeth, Augusta and Mary, made their appearance in the Duke of Newcastle's gallery. Her Majesty was dressed in a fawn-coloured satin, her head-dress plain, with a very slender sprinkling of diamonds. The Royal box was graced with the Duchess of Gloucester and the young prince. The ladies were all in morning dresses; a few with feathers and variegated flowers in their head-dress, but nothing so remarkable as to attract public attention" (*HTH*, vol. 1, p. 1). While such details are indeed the stuff through which contemporary newspaper reporting attempted to humanize the portentous issues of the deliberation, the *History*'s literariness calls attention to the strategic placing of women in its narrative: they enter as the picturesque audience to the theater of sublimity, but their demeanor cannot be allowed to interrupt the real drama of desire at hand, or the deathly erotics enacted in the battle between Burke and Hastings.

For women, after all, were to supply Burke with one of his most powerful rhetorical weapons against Hastings, particularly in his opening speeches at the trial. Lurid descriptions of the physical tortures performed by Hastings's minions make such speeches disturbing reading, as they concentrate colonial practice into a symbolic body available to punishments both highly inventive and furthermore impossible to visualize:

> The treatment of females could not be described:— dragged forth from the inmost recesses of their houses, which the religion of the country had made so many sanctuaries, they were exposed naked to public view; the virgins were carried to the Court of Justice, where they might naturally have looked for protection; but now they looked for it in vain; for in the face of the Ministers of Justice, in the face of the spectators, in the face of the sun, those tender and modest virgins were brutally violated. The only difference between their treatment and that of their mothers was, that the former were dishonoured in the face of day, the latter in the gloomy recesses of their dungeons. Other females had the nipples of their breasts put in a cleft bamboo, and torn off. What modesty in all nations most carefully conceals, this monster revealed to view, and consumed by slow fires. . . . Here Mr. Burke dropped his head upon his hands a few minutes; but having recovered himself, said, that the fathers and husbands of the hapless females were the most harmless and industrious set of men. Content with scarcely sufficient support of nature, they gave almost the whole produce of their labour to the East-India Company: those hands which had been broken by persons under the Company's authority, produced to all England the comforts of their morning and evening tea. (*HTH*, vol. 1, pp. 7–8)

In this extraordinary catalog, Burke first gives colonialism a body and then strips it; subjects it to rape in a court of law; damages it further in sundry fashions, and then proceeds to collapse it into the pathos of a cup of tea in England. A very dangerous pattern of domestication is established here, for the female body is ushered in only to be transmuted into a figure for the damage Burke wishes on Hastings's political credibility.

The narrator of the *History* itself, however, is seduced by the wounds on Burke's female bodies. "In this part of the speech," the annotation reads,

"Mr. Burke's descriptions were more vivid—more harrowing—and more horrific—than human utterance on either fact or fancy, perhaps, ever formed before. The agitation of most people was apparent—and Mrs. Sheridan was so overpowered, that she fainted. On the subject of the Ministers of these infernal enormities, he broke out with the finest animation!" (*HTH*, vol. 1, pp. 7–8). Here, the *History* unwittingly replicates that strategy of sexual sensationalism through which Burke evokes rape as a figure for colonial practice in order to render it analogous to a rhetoric of unspeakability. Not only is the unspeakable a useful conduit into the darkness and obscurity of sublimity, but it further diverts attention from the discursive homoeroticism that characterizes the struggle between Hastings and Burke. For the latter's will to violate the former governor-general cannot be read simply as a literal example of the nature of Burke's obsessions, and presents itself instead as the formation of a paradigm of considerable colonial significance. When the colonial dynamic is metaphorically represented as a violated female body that can be mourned over with sentimentality's greatest excess, its rape is less an event than a deflection from a contemplation of male embattlement, the figure of which more authentically dictates the boundaries of colonial power. No agonistic struggle impels such embattlement, which cannot make the imperial gesture of claiming another man's power for his own: instead, it invents an arena for transfers of power that must always take place offstage, complicating for its antagonists—caught in the throes of a colonial intimacy—a sense of the spoils for which they fight.

When the *History* demonstrates its avid interest for the bodily harm cataloged by Burke's opening speeches, it offers to the popular imagination both the sensational detail necessary to the sensibility of eighteenth-century England and a more inchoate acknowledgment of the sexual metaphorics implicit in the Hastings trial. Even when the narrator attempts to maintain a consistent sympathy for Hastings, his engagement in Burke's rhetoric demonstrates a complicity in the guilt of spectatorship shared equally by the entire audience of the trial. As Fanny Burney—another firm believer in Hastings's innocence—records in her diary, to be witness to such high drama was to pay an exacting psychic price: "[Mr. Hastings] turned about and looked up; pale looked his face—pale, ill, altered. I was much affected by the sight of that dreadful harass which was written on his countenance. . . . I felt shocked, too, shocked and ashamed, to be seen by him in that place. I had wished to be present from an earnest interest in the business, joined to a firm confidence in his powers of defence; but *his* eyes were not those I wished to meet in Westminster Hall."[14] Later, after listening to Burke deliver his mighty denunciations, Burney again describes her inability to look at the prosecutor: "In a minute, however, Mr. Burke himself saw me, and bowed with the most marked civility of manner; my courtesy was the must ungrateful, distant, and cold; I could not do otherwise; so hurt I felt to see him the head of such a cause, so impossible I found it to utter one word of admiration whose nobleness was so disgraced by its tenour, and so conscious was I the whole time that at such a moment to say nothing must seem almost an affront, that I hardly knew which way to look, or what to do with myself."[15] Here, her difficulty is no mere gentility, but points to the colonial spectator's implication in a circuit of guilt far too amorphous to be contained in the body of one man. To be unable to look at either the object of prosecution or the prosecutor himself is to record a moment in which the colonial gaze is forced to retreat into blindness: such complicated acts of unseeing that mark both Burney's and the *History*'s narratives of the trial are testaments to their guilty recognition of the intimacies of colonial violation. Even as Burke represents India as a hapless virgin despoiled at the will of British malignancy, his audience knows that a more accurate representation of colonialism would examine the shared responsibility that obtains between Hastings and Burke.

Burke concluded his opening speeches on 19 February 1788, the sixth day of the impeachment proceedings. The *History*'s narrative is at pains to convey the power of this rhetorical moment, and replicates Burke's discourse of excess without commentary on its tendency to exceed the language of the law. Instead, the speech is quoted as high theater of such eloquence that it has a nearly disempowering effect on its audience:

> "I charge (cried he) Warren Hastings, in the name of the Commons of England, here assembled, with High Crimes and Misdemeanours!—I charge him with Fraud, Abuse, Treachery, and Robbery!—I charge him with cruelties unheard-of, and Devastations almost without a name!—I charge him with having scarcely left in India—what will prove Satisfaction for his guilt!"
>
> "And now, (added he, in language which faintly hearing, we almost tremble to convey) and now, (added he) I address myself to this Assembly, with the most perfect reliance on the justice of this High Court. . . . I impeach, therefore, Warren Hastings, in the name of our Holy Religion, which he has disgraced.—I impeach him in the name of the English Constitution, which he has violated and broken.—I impeach him in the name, and by the best rights of Human Nature, which he has stabbed to the heart. And I conjure this High and Sacred Court to let not these pleadings be heard in vain!" (*HTH*, vol. 1, pp. 8–9)

The theatricality of such a catalog notwithstanding, its rhetoric is most crucially self-disempowering, escaping the confines of a criminality that can be attached to specific acts. Instead, its zeal for "Devastations almost without a name" imbue the accusations with an unspeakability that both dismantles the particularity of each charge and leaves the orator lost in the claustrophobia of the sublime. Neither can Burke's concluding personification of "Human Nature" lend any coherence to the catalog, for, as the actual drafting of the charges had revealed, the enactment of colonial criminality had proven the obsolescence of Burke's commitment to the idea of "natural law." When he accuses Hastings of having "stabbed to the heart" the rights of human nature, Burke rhetorically performs a similar act of slaughter; in that he unwittingly displays the redundance of such a figure to the details of colonial discourse.

The narrator of the *History*, however, is unprepared to examine the incipient posthumanism of Burke's political passion. While the popular imagination remains aligned to Hastings, it is still prepared to serve as a generous audience to Burke's eloquence, even when it cannot recognize the implications of his rhetoric. The more radical such references, the more lost they must be in an admiration of their power to move. Burke thus becomes the rhetorical reference point for all the ensuing oratory of the trial; no speaker takes on the stage without being judged by the litmus test of Burke's sublimity. When Charles Fox succeeds Burke to deliver the Benares Charge, his speech elicits the inevitable comparison: "For individual passages, separable from their novelty, or their original importance, in idea or diction, Mr. Burke is the mighty master. This speech of Mr. Fox was not so distinguished. It abounded, however, in distinctions of its own kind, of which the best was vehemence; the worst, unnecessary repetition of preliminary words. The SARCASTIC REFERENCE to opinions in another place, was very artfully conveyed. . . . The short mention of Mr. Burke found ready reception with all who heard it:—'If we are no longer in shameful ignorance of India; if India no longer makes us blush in the eyes of Europe; let us know and feel our OBLIGATIONS to HIM—whose admirable resources of opinion and affection—whose untiring toil, sublime genius, and high-aspiring honour, raise him up conspicuous among the most beneficent Worthies of Mankind' " (*HTH*, vol. 1, p. 17). Such instant memorialization, however, can have deathly effects, in that it elevates to embalm: the rhetorical overexposure of the opening year of the trial unconsciously tolls a dirge for its own discourse, suggesting that its energies would be as short-lived as the trial long. In popular readings, Burke was already a monument six months into the trial; in the ensuing years, he would be increasingly regarded as a relic of his own rage, while his proleptic understanding of colonial difficulty would be put away unread.

After Burke's opening oration, Sheridan's speech on the Begums Charge was generally judged to be the rhetorical high point of the trial. From this point on, according to Macaulay, "The great displays of rhetoric were over. . . . There remained examinations and cross-examinations. There remained statements of accounts. There remained the reading of papers, filled with words unintelligible to English ears, with lacs and crores, zemindars and aumils, sunnuds and perwannahs, jaghires and nuzzurs."[16] While Macaulay's essay on Hastings tends to make too seamless a narrative of the trial, it represents the contemporary view of the rapidity with which Burke was broken down by his own discourse: after the great brotherhood of the opening year, the Managers fell apart over their sharp divergences concerning the French Revolution and Burke was left in rhetorical isolation. "Conscious of great powers and great virtues," writes Macaulay, "he found himself, in age and poverty, a mark for the hatred of a perfidious court and a deluded people. In Parliament his eloquence was out of date. A young generation, which knew him not, had filled the House."[17] Seeking to plot out a similar collapse, the *History* too focuses its latter sections on Burke's excess rather than his eloquence, appending to part 7 a catalog of Burke's more colorful accusations against Hastings: "He has gorged his *ravenous maw* with an allowance of 200£ a day. He is not satisfied *without sucking the blood* of 1400 nobles. He is never *corrupt* without he is *cruel*. He never *dines without creating a famine.* He feeds on the *indigent,* the *decaying,* and the *ruined . . .* not like the generous eagle, who feeds upon a *living, reluctant, equal prey:* No, he is like the *ravenous vulture,* who feeds upon the *dead. . . .* Mr. Hastings feasts in the dark alone; *like a wild beast he groans in a corner over the dead and dying . . . .* He comes as a *heavy calamity* to the nation, as we say a country is visited by *famine* and *pestilence"* (*HTH,* vol. 7, pp. 152–53). Rather than be credited with the formation of an novel idiom powerful enough to take on the gratuitous violence of colonialism, Burke in the eyes of the popular imagination is an angry anachronism already outmoded in his own day.

If Burke's role in the Hastings trial is generally read as a humanism driven to the end of its tether, such a reading in itself begs a further question: in the context of political discourse, what were to the orator the uses of excess? Why did he need to address an issue of high novelty in an idiom deemed outdated both by the legal and popular views of the times? Here, the energy of obsolescence requires closer attention, for in insisting that the language of the past was the only appropriate mode of addressing the future, Burke does not offer an ineffectual discourse, but a strategy through which he can with violence disrupt the continuities of historical and political narrative. To be obsolete is therefore to belong to that era of colonial time in which the obsolescence of humanistic discourse is an openly acknowledged fact, when the orator need no longer invent the hideousness of Hastings in order to construct a catalog of colonial excess. Encoded in the hysteria of Burke's attack on Hastings is a secret consciousness that colonialism could not but generate a fundamentally hysteric discourse, or a language unable to locate its relation to the politics of cultural fear. The ravening beast that Burke makes of Hastings is thus a figurative recognition of the former's greater fear—his sense that he would be unable to chart the extremity of colonial excessiveness. As Hastings descends, rung by tropological rung, Burke's great chain of being, his descent signifies the dismantling of the chain rather than the person. It leaves Burke in contemplation of a decayed sublime, one more closely aligned to death than any he had previously regarded.

In nineteenth-century rereadings of the Hastings trial, Burke's hysteria is stressed less than his voluminous knowledge of the subcontinent. Macaulay's paradigmatic evaluation of his labor singles out Burke's "industry" and his "sensibility" for particular praise:

> He had studied the history, the laws, and the usages of the East with an industry such as is seldom found united to so much genius and so much sensibility. Others have perhaps been equally labourious, and have collected an equal mass of materials. But the manner in which Burke brought his higher powers of intellect to work on statements of facts, and on tables of figures, was peculiar to himself. In every part of those huge bales of Indian information which repelled all other readers, his mind, at once philosophical and poetical, found something to instruct or to delight.[18]

Burke's engagement with India is here aestheticized to omit his more horrific realizations of what the colonization of the subcontinent would entail, much as his reliance on the disturbing power of excess is read as a sign of imaginative energy. "His reason analysed and digested those vast and shapeless masses," claims Macaulay, "His imagination animated and coloured them. Out of darkness, and dullness, and confusion, he formed a multitude of ingenious and vivid pictures. He had, in the highest degree, that noble faculty whereby man is able to live in the past and in the future, in the distant and in the unreal. India and its inhabitants were not to him, as to most Englishmen, mere names and abstractions, but a real country and a real people."[19] Despite his perceptive recognition of Burke's ability "to live in the past and in the future," Macaulay's tendency is to recast Burke as an animating spirit embuing the obscurity of India with its shaping power, and to ignore Burke's contrary aim of keeping the obscurity of the subcontinent intact. To explain away the difficult would be to obliterate his keen sense of the alternative social and political structures represented by India: Burke was never impelled to take the "unreal" and convert it into "vivid pictures," but instead fiercely insisted on the prior reality of a place that resisted translation into Western images.

As the author of the "Minute on Indian Education," however, Macaulay had his own ambivalences toward the obscurity of India, many of which are apparent in his need to turn Burke's sublime into the picturesque. This influential conversion still colors such contemporary interpretations of the Hastings trial as David Musselwhite's, whose reading of Burke's "Orientalism" relies heavily on Macaulay's more fanciful passages, allowing Musselwhite to conclude: "Burke's 'India' was a magnificent imaginative achievement. No one has more glowingly appreciated it than Macaulay. . . . Macaulay knew India, of course, and we might take the foregoing [passage] as his testimony to the veracity of Burke's image of India, but what it is more important to realize is that here Macaulay's India is precisely that romantic and exotic India that Burke had done so much to construct."[20] Rather than discriminate between Macaulay's superimposition of a picturesque India on the dynamic of Burke's Indian sublime, Musselwhite accepts this nineteenth-century misreading of Burke in order to study the Hastings trial as an Orientalist paradigm, with the Managers functioning as the cultural villains. Headed by Burke, the Managers seek to represent the East in the discourse of the West; to judge it by their own systems of value; to make fictional characters out of its people: "The effect of all these strategies is to render India radically 'different' while at the same time making it readily imaginable. The Orient has to be, as Said puts it, 'Orientalized'. . . . Paradoxically, what can be given a high degree of imaginative coherence becomes, for that very reason, wholly alien, unmediated—one of the consistent problems of the trial was that of interpretation: how does one interpret the interpretation?"[21] Such an alteritist reading fails to acknowledge how much unimaginability Burke willed on his representations of India, and how little the trial was ultimately concerned with a battle between East and West. If the impeachment of Hastings is indeed a crucial site for the study of cultural interpretation in the late eighteenth century, then some self-reflexivity must also be allowed to the Managers' discourse: however obsessive became Burke's idiom of magnification, its impulse was less to Orientalize than to exemplify his passionate apprehension of the failures of colonial interpretation.

In demonstrating the temporal invalidity of both impeachment and of the urge to locate colonial responsibility in a single figure, the Hastings trial represents that theater upon which the rhetoric of English India loses a body to gain a language. However much Burke's insistence on the difficulty of the Indian question was repressed in the popular colonial imagination, it remains as a hidden anxiety even in the colonialist complacencies that dominate the nineteenth century. When James Mill passes judgment on the trial in his *History of British India,* his final assessment of Burke is cannily ungenerous: "[Mr. Burke] neither stretched his eye to the whole of the subject, nor did he carry its vision to the bottom. He was afraid. He was not a man to explore a new and dangerous path without associates. Edmund Burke lived upon applause—upon the applause of the men who were able to set a fashion; and the applause of such men was not to be hoped for by him who should expose to the foundation the iniquities of the juridical system."[22] Burke was indeed afraid, but his fear was one in which James Mill would have done well to collaborate, as it anticipated the excesses upon which the colonization of India would continue to be based. When Burke is "afraid" of the inefficacy of colonial law he does not stop to tremble, but proceeds to articulate a damning catalog of its consequences, thereby linking the idiom of colonial fear to the vertiginous terror of sublimity. Mill, however, cannot confront the implications of such a linkage, which would further force him into an examination of his own Indian anxiety; he therefore chooses to conclude that Burkean fear operates beyond the realm of the ethical: "Mr. Burke had also worked himself into an artificial admiration of the bare fact of existence; especially ancient existence. Every thing was to be protected; not, because it was good, but, because it existed. Evil, to render itself an object of reverence in his eye, required only to be realized."[23] Considering the years of discursive energy Burke had expended in reverencing Hastings, it is clear that Mill cannot afford to read accurately the political disruptiveness of the Hastings trial, nor its hidden impact on his own historiography.

Both from the perspective of its contemporary impact and from that of the later readings it elicited, the trial of Warren Hastings is thus always more loaded than a mere legal happening, continually implying that its most significant influence occurs troublingly elsewhere, and even there, offstage. However readily eighteenth-century England seemed to bury such a trial on its imperial imagination, the impeachment was to make one literal return and, in a complex act of cultural barter, pay back to the theater what it had borrowed of its mode. For Sheridan, famed orator of the Begums Charge, would four years after Hastings's acquittal return to the idiom that had so fraught Westminster Hall: centerpiece, in 1799, not of the Managers of impeachment but of the Drury Lane.

RICHARD BRINSLEY SHERIDAN'S INVOLVEMENT IN THE IMPEACHMENT PROCEEDings suggests a rhetorical register other than that of Edmund Burke. Known to have expressed as early as 1788 the endearing wish that "Hastings would run away and Burke after him,"[24] Sheridan's relation to the trial lacked the intensity of Burke's tragic embattlement. Instead, as playwright he was able to internalize the theatricality of the proceedings and, after the reception of his Begums speech, realize that spectacular success deserves repetition. When *Pizarro, A Tragedy* opened in 1799, it was immediately judged a complete anomaly in Sheridan's career: why had the author of *The School for Scandal* and *The Critic* chosen the lugubrious mode of political melodrama, and a subject so distant as the Spanish oppression of the Incas in Peru? The play was consequently interpreted as a piece of Whig oratory, an allegory for Sheridan's views on the threat of a French invasion, while the contiguities between its oratory and that of the Begums speech were frequently remarked: when William Pitt was asked his opinion of *Pizarro*, he is reputed to have replied, "If you mean what Sheridan has written, there is nothing new in it, for I heard it all long ago at Hastings's trial."[25] As a text, however, *Pizarro* is too easily dismissed at best as an act of rhetorical self-borrowing or at worst as an exercise of sensationalist propaganda, for Sheridan's accomplishment suggests disturbingly novel implications. By collapsing colonial space into melodramatic space, *Pizarro* dramatizes a somber realization of the inefficacy of discourse to halt colonial logic: henceforth, dialogue—the substance of Sheridan's former plays—would be subordinated to machinery, to the mechanizing ability of the theater to produce more and more spectacular effects. If the play does indeed essentialize the Hastings trial, it demonstrates that even the excessive language of melodrama must be deemed peripheral to the brute force of side effects. As a rewriting of the trial, *Pizarro* represents a retrospective acknowledgment of the naivete of eloquence within a colonial framework, even as it pays a final compliment to the eloquent Begums Charges and a more hidden compliment to the futile sublimity of Burke.

As the black sheep of Sheridan's dramatic works, *Pizarro* continues to receive scant critical attention, despite its considerable opening success and subsequent influence on the shape of British drama in the nineteenth century.[26] But to read a play of such loaded political and dramaturgical consequences solely for its literary merits is to misapprehend its status as a cultural artifact. Sheridan's last play is on a literal level a politically significant document, in that it disseminates the colonial guilt surrounding a trial whose implications were too soon repressed, converting them into a spectacle hugely to be enjoyed for the next hundred years. More significantly, however, *Pizarro* represents a dramaturgical decision through which Sheridan forced the English theater to become a stage for the enactment of the mechanization of power. From *Pizarro* on, theatergoers would watch contemporary drama not for poetics alone, but also for its cumbersome enactment of illusion: for bridges to break down, for castles to collapse, for monstrosities to descend from the heavens.[27] This conversion of theatrical power into the sum of its effects is of course too overdetermined to be attributed simply to Sheridan, but his metaphorization of the Hastings trial plays a crucial part in such a shift in theatrical sensibility. Much as the proceedings unfolded to indicate the outdatedness of impeachment, or the proliferating impersonality of colonial responsibility, so *Pizarro* transfers dramaturgical attention from the actors to the enactment of political spectacle. In so doing, the play curiously suggests that as a language melodrama is insufficient in its extravagance, requiring literalized structural appendages to illustrate the emptiness of its power.

Genealogically speaking, *Pizarro* has a complicated history: Sheridan's play is an adaptation from an English translation of August von Kotzebue's *Die Spanier in Peru*, which is in turn derived from Jean-François Marmontel's historical romance, *Les Incas, ou la destruction de l'empire du Pérou*. Given such hybridity, readers of Sheridan have tended to dismiss the play as a latter-day collaboration with German theatrical sensationalism and consequently as an aberration to his contribution to the English stage. The translated quality of the play, however, adds to its interpretative interest, as it represents an aesthetic corollary of Sheridan's belief in the necessary interpolations that colonialism implies. By taking and reshaping an already familiar text, Sheridan draws attention to the additional familiarity of his work: its congruence with the trial of Warren Hastings. Hastings returns as the implacable Pizarro, wreaking vengeance on Peruvian innocence; Burke reappears as the Spanish ecclesiastic, Las-Casas, denouncing Pizarro with indignation and horror; while to the Peruvian general, Rolla, Sheridan makes the gift of his Begums speech. While the lines of historical simplification are very severely drawn—Spanish corruption neatly parallels Peruvian virtue—

a hidden sense of the failure of melodrama complicates the text, even at its ostensibly triumphant ending. The colonial stereotype that *Pizarro* seeks to maintain is thus fraught with an internal anxiety about the fixity of its cultural formations, implying that the trial cannot be merely romanticized into an exotic adventure but that its rewriting must inevitably involve a repetition of interpretative defeat.

In the Begums Charges, Hastings was accused of extorting payments from the widow and the mother of the late ruler of Oudh, an independent state, and further of supplying company troops to the current ruler, who was commanded to invade the Begums' estate and confiscate their treasure. The accusation in itself was sensational enough, but in Sheridan's hands, it grew to proportions of high colonial hysteria. He was able first to draw on the occult sanctity he ascribed to the female sanctuary that the Company's troops ransacked, and then to expatiate at length on the symbolic violation of the Begums at the hands of the East India Company. The vulnerability of the women is somewhat belied by Sheridan's acknowledgment of the independence and political sophistication that the Begums demonstrated in their negotiations with Hastings, but he nevertheless is able to stress their pathos rather than their power. Finally, in reference to the younger Nawab's collusion with the Company, Sheridan's eloquence can turn to highly moving apostrophes to filial piety, completely disregarding the enmity that obtained between the Nawab and the Begums. Despite the obviousness of such stereotypical oppositions, however, the Begums speech contains some curious ambivalences in relation to its own sexual symbolism, reversing thereby the rigidity with which it maps out the location of colonial will.

Much horror had Sheridan to express over the invasion of the Begums' estates. It was not, he took pains to point out to the House of Lords, an issue of conquest and plunder, but an unimaginable crossing of psychic boundaries, the costs of which England could not assess: "A threat," he declaimed, "to force that residence, and violate its purity by sending men armed into it, was a species of torture, the cruelty of which could not be conceived by those who were unacquainted with the customs and notions of the inhabitants of Hindostan. A knowledge of the customs and manners of the Musselmen in Turkey, would not enable one to judge of those of Musselmen in India. . . . The confinement of the Turkish ladies was in great measure to be ascribed to the jealousy of their husbands; in Hindostan the ladies were confined, because they thought it contrary to *decorum* that persons of their sex should be seen abroad . . . their sequestration from the world was *voluntary* . . . they were *enshrined* rather than *immured;* they possessed a greater *purity* of *pious prejudice* than the Mahomedan ladies of Europe and other countries, and more zealously and religiously practiced a more *holy* system of *superstition*" (*HTH*, vol. 1, pp. 77–78). The will for confinement peculiar to subcontinental women, in other words, suggests a power of its own, making of the veil as much a weapon as the bayonets that attacked it. In attempting to stress the vulnerability of the subcontinent in its feminine manifestation, Sheridan unwittingly depicts his own phantasmagoric interpretation of how empowering it is to be unreadable. While such hidden recognition could be regarded as standard Orientalist apprehensions of otherness and its attendant mystery, the fluctuations of Sheridan's discourse indicate that he is less interested in the mystification of violation than in the Begums' ability to represent precisely the authority of the unread.

In *Pizarro*, such authority is replicated by the female characters' ability to bring death rather than life onto the stage: both the Spanish Elvira and the Peruvian Cora are the instruments whereby the villain Pizarro and the hero Rolla are respectively slain.[28] The vulnerability of the women is thus more deathly than it is innocent: like the Begums, their very bodily presence suggests an invisible territorial integrity impervious to the literal ambitions of the marauding invader. While the play's reference to the Begums Charge is an attempt to underscore the natural goodness of the Peruvians, Sheridan's ambivalent relation to the trial complicates the ostensibly clear-cut stereotypes that the play presents. As has been frequently noted, Sheridan's two major additions to Kotzebue's text are pointed footnotes on the impeachment—the first is Rolla's speech to the Peruvian forces, which repeats the texture of the Begums speech, and the second is the stronghold of the Peruvian women. James Morwood points out that "in Kotzebue, the hiding place of the Peruvian women is merely an 'open Space in a Forest' . . . Sheridan makes it an 'unprofan'd recess'. . . . Through these additions, Sheridan wishes to call to mind the *zenanas* or private quarters of the Begums, the sanctity of which he had emphasized in Westminster Hall as he argued that any treasures 'given or lodged in a *zenana* of this description' could be 'snatched thence only by sacrilege.' "[29] The untouchability of such a feminine stronghold, however, is powerful enough to adulterate the natural law that it is designed to represent, becoming—like the process of impeachment—an extralegal space that cannot be confined to the ruling of known law.

During a powerful moment in the Begums speech, Sheridan savagely attacked Sir Elijah Impey, Hastings's chief justice, for urging the Nawab of Oudh to invade his mother's territory, but his pious rage is unconsciously ironized by the references on which the speech draws: "When on the 28th of November, [Impey] was busied at Lucknow on that honourable business, and when three days afterwards he was found at Chunar, at the distance of 200 miles, prompting his instruments, and like Hamlet's Ghost exclaiming— 'SWEAR!'—his progress on that occasion was so whimsically sudden, when contrasted with the gravity of his employ, that an observer would be tempted to quote again from the same scene,—*Ha! Old* Truepenny, *canst thou mole so fast i' the ground?'*—Here however the comparison ceased—for when Sir Elijah made his visit to Lucknow, '*to whet the almost blunted purpose*' of the Nabob, his language was wholly different from that of the Poet:—it would have been much against his purpose to have said, 'Taint not thy mind, nor let thy foul contrive / Against thy MOTHER aught!' " (*HTH*, vol. 1, p. 97). Even as Sheridan seeks to establish the Begums' innocence, he is irresistibly drawn to refer to a familial configuration in which the location of guilt is as difficult to pin down as the execution of revenge, while the guilty implication of the female is made more powerful by its very passivity. Similarly, *Pizarro* cannot but question the model of female virtue that it seeks to uphold: the interpretative seclusion of the women is both more abstracted and more dangerous than Pizarro's stated rage.

    Pizarro's most celebrated use of the Hastings trial occurs in the second scene of act 2, where the general Rolla rallies the Peruvian forces to the justice of their cause. While its rhetoric makes specific reference to the Begums speech, it further essentializes all the Managers' manners of indictment:

> THEY, by a strange frenzy driven, fight for power, for plunder, for extended rule—WE, for our country, our altars, and our homes.—THEY follow an Adventurer whom they fear—and obey a power which they hate—We serve a Monarch whom we love, a God whom we adore. . . . They boast, they come but to improve our state, enlarge our thoughts, and free us from the yoke of error! Yes—THEY will give enlightened freedom to *our* minds, who are themselves the slaves of passion, avarice and pride.—They offer us protection—Yes, such protection as vultures give to lambs—covering and devouring them! (Act 2, scene 2, lines 25–32)

Here, a rigid imperial binarism obtains between "us" and "them," drawing on the Burkean rhetoric through which the managerial "we" sought to locate all colonial malfunction in the iniquitous "he" of Warren Hastings. Even more significantly, however, the self-quotation of the tirade is historically marked, returning to the fourth and final day of Sheridan's Begums speech, when he moved Westminster Hall to tears with a similar exclamation:

> This was *British* Justice! this was *British* Humanity! Mr. Hastings ensures to the Allies of the Company in the strongest terms their Prosperity and his Protection;—the former he secures by sending an army to plunder them of their wealth and desolate their soil!—his protection is fraught with a similar security; like that of a Vulture to a Lamb—grappling in its vitals! thirsting for its blood!—scaring off each Petty Kite that hovers round—and then, with an insulting perversion of terms, calling sacrifice, *Protection*! (*HTH*, vol. 1, pp. 97–98)

While one of Sheridan's earliest biographers, Thomas Moore, justifies such self-plagiarism on the grounds of the haste with which *Pizarro* was written, it is clear that such a gesture of recall is of more loaded symbolic significance to the playwright himself.[30] Not only does its dramaturgical flair take him back to a moment of great oratorical triumph, but it more crucially serves as an epitaph for a political drama in which the dividing lines between "they" and "we" became increasingly impossible to maintain.

Despite Rolla's celebration of the Peruvian state of "natural law," the play itself is an incipient self-questioning of such easy distinctions between the natural and the civil. If the Hastings trial had brought clarity to any issue at all, it was to the necessary redundancy with which the idea of the natural could function in a colonial setting. In the context of *Pizarro*, the trial returns to allow Rolla his eloquence but also to ensure that as the epitome of natural law, he will die at the end of the play: even though Pizarro is slain and the Spanish troops defeated, the converted Spaniard Alonzo remains in Peru, offering its inhabitants yet another version of colonial superimposition. As a rehearsal of the Hastings trial, *Pizarro* thus tacitly acknowledges the Managers' rhetorical failure to produce an alternative protection to the one that Hastings offered India, dramatizing in the process the newly learned anachronism of eloquence. For early in the first act of *Pizarro* Edmund Burke quits the stage, demonstrating in his theatrical return a greater foreknowledge of defeat than did the historical man: Las-Casas denounces Pizarro in sublimely familiar locutions, but soon comes to realize the futility of his speech. "Oh, men of blood!" exclaims Las-Casas, "I leave you, and for ever! No longer shall these aged eyes be seared by the horrors they have witnessed. In caves, in forests, will I hide myself; with Tigers and with savage beasts will I commune: and when at length we meet again before the bless'd tribunal of that

Deity, whose mild doctrines and whose mercies ye have this day renounced, then shall YOU feel the agony and grief of soul which tear the bosom of your accuser now!" (act 1, scene 1, p. 27).

Much as, in the actual proceedings of the impeachment, Burke obsessively likened Hastings to the predators of the Indian jungle, Sheridan allows his dramatization of the indignant Manager a latter-day understanding of his possible intimacy with the object of his accusations. As Las-Casas strides off to commune with tigers and savage beasts, the "High Crimes and Misdemeanours" for which they were the tropes dismantle into new configurations of colonial responsibility, configurations of a complexity not to be contained by either the court or the theater of the trial of Warren Hastings.

4

The Feminine Picturesque

W HEN R OSAMUND L AWRENCE ARRIVED IN THE PROVINCE OF S INDH IN 1914, one of the first sentiments she recorded in the journal later to be published as *Indian Embers* is the exclamation, "What sketching I shall do!"[1] Rather than suggest any uncomplicated aesthetic self-gratification, her remark reflects a long-standing nineteenth-century tradition through which British women in the colonized subcontinent were required to remain on the peripheries of colonization, collecting from that vantage point peripheral images of people and place. From the extensive body of journals, memoirs, letters, and fiction written by Anglo-Indian women, it becomes evident that outside the confines of domesticity, one of the few socially responsible positions available to them was the role of female as amateur ethnographer. They could sketch landscape and capture physiognomy as long as they remained immune to the sociological conclusions of their own data, entering the political domain in order to aestheticize rather than to analyze. Such a colonial immunity, however, was arduous to sustain in the infectious imperial climate of nineteenth-century India, where the psychic strains of self-censorship were far more the burden of the Anglo-Indian female than of the male. If the latter had the bureaucracy of the Raj to supply a semblance of narrative coherence to his Indian sojourn, the former was granted very little stability other than perpetual reminders of her cultural redundancy on the Indian landscape. Living on an elite island that was nevertheless rife with domestic politics, dwelling in a protection hysterically conscious of how much protection was necessary, the Anglo-Indian woman persistently became a symbolic casualty to the deranging costs of colonial power.

She could, however, sketch. Her function was to produce both visual and verbal representations of India that could alleviate the more shattering aspects of its difference, romanticizing its difficulty into the greater tolerability of mystery, and further regarding Indian cultures and communities with a keen eye for the picturesque. For the female as colonizer, the picturesque assumes an ideological urgency through which all subcontinental threats could be temporarily converted into watercolors and thereby domesticated into a less disturbing system of belonging. Its aesthetic contributes to what Francis Hutchins calls the "illusion of permanence" in British imperialism: the picturesque becomes synonymous with a desire to transfix a dynamic cultural confrontation into a still life, converting a pictorial imperative into a gesture of self-protection that allows the colonial gaze a license to convert its ability not to see into studiously visual representations.[2] The liberty of censorship, however, exacts a price of its own; it calls attention to the colonial reliance on secrecy through an overly efficient obliteration of the possibility that the objects to be represented could pose to their author an unread cultural threat. When the Anglo-Indian woman is confined to such modes of representation, her serenity itself takes on the patterns of a hysteria all too secretively aware of the dangers in an unrelenting assumption of cultural and psychic safety.

To read the feminine picturesque as it develops in nineteenth-century Anglo-Indian narrative is to be continually confronted with the question of degree: to what extent is the British woman implicated in the structures of colonialism, and what lines can be drawn between her collusion with, and confinement in, the colonization of the subcontinent? Does such collusion inevitably suggest confinement, much as Burke's feminized idea of beauty implies that the beautiful is that which is imprisoned within itself? The picturesque represents the site on which the Anglo-Indian woman herself attempts both to raise and to repress such questions, and thus is converted from its status as confessedly "minor art" into a dense tale of colonial incertitude. While the importation of British women to serve as wives certainly establishes their more contingent relation to colonialism, their very entry into the world of rigidly maintained stereotypes points to a political engagement of an order other than that of the male colonizer. The hesitancies attendant on such complicity can be attributed to the female's peculiarly tropological relation to the tangibilities of colonization: she was in India as a symbolic representative of the joys of an English home; she was the embodiment of all that the Englishman must protect; most significantly, she was a safeguard against the dangers posed by the Eastern woman. As Kenneth Ballhatchet's succinct study *Race, Sex and Class under the Raj* has demonstrated, such dangers have less to do with Orientalist images of the subcontinent veiled as an Eastern bride and more with the literal control of venereal diseases among the British troops and the widespread fear that Indian mistresses among the ruling classes would dilute the whiteness of colonial power.[3] Even though she arrived as a protection against such dire consequences, however, the Anglo-Indian woman could not be protected from her own fear of native women—a fear of proximity rather than of difference—which she must urgently work to transform into the obscure discourse of the picturesque.

Representations of the picturesque are not only important documents of the female anxiety generated by colonialism, but further serve as an implicit critique of the metaphorical heterosexuality with which the colonial project is traditionally imaged: while the Anglo-Indian woman writer has much invested in maintaining standard Orientalist stereotypes to mystify the East, her work, far more than that of her male counterpart, engages in an incipient questioning that dismantles colonialism's master narrative of rape. From the energy of Fanny Parks's *Wanderings of a Pilgrim in Search of the Picturesque* to Harriet Tytler's calmly deranged Mutiny memoir, the woman writer seems to be at a better vantage point to assess how much the colonial encounter depends upon a disembodied homoeroticism rather than on the traditional metaphor of ravishment and possession. Here, their nineteenth-century texts anticipate the achievement of *A Passage to India,* in which Adela Quested must experience a delusional rape in order that her body may be transmogrified into that legal space over which Fielding and Aziz can stake out the overdetermination of their mutual loyalty. Their narratives preempt as well the alternative twentieth-century reading offered by V. S. Naipaul, who claims that "the British had possessed the country so completely" that their withdrawal was irrevocable: "No other country was more fitted to welcome a conqueror; no other conqueror was more welcome than the British. What went wrong? Some say the Mutiny; some say the arrival in India afterwards of white women. It is possible."[4] The writings of such arriving women would supply Naipaul with a very different sense of colonial possession, in which to rule was simultaneously to be dispossessed; to be forced to evolve an aesthetic in which the working of such power became synonymous with the metaphorical redundancy of femininity. In implicitly rejecting the paradigm of colonialism as rape, the Anglo-Indian woman writer evinces a powerful understanding of the imperial dynamic as a dialogue between competing male anxieties, even when such an exchange compels her to retreat deeper into the thin language of the picturesque.

Here, the Anglo-Indian woman performs a symbolic function in colonial discourse that is closely aligned to that of her Indian counterpart. As Lata Mani has convincingly demonstrated, the Indian woman in nineteenth-century British India was officially evoked as a repository of tradition: "Debates on women, whether in context of *sati,* widow remarriage, or *zenanas,* were not merely about women, but also instances in which the moral challenge of colonial rule was confronted and negotiated. In this process women came to represent 'tradition' for all participants: whether viewed as the weak, deluded creatures who must be reformed through legislation and education, or the valiant keepers of tradition who must be protected from the first. . . . Given the discursive construction of women as either abject victims or heroines, they frequently represent both shame *and* promise."[5] With similar ambivalence, the Anglo-Indian woman enters the colonial dynamic to supply an aesthetic context to the myriad workings of imperial power. She brings both amelioration and conversely an intensification of cultural fear, since the domesticity of her presence further signifies how much protection is required to keep her aesthetic segregated from native tradition.

Even while it is thus sequestered, the feminine picturesque develops as a peculiarly dual discourse: on one level, it is obedient, and follows the strictures of sentimentality in complete acceptance of its own minority status. On a more subversive level, it manipulates the terminology of the picturesque to lend a new violence to fragility, implicitly questioning the symbolic relevance of women to a colonial discourse. Here, it establishes lines of contiguity between the position of both Anglo-Indian and Indian women and the degrees of subordination they represent, for even when her writing seeks to enclose the Indian into a picturesque repose, the Anglo-Indian is simultaneously mapping out her own enclosure within such an idiom. When the female revision in the publicity of official Anglo-Indian narrative is read for its deep cultural contradictions, it clearly indicates how little its privacy has to do with popular interpretations of the "Mem Sahib" generated by Raj revivalism, which has tended toward dangerous misreadings of female function in Anglo-India. In the context of general scholarly studies, Pat Barr's historical survey *The Memsahibs* attempts to supply a more sympathetic account of British women's social function in Anglo-India, while the more recent *Women of the Raj* by Margaret MacMillan makes an unfortunate return to the incipient Orientalism that elevates the *Mem Sahib* to an icon of absolute power:

> Sometimes they were magnificent. Sometimes, on the other hand, they were awful, as only people who are afraid can be. When a conviction of superiority goes with the fear, then the arrogance is heightened and sharpened. The memsahibs (roughly translated 'the masters' women')—even those who know nothing of the British Raj have heard of them. . . . Over the years, their ringing voices have pronounced Indian painting garish, Indian music cacophonous, Indian ways barbaric. . . . In-

dians themselves were useful when they were servants—
servants who of course had to be treated like wayward children.
Otherwise they existed, millions upon millions of them, to serve
as extras in the great drama of the Empire.[6]

Alteritist before it addresses otherness, the attempted chastisement of such a
generalization reinforces rather than questions the popular stereotype, in
which the trappings of the Raj function as unquestioned symbols of monolithic empowerment.

When an alteritist critical strategy measures the Anglo-Indian woman
against an unread Indian otherness, the subject's implication in concrete specificities of colonial guilt is as a consequence mitigated or at least displaced by
universalist questions of identity and difference. She becomes a paler counterpart of the greater otherness of the Indian woman, rendering indistinct
her location in the expected trinity of culture, race, and gender. Since the
imbrication and interplay of such categories are equally significant to a feminine picturesque, it becomes necessary to dismantle the paradigm of alterity
in order that both similarities and differences in the colonial iconography of
British and Indian women may be properly stressed. They serve subordinate
but vastly different symbolic functions in the structure of colonial discourse:
the tradition of one is pitted against the aestheticism of the other, causing the
Indian to embody intuitively what the European presents concomitantly as
the refinement of culture. To the male colonial imagination, oppressed Indian
and elite European join to provide a Darwinian map of the gendering of
culture, or a hierarchy more disturbing than one implied by readings in the
gradations of otherness. Too focused an attention on the latter disregards the
complexity of subordination represented by the former, as exemplified in a
recent reading of Kipling's representation of Indian women:

> In being doubly "other," the Indian woman was, to the An-
> glo-Indian, potentially a two-fold impediment to British rule.
> The ideology of this rule puts a man's work, the white man's bur-
> den in India, above all else. . . . [Women] are powerfully
> distracting; and for men to do their best work, they must be
> shifted to the peripheries of men's vision. The English wife con-
> stitutes a *kind* of menace, for she can and, in Kipling's eyes, often
> does domesticate the energies better spent on government. But
> the danger she represents sexually is effectively cancelled by her
> racial and national identity to the Englishman. On the other
> hand, the Indian woman, because she is both Indian and female,

presents the direst possible threat to the homosocial solidarity of
district officer, soldier, and intelligence agent.[7]

Such a reading aptly recognizes the "homosocial solidarity" of Anglo-India,
but by overstressing the complete alterity of the Indian woman, tends to ro-
manticize the pragmatics of how cultural difference functions in a colonial
world. In contrast, the seeming serenity of the picturesque provides a
densely detailed documentation of the imaginative strains engendered by
such pragmatics.

In the homosocial world of the early nineteenth century, the Anglo-
Indian woman manipulates the picturesque into a complex cultural expression of ambivalence about her role as a segregated and a segregating
presence. As Kenneth Ballhatchet points out, "Improved conditions encouraged more Englishwomen to live in India, and in various ways their presence
seems to have widened the distance between the ruling class and the
people. . . . As wives they hastened the disappearance of the Indian mistress. As hostess they fostered the development of exclusive social groups in
every civil station. As women they were thought by Englishmen to be in
need of protection from lascivious Indians."[8] If the latter fear prevailed
throughout the century, then it was further exacerbated into an extreme hysteria over the events surrounding the great rebellion of 1857: pre- and post-
Mutiny narratives of the picturesque reflect such an intensification by evincing increasing helplessness in the face of their own feminine vulnerability.
Writing in cultural and social segregation, the Anglo-Indian woman conversely develops an idiom of greater and greater powerlessness just as the Raj
consolidates its power in 1858. During an era obsessed with public displays of
authority and spectacles of power, the Anglo-Indian woman locates a language in which to disempower such authority, focusing instead on the
domestic limitations of the picturesque.[9] In the seclusion of its aesthetic, she
constructs a discursive equivalent to the Indian woman's *zenana*, that space
which both draws and repels her, and about which she is obsessively impelled
to write.

Here, the Anglo-Indian aesthetic turns to the Indian tradition to record
what extremities of familial disruptions the Raj demanded of her. The
zenana, after all, was possessed of one advantage denied to British women: it
could include children within its space. Throughout Anglo-Indian narrative,
the separation of parent and child is a sentimentalized motif that repetitively
reveals the extent of its traumatic betrayal: Flora Annie Steel's *On the Face
of the Waters* represents colonial maternity's attempts to maintain a solemn

sadness at the absence of its child, but the narrative bereavement it exudes indicates a more severe psychic damage, much as Kipling's autobiographical story "Baa Baa Black Sheep" darkly maps out the casualties experienced by those imperial children who were shipped back to England, often for several years of separation from whatever originary home Anglo-India had represented to them. In their infancy too these children had been symbolically closer to the *zenana* than to their actual mothers: nurtured by wet nurses and *ayahs*, they were, Kipling records, the true intimates of the colonial world. Such intimacy, however, can be expensive, generating a thick interchange of psychic cost for both biological and surrogate mother. While the women maintained their strictly defined cultural positions of mistress and menial, a metaphoric fluidity as disturbing as that of milk had entered their dynamic: they were bound in identical postures of erotic tenderness toward an infant whom they temporarily shared, and whose absence signified emotional and economic loss to both. The intimacy that such loss represented is further literalized by the arresting parable of colonial barter through which, most simply put, the lactating Indian feeds another's child and loses her own, in order that the economic unit of her entire family may be equally fed. The bond of nurturing between ruler and servant is quite pragmatically a bond of death, as Mrs. Sherwood, a nineteenth-century diarist and wife to a British army officer, records in costly self-expiation:

> Each person who had anything to do with [the] nursery agreed that dayes, or wet nurses, must be had for delicate children in India, even should the white mother be able to nurse her children for a time. I asked what was done with the little black infant. "Oh," replied the amiable white woman, "something handsome is always paid for their being reared, but they commonly die." And she added, "My lady has had six dayes for different children, and the babies have one and all died."
>
> "Died!" I remember I exclaimed, "but this is murder."
>
> She answered coolly, "It can't be helped. The mothers never fret after them; when they nurse a white baby they cease to care for their own. They say, 'White child is good, black child is slave.'"[10]

Submerged in such narrative calm, the picturesque continues to pay necessary dues to the economy of the borrowed breast, establishing a silenced intimacy between the conflicted participants in motherhood within the colonial system.

My reading of the nineteenth-century picturesque addresses the following questions: given the censored status of their discourse, what literary modalities allow even nonfictional texts by women writers to embody the veiled realities of colonial panic? How, furthermore, does the act of auto-biography dilute or reify male historiography, as it inscribes a female and foreign body onto an Indian landscape? Despite the ostensible privacy of the picturesque—its impulse to be anecdotal rather than historical—could such a genre signify an Anglo-Indian breakdown of the boundaries between offi-cial and intimate languages? If so, the figure of woman writer as amateur could emblematize an unofficial fear of cultural ignorance shared equally by male and female imperialists, converting amateurism into an elaborate alle-gory through which Anglo-India examines in hiding colonialism's epistemo-logical limits.

I will weigh such questions through a juxtaposed reading of three para-digmatic texts: Fanny Parks's pre-Mutiny journal, Harriet Tytler's post-Mutiny memoir, and finally, the ethnographic project of *The people of India.* Parks's narrative exemplifies the picturesque impulse to transmute coloni-alism into a literary document, conflating British romanticism with a ready assimilation of exotic mysticism in order to construct a striking account of colonial hybridity. Tytler, on the other hand, represents a casualty of the picturesque mode: her straining toward Anglo-Indian stereotypes and a complete narrative calm bespeaks a disequilibrium that keenly images the dislocations of plot dictated by the Mutiny era. And finally, *The people of India* signifies a massive official attempt to replicate the structure and design of the feminine picturesque: its arbitrary catalog of what it deems to be the more interesting racial types of the subcontinent randomly collapses social, religious, and regional divisions into a fixed grid of colonial misapprehen-sion. Both photographic image and the accompanying text freeze the complex dynamic of Indian social structures into a misreading that ex-emplifies the amateurism of official Anglo-Indian discourse; and further illustrates the crucial part played by the picturesque in colonialism's misin-terpretation of caste.

The sequestering capacity of the picturesque thus calls to be read both as a denial of the violence with which Anglo-India lived daily and as a dis-course of difficulty in its own right: its opacities serve as a corollary to Burke's perception of colonial terror, adding to the rhetoric of English India fresh refinements of fear.

IN 1850, FANNY PARKS PUBLISHED A TWO-VOLUME JOURNAL ENTITLED *Wanderings of a Pilgrim in Search of the Picturesque, during Four-and-*

Twenty Years in the East; with Revelations of Life in the Zenana. Seventeen
years earlier, her father—a major in the British army in India—had published his own journal, *Tours in Upper India, and in Parts of the Himalaya
Mountains; with Accounts of the Courts of Native Princes, Etc.*[11] The titles
nicely mirror Anglo-Indian gender distinctions, causing the father to tour
while the daughter wanders; to provide accounts rather than revelations; to
examine princely courts rather than *zenanas*. While Maj. Edward Archer is
indeed admiring of the Himalayas, his diary tends to be more drawn to the
pragmatics of colonization in the subcontinent, criticizing the East India
Company with a military bluntness: "It is not to be denied that the power of
the British has been obtained more by force than by other and fairer
means. . . . Those of former Governors-General, whose exactions and
grasping seizures have acquired to the perpetrators such damning shame,
have been accounted the greatest of Indian statesmen. Among these names
are those of Lord Clive and Mr. Hastings."[12] As wife to a member of the
Bengal Civil Service, Fanny Parks is denied the scope of such critiques of the
Company, and turns instead to the alternative politics of the picturesque.
Her title clearly announces the quasi-religious aspirations of the genre: if her
father tours Upper India simply as a major, Parks insists on her greater metaphoricity. She is the pilgrim; India, the shrine.

Much as the picturesque is conscious of its nearly outmoded
quaintness, so the shrines that Fanny Parks seeks out are already relics, experiences to be represented with an elegiac acknowledgment of their vacated
power. While her narrative energetically collects and preserves these cultural
encounters, it is compelled into a defensiveness that Major Archer did not
have to face: his competent discourse needed no accompanying apologia
about why such an account of his tours should exist. Parks, however, is from
the outstart troubled by the potential narcissism of which she may be accused, and tellingly anticipates such charges in her inscription of dedication:
"To the memory of My Beloved Mother, at whose request it was written,
This Narrative is Dedicated: And if any of the friends, whose kind partiality
has induced them to urge its publication, should think I have dwelt too much
on myself, on my own thoughts, feelings, and adventures, let them remember that this journal was written for the affectionate eye OF HER to whom
nothing could be so gratifying as the slightest incident connected with her
beloved and absent child."[13] The woman chronicler of Anglo-India knows the
dubiety of her claim to represent both its geography and its politics; she is
conscious that her person may too much intrude upon the sequence of colonial narrative. The picturesque is therefore cast as an aberration from

historiography, while its validation turns to the pathos with which it can mirror the address to parent from an absent child.

Parks's introduction to her memoir is further evidence of the Anglo-Indian woman writer's will to put her own discourse on trial: since she cannot question the course of Anglo-Indian history, Parks must find an alternative expression for the hybridity that supplies her peculiar context. In an overwrought urge to image the tropological density that her narrative demands, Parks turns to the image of Ganesh, the elephant god, as a surrogate for her own cultural amalgamation. The picturesque retells the myth of Ganesh's birth: Parvati the mountain goddess gave birth to Ganesh, and asked the gods to assemble in congratulation of his beauty. Shiva the destroyer paid compliments but would not even look at the child. On Parvati's reproof, his anger withered away the head of the infant. In compassion for the mother's distress, Brahma commanded Shiva to bring "the head of the first animal that he should find living with its head to the north." When Parvati objects to the elephant head with which Shiva returns, Brahma responds, "Lament not the fate of your child:—with the head of an elephant he shall possess all sagacity. In puja Ganesh shall be invoked ere any other god be worshipped, hence shall he be greater than all the gods. Ere a pious Hindu commences any sort of writing, the sign of Ganesh shall he make at the top of his page, otherwise his words shall be folly, and his traffic a matter of loss. He shall be patron of learning, his writing shall be beautiful" (*WP*, vol. 1, pp. viii–ix).

In the context of Parks's appropriation of this image, Ganesh serves as a trope for the cultural hybridity that a feminine picturesque must both record and lull into repose. The god is thus emptied of any mythological violence to represent instead an aesthetic object both collectible and transportable. Here, Parks literalizes the acquisitive quality of a sentimental narrative by illustrating that its narrator is not only emotionally demanding of its reader but is further materially demanding of the culture that it transcribes. The deity originally invoked as a metaphor for the Anglo-Indian woman's defense of her own hybridity is soon transmuted into an artifact that she alone can possess:

> Although a *pukka Hindu*, Ganesh has crossed the *Kala Pani*, or Black Waters, as they call the ocean, and has accompanied me to England.
> There he sits before me in all his Hindu state and peculiar style of beauty—my inspiration—my penates.
> O Ganesh, thou art a mighty lord! thy single tusk is beau-

tiful, and demands the tribute of praise from the Haji of the East. Thou art the chief of the human race; the destroyer of unclean spirits; the remover of fevers, whether daily or tertian! Thy pilgrim sounds thy praise, let her work be accomplished! SALAM! SALAM! (*WP*, vol. 1, pp. x–xi)

While such an excessive apostrophe attempts to resolve both religious and colonial antagonisms into an eerie harmony in which Hindu, Muslim, and colonizing Christian jointly revere the god of writing, its will to serenity is also menacingly consuming. Much as Parks's picturesque dehistoricizes the subcontinent into an amorphously aesthetic space, it further desacralizes each icon that Parks represents into an allegory of colonial ownership: at the end of the pilgrim's wanderings, Ganesh sits in Great Britain with a zoological composure, god no longer of writing but of the literal appropriation that Parks's narrative delineates.

The opening chapter of the text, "Departure from England," offers an ostensibly realistic diary of the colonialist's journey by sea, the tone of which follows the demands of a feminine decorum. Parks presents herself as a young woman who, in the protection of her husband, is out on an adventure; she is embarked on a tour rather than on an engagement in the colonial project. Despite her inability to address the latter subject directly, however, the diarist rapidly supplies a set of subterranean reference points that disturb the repose of the picturesque, suggesting a tropological anticipation of the psychic strains that lie at the journey's end. After describing a masque the ship's crew performed for the entertainment of the travelers, in which a boatswain's mate played the part of Neptune and ended the ceremonies with a rendition of "Rule Britannia," Parks adds, as if by chance, "Neptune was accompanied on board by a flying-fish that came in at one of the ports, perhaps to escape from an albicore: a lucky omen. The gentlemen amuse themselves with firing at the albatross, as they fly round and round the vessel; as yet, no damage has been done—the great birds shake their thick plumage, and laugh at the shot" (*WP*, vol. 1, p. 7). As the woman watches the men at predatory sport, she maintains her calm, but an ominous possibility of destruction has entered her narrative: the world of the picturesque veers dangerously close to that of the Ancient Mariner.

If Parks's incipient colonial apprehensions are aestheticized into the literary safety of Coleridge's allegory of guilt, her reading of impending alienation draws obsessive attention to the potentially deathly costs of calm. For the rest of the voyage, her journal is divided between lamentations of the ship's slow progress and composed catalogs of the spoils brought in by the

hunting men: "A dead Calm! give me any day a storm and a half in preference! It was so miserable—a long heavy swell, without a ripple on the waves;
the ship rolled from side to side without advancing one inch; she groaned in
all her timbers. . . . This day, the 28th of August, was the commencement of
the shooting season: game was in abundance, and they sought it over the
long heavy swell of the glasslike and unrippled sea. The sportsmen returned
with forty head of game: in this number was an albatross, measuring nine
feet from the tip of one wing to that of the other. . . . When the boat returned, it brought good fortune, and we went on our way rejoicing" (*WP*,
vol. 1, p. 9). By this point, Parks's picturesque narrative is following the plot
of "The Ancient Mariner" with such fidelity that her opening chapter calls to
be read as an uneasy parable, in which the precursor text is both literalized
and retold as a proleptic mapping of the structure of colonial guilt. While the
feminine decorum of Anglo-India prevents the narrative from an overt statement of such a connection, Parks's disempowered relation to imperial action
and its attendant sport cannot save her from having the bird strung figuratively around her neck: "Another calm, and another battue: the gentlemen
returned from the watery plain with great eclat, bearing seven albatross,
thirty pintados, a Cape hen, and two garnets. One of the albatross, which was
stuffed for me, measures fifty-three inches from head to tail, and nine feet
ten inches across the wings" (*WP*, vol. 1, p. 10). Much as Ganesh must be
domesticated from icon to artifact at the close of Fanny Parks's journeying,
her voyage out supplies her with a sign equally loaded with ambivalence even
after it has been emptied—confined in the calm of the picturesque, she travels with her stuffed albatross deeper into the idiom of colonial guilt.

In a feminine picturesque, the repression of a sense of historical responsibility and its transmutation into the domain of the literary produces
an aura of unnatural calm through which the narrative glides in limpid suspension. It lends an increasing fatigue to Parks's language ("Sept. 25th—
Another calm allowed for more shooting, and great was the slaughter of the
sea game" *WP*, vol. 1, p. 10), particularly in its consciousness of the Cole-
ridgean surrealism that surrounds her account of the voyage. As her
narrative quietly records rather than comments on the literariness of such a
surreal, its self-censoring capacity demonstrates the hidden menace of equanimity: in the subversion of its own serenity, calmness is translated into the
"dead calm" that halts the ship, or the immobility that converts its decks into
a literal arena for slaughter. The calms and the lulls that Parks describes are
thus increasingly lacunae for the enactment of tyranny, both on the level of
gratuitous killing and, more significant, on the symbolic level of narrative

self-examination, through which Parks is able to locate her growing sense of the oppression of decorum. Her discourse will remain decorous, but henceforth cannot but be totally mistrustful of the dangers encoded in propriety: oppositions between states of peace and violence are rendered indeterminate, as Parks intuits even before her arrival on the subcontinent the secret cost of colonial calm. Even as the pilgrim wanders off in search of the picturesque, she tacitly acknowledges the discursive burden of an idiom that cannot retreat from the aesthetic imprisonment that equanimity signifies, allowing her narrative to admit to the inconsolable quality of its consolation. "The sunsets on and near the line are truly magnificent," claims the diary; "nothing is more glorious—the nights are beautiful, no dew, no breeze, the stars shining as they do on a frosty night at home, and we are gasping for a breath of air! A sea-snake of about a yard and a half long was caught—many turtles were seen, but they sank the moment the boat approached them" (*WP*, vol. 1, p. 12). In the breathless immobility of colonial arrival, which has simultaneously become a reinscription of the Ancient Mariner's enactment of the unlimitability of guilt, water snakes are to be drably caught as empty signs of history's distance from the archaism of absolution.

The water snake that entered *The Rime of the Ancient Mariner* to foreshorten the event of guilt into the more complicated narrative of perpetually deferred expiation must serve a perfunctory purpose for Fanny Parks: she observes the snake, watches its confinement, and can have no further dealings with it as an emblem of tentative absolution. Instead, her nostalgia for a literary world in which epistemological guilt can somehow be transformed into a provisional serenity is replaced with grim honesty by a historical foreboding that, in a colonial environment, equanimity will be continually self-subverting, allowing for no narrative frame to which the picturesque may anchor its plot. In such an absence of romanticism's ambivalent offering of a possible serenity, Parks anticipates her engagement in the other order of colonialism, where to be becalmed is to know further guilt:

> Becalmed for eighteen days! not as when off the Cape; there it was cool, with a heavy swell, here there is no motion, the sun vertical, not a breath of air, the heat excessive. At length a breeze sprang up, and we began to move: one day during the calm we made seven knots in the twenty-four hours, and those all the wrong way!
> "Day after day, day after day
> We stuck, nor breath nor motion;
> As idle as a painted ship

Upon a painted ocean."
Our voyage advanced very slowly, and the supply of fresh water
becoming scanty, we were all put on short allowance; anything
but agreeable under so hot a sun. (*WP*, vol. 1, pp. 12–13)

The mariner crucial to Parks's anticipations of a colonial experience is finally
cited overtly, but in the context of a rigidity that forces the picturesque into a
self-questioning fearfully cognizant of its own implications. Its peace is idle;
its geographical apprehension is more in tune with the surface of a canvas
than soil; it further knows the redundancy of seeming painterly upon an already painted colonial surface. The mariner in Parks's narrative is a woman
urgently negotiating with the terror that Anglo-India signifies to her intuitive prefiguration of the potential violence in discourses of imperial peace.[14]

If Fanny Parks arrives in India with an intimate understanding of the
nightmare life-in-death, such prescience does not prevent her monumental
narrative from accomplishing exactly the agenda that its title announces:
her two volumes map out an omnivorous and often maniacal consumption
of the picturesque in all of its manifestations, ranging from race, religious
practice, landscape, towns, and tombs to appendixes that include a compendium of Oriental proverbs and a helpful catalog of how ice cream can best be
made in the subcontinent. Parks's text is lavishly illustrated, both with her
own sketches and with those of her friends, replicating her narrative's self-
interrupting style in order to quote voluminously from others' letters,
journals, and newspaper articles. The result is a bewildering document so
overloaded with information—in which vignette so relentlessly follows
vignette—that colonial history empties into vacuity even as its domestic
details are being abundantly transcribed. It would however be too simple to
read such a consumptive text as illustrative merely of the privilege with
which Anglo-Indian women could live in India, for its narrative more crucially embodies a sense of historical and cultural unhinging that impedes the
development of plot. Instead, the picturesque constructs a metonymic chain
which, confounding all notions of narrative coherence, bespeaks its own distraction: with the impulse of a collector, it barely finishes narrating one of
India's charms when its attention is displaced onto another. Parks herself is
conscious of this discursive scattering, and tellingly ascribes it to the social
burdens of femininity. "I am reading Captain Mundy's 'Sketches in India,'"
she writes, "a much more amusing journal than I can write. I have no tigers
to kill, no hurdwar to visit; nor have I even seen the taj. His journal is very
spirited, very correct, and very amusing" (*WP*, vol. 1, p. 268). Her narrative,

on the other hand, must remain sequestered in its own serenity and in detail's habit of proliferation even when it apparently desires the greater precision of cultural and ethnic discrimination.

Where Parks will discriminate, however, is in her representation of "the natives." In the tradition of Anglo-Indian narrative, she is highly interested in distinctions of caste and class, examining racial and social difference as metaphoric artifacts that can be added to her collection. As she looks at the populations of the subcontinent with an eye to aestheticize them, her narrative exhibits a curious urge to be drawn into catalogs of bodily mutilation. Apart from the stereotypical accounts of crowds and contagion that Parks offers, her colonial gaze focuses with cinematic intensity on physical aberrations, the cumulative effect of which causes bodily malfunction to become synecdochical of "the native":

> Some of the natives are remarkably handsome, but appear far from being strong men. . . . I knew not before the oppressive power of the hot winds, and find myself as listless as any Indian lady is universally considered to be; I can now excuse, what I before condemned as indolence and want of energy—so much for experience. . . . The elephantiasis is very common among the natives; it causes one or both legs to swell to an enormous size, making the leg at the ankle as large as it is above the knee; there are some deplorable objects of this sort, with legs like those of the elephant—whence the name. Leprosy is very common; we see lepers continually. The insects are of monstrous growth, such spiders! and the small-lizards are numerous on the walls of the rooms, darting out from behind pictures, etc. Curtains are not used in Calcutta, they would harbour musquitos, scorpions, and lizards. (*WP*, vol. 1, p. 26)

In an unconscious allegorization of the Anglo-Indian experience, this passage is paradigmatic of Parks's inability to keep the picturesque aesthetic from mutating into cultural nightmare. The catalog begins with a calm evocation of Indian beauty; it then Indianizes the narrator into a treacherous serenity out of which she must immediately break in order to maintain her sense of racial and cultural differentiation. The picturesque is displaced by Parks's horrified reading of the Indian as a body out of control, swelling with an internal evil or wearing evil on its skin in a hideous reminder of the grotesquery encoded within the colonial will to aestheticize. Parks's narrative will attempts to read bodily mutation as a purely Indian property, in order that the infection of India can be confined to the Indian race, but its threat cannot be so easily quarantined: the Anglo-Indian domestic space is itself infested with tiny but deadly literalizations of India's power to inspire fear.

The Indian fear into which the picturesque yields is represented both by the native body's tendency to slip into bestiality or emanate infection and by the structures of confinement that Anglo-India imposed upon its women. While Parks can travel much in order to expand her compendium of colonial experiences and artifacts, her journal is perforated with evocations of oppression usually expressed in terms of a psychic climatology: "O! Western shore! on which I have passed so many days; what I would not give for your breezes, to carry away this vile Indian languor, and rebrace my nerves? In front of the thermantidote, and under a pankha, still there appears to be no air to breathe! This easterly wind is killing . . . this heavy, unnatural atmosphere overpowers me. . . . The air is so oppressive, it appears full of dust, so white, so hot! this atmosphere is thick and dull,—no rain!" (*WP*, vol. 1, pp. 273–75). Along with the insects that run through it, the heat that weighs upon typical Anglo-Indian women's writing is one safe way of recording colonial claustrophobia without transgressing onto the overtly political terrain of the male Anglo-Indian. Sunlight and scorpions are to be equally dreaded as speakable fears; they supply a tropology through which the female writer can disguise her odes to colonial dejection, which remain confined to the bodily rather than overtly spill over into the psychic or political realms.

When writing is thus made synonymous with bodily confinement, its evocation of all embodiment implies a self-replicating narcissism that deranges boundaries of racial demarcation even where the feminine picturesque works most stringently to maintain them. Parks's reading of speakable difference screens a delusional fear that the mutations she records are none other than her own: if her cultural dispersal into Anglo-India leaves her nothing but a bodily context, each mutilation she is compelled to describe literalizes the psychic malformation she will endure as a collaborator in the colonial project. Her obsessive catalogs of Indian difference and disease point to the strained tropology through which Parks staves off a contemplation of the unspeakable similitude suggested to her by the Indian body. The intricacy of colonial embodiment thus cannot be simply reduced to an alteritist apprehension of how the dominating self regards the subordinated other, as, for example, in Margaret MacMillan's attempt to explain the Anglo-Indian woman according to such a stereotypical dynamic: "They did not come to India for India's sake. They came, the great majority, to be wives; and they found in existence a tightly-knit community which gave them the simple choice of joining or staying outside. It was not much of a choice. Outside meant loneliness or India, and India frightened them. In any case Indian society would probably not have accepted them. . . . The British, like all other foreign invaders of India, were Untouchables."[15] Parks's narrative does not lend itself to such easy metaphorizations of caste, for it is too fraught with a secret knowledge that psychically speaking, Anglo-India gave her no inside to which she could belong. Otherness is too much the provenance of domination for Parks to forget the expenses of power, particularly in a female narrative tradition obsessed with its confinement to the body.

That heat and dust would be its most immediate expression of confinement is unsurprising: climatology provides a miasmic alternative to the specificities of matured disease that characterize for Parks the Indian and potentially her own constitution. "Those Indian fevers!" she exclaims; "I have scarcely enough energy to write. . . . The damp air renders me so heavy and listless, it is an exertion either to eat or drink, and it is impossible to sleep, on account of the heat. . . . Nothing is going forward, stupid as possible, shut up all day, languid and weary. . . . Woe is me that I sojourn in this land of pestilence, that I dwell afar from the home of my fathers!" (WP, vol. 1, pp. 302–3) The pestilential omnipresence of the subcontinent supplies Parks with a natural vocabulary to address the cultural disease in which she is incriminated: her availability to literal infection deflects narrative attention from its submerged subject, or the already contaminated context of colonial embodiment. In the feminine picturesque such embodiment is of course anti-erotic, confining itself to viral as opposed to sexual invasion and consigning glamor to the homoeroticism of the male colonial dynamic. Apportioning colonial pleasure and pain, however, is a complicated task: if Parks gestures at it in her catalog of Indian grotesqueries, she is brought dangerously close to a recognition of colonial narcissism in her reading of what the Indian woman signifies to colonial narrative, as body either too much hidden or too much exposed.

In nineteenth-century Anglo-Indian narrative, the body of the Indian woman dictates the limits and excesses of what a colonial epistemology allows itself to know. Where the latter decades of the Raj were to see her as a body completely tropologized into a figure for the colonized land upon which the colonizer performed predictable rape, the prior century evinced a more ambivalent awareness of the multiple tropologies that Indian women could figurally supply. To a male imperial imagination, they epitomized what a surface-level picturesque signified to the colonizing imagination: in 1832, Capt. Thomas Skinner records his appreciation of Indian difference by claiming, "Nothing can be more picturesque, and to our fancies more thoroughly oriental, than the moment, when 'the daughters of the men of the city come out to draw water.' Their graceful robes and fine straight figures, with the various positions in which they are arranged, make the most interesting picture possible—some approaching with their empty pitchers lying on the sides upon their shoulders, while their children sit astride their hips; others return laden, with the pitchers on their heads, supported by the right hand, while the left is ready to draw the veil over the face lest any stranger should approach."[16] In such a narrative, the Indian woman is nothing other than the sentimental erotic, a figure over which the colonizer can exercise an appreciation of the aesthetic dividends of power. The picturesque further serves as a measure of sexual protection, veiling the woman in an inviting but still uncrossable difference. In a more revelatory pattern of embodiment, however, Anglo-Indian narrative schematizes the Indian woman into two parallel images: she is either sequestered in the unknowability of the zenana or all too visible in the excessive availability of the professional courtesan, known in Anglo-Indian lingo as the "nautch-girls."

These women emblematize a peculiarly Indian threat to both male and female writers in Anglo-India, for their attraction has less to do with an Oriental mystery than with the potential vengeance of cultural contagion. "The influence of these nautch-girls over the other sex, even over men who have been brought up in England," Mrs. Sherwood laments in her diary, "is not to be accounted for. . . . I have often sat by the open window, and there, night after night, I used to hear the songs of the unhappy dancing-girls. . . . All these Englishmen who were beguiled by this sweet music had had mothers at home, and some had mothers still, who, in the far distant land of their children's birth, still cared, and prayed, and wept for their once blooming boys, who were then slowly sacrificing themselves to drinking, smoking, want of rest, and the witcheries of the unhappy daughters of heathens and infidels. I cannot describe the many melancholy feelings inspired by this midnight music."[17]

The infection of such women inheres in their promise of the erotics of cultural intimacy rather than in their otherness, particularly since the colonial sexual dynamic that Mrs. Sherwood sketches places the Anglo-Indian woman in a position of far greater confinement than that of her Indian counterpart. The accomplishment of the courtesan allows her a greater intellectual and erotic liberty than the Englishwoman could hope for, thus further confining the latter to the periphery of colonial exchange. For the dancing girls were transgressive only in the context of Anglo-India: as Ketaki

Dyson points out, they "were not only educated but also received government protection. They were free from stigma, recognized as a distinct professional class, and taxed according to their incomes. No religious occasion was thought to be complete without their attendance."[18] The clash of social codes generated by the courtesan's respectability was not easily aligned with the aesthetic of a feminine picturesque, in which the body signified a neurasthenic privacy rather than a public and viable medium of economic exchange. If the picturesque perspective turns away in horror at the prospect of the nautch-girl, it expresses less a fear of her sexual power over the Anglo-Indian man and more a hidden recognition that the Indian courtesan provided an uncannily literal replication of the part Anglo-Indian women had been imported to perform.

The feminine picturesque is thus forced to categorize the nautch-girl according to its own hierarchy of caste, seeing her as the new untouchable in the Anglo-Indian world. As a consequence, the *zenana* becomes the essential space of Indian femininity and it is only after such a sanctum has been penetrated that the Anglo-Indian can claim to "know" the Indian. That such a desire repeats in miniature the entire structure of the colonial project could be seen as part of its impulsion: the female repeats in diminution proportions of the male sublime. In Fanny Parks's narrative, the *zenana* soon becomes central to her discourse, signifying the picturesque's narcissistic urge to see itself through the eyes of other modes of confinement. "The perusal of Lady Mary Wortley Montague's work has rendered me very anxious to visit a *zenana*, and to become acquainted with the ladies of the East," she records, adding the startling list, "I have now been nearly four years in India, and have never beheld any women but those in attendance as servants in European families, the low caste wives of petty shopkeepers, and *nach* women" (*WP*, vol. 1, p. 59). Much as Adela Quested and Mrs. Moore set off on an unlikely picnic to the Marabar Caves in order to experience the "real" India, so Parks concentrates her expectation of the reality of Indian women into a similarly enclosed and peripheral space, illustrating the persistence with which Anglo-Indian narrative has looked for India in the wrong places and instead found disappointment. When Parks is finally granted her desire—she is invited to visit the *zenana* of "an opulent Hindu in Calcutta"—her experience brings little satisfaction:

> He led me before a large curtain, which having passed I found myself in almost utter darkness: two females took hold of my hands and led me up a long flight of stairs to a well-lighted room, where I was received by the wives and relatives. Two of the

ladies were pretty; on beholding their attire I was no longer surprised that no other men than their husbands were permitted to enter the zenana. The dress consisted of one long strip of Benares gauze of thin texture, with a gold border, passing twice round the limbs, with the end thrown over the shoulder. The dress was rather transparent, almost useless as a veil; their necks and arms were covered with jewels. The complexion of some of the ladies was of a pale mahogany, and some of the female attendants were of a very dark colour, almost black. Passing from the lighted room, we entered a dark balcony, in front of which were fine bamboo screens, impervious to the eye from without, but from the interior we could look down upon the guests in the hall below, and distinguish perfectly all that passed. . . . I was glad to have seen a zenana, but much disappointed. (*WP*, vol. 1, pp. 59–60)

Parks's disappointment suggests a narcissistic failure to locate a cultural mirror-image for her oppression in the picturesque: the *zenana* as a figure of imprisonment must now be substituted by a more complex understanding of how such a space could signify the possibility of mobility within secrecy. As a secret community within a community, the *zenana* opens onto itself in order to supply its residents the empowering ability to observe from a position of absence, while the erotic advantage of remaining unseen is maintained intact. To the penetrating eye of the Anglo-Indian woman, even the *zenana* registers as an image offering more bodily liberty than a solitary confinement in the picturesque.

Parks's most extensive "revelations of life in the zenana" occur through her acquaintance with Colonel Gardner, one of the several colonials who had married into Indian nobility, and with the family of the Maratha princess, Baiza Bai. Her sojourns in these homes provide her a more realistic if elitist perspective of the gender divisions in Indian domesticity, but her accounts of the population at large remain uniformly imagistic. Her hidden apprehension of the Anglo-Indian woman's victimization at the hands of the colonial project prevents her from acknowledging the greater victims that surround her, for an ability to look at them would necessitate an overt confrontation with her own confinement. She must thus write out of a strange half-absence, transforming cultural difference into acts of cultural collection, and reifying colonial terror into the safety of the collectible thing. Whether Parks is visiting a *sati*-ground or a Mughal tomb, she will record the experience with a decorous curiosity that must remain impervious to the art of discrimination. On occasion, however, the collected image threatens to break down the repose of the cultural connoisseur, calling to be read too much in its own light: "At Benares I purchased thirty-two paintings of the Hindoo deities for one rupee! and amongst them was a sketch of the goddess Kalee" (*WP*, vol. 1, p. 164). The image may be bought, but how will such symbolic violence be further sketched into a narrative of the picturesque?

In Parks's visits to the *zenana* and in her depiction of the Indian woman at large, her primary mode of interpreting femininity is through descriptions of female adornment. Rather than feature, she looks first at pigmentation and then at jewels, constructing her private system of caste in the gradatons that she notes. When faced with Kali, Parks accords her similar treatment, which, almost against its own narrative will, quickens her language with the weight of what she must represent:

> The goddess is represented as a black female with four arms, standing on the breast of Shivu. In one hand she carries a scymitar; in two others the heads of giants, which she holds by the hair; and the fourth hand supports giants' heads.
>
> She wears two dead bodies for ear-rings, and a necklace of skulls. Her tongue hangs down to her chin. The heads of giants are hung as a girdle around her loins, and her jet black hair falls to her heels. Having drunk the blood of the giants she slew, her eyebrows are bloody, and the blood is falling in a stream down her breast. Her eyes are red, like those of a drunkard. She stands with one leg on the breast of her husband Shivu, and rests the other on his thigh.
>
> Men are pointed out amongst *other animals* as a proper sacrifice to Kalee: the blood of a tiger pleases her for 100 years; the blood of a lion, a reindeer, or a man, for 1000 years. By the sacrifice of three men she is pleased for 100,000 years. (*WP*, vol. 1, p. 165)

Where the *zenana* disappoints, Kali cannot. The pleasure that Parks takes in constructing this catalog brings her narrative precariously close to repudiating its picturesque confines: while her introductory apostrophe to Ganesh made the elephant god as demure as the other curios that Parks collects, Kali remains a deity symbolizing what could be for the writer a new internalization of colonial consumption. As Partha Mitter points out in a valuable study of European reaction to Indian art, *Much Maligned Monsters*, "The reason for the several heads and arms of the Indian gods . . . was to explain all by multiplying the attributed up to infinity. . . . Piling signs upon signs and symbols upon symbols these images aspired to obtain the sublime plenitude of the divine. These images which reflected the desire and at the same time the impossibility of representing the totality, warned the believer that the right to penetrate the unattainable profundities belonged only to pure intelligence."[19] For the picturesque intelligence, Kali's excessive signification disrupts her narrative by embodying not only the dangers of divinity but, more crucially, a colonial and a feminine sublime.

If Parks's picturesque has been consistently drawn to representations of Indian women as her emblem of the absence encoded in colonial encounters, then her obsession with the image of Kali signifies a moment of ideological self-questioning quickly repressed in the logic of the text. The goddess's menacing enigma extends both to her gratuitous violence and to the bewildering liberty which, even though she has made it her own, will not let her rest. As an image of intense empowerment, she conjures up the Indian threat repetitively perceived as impinging on Anglo-Indian women's bodies, while simultaneously embodying the redundancy of rape to what that threat may signify. The goddess's bodily demeanor suggests a frenzy beyond the heterosexual, converting her into an icon for the unlocatable aura of colonial threat. When the Anglo-Indian woman confronts the laboring glee that Kali represents, her confinement in imperial calm is suspended into a momentary recognition: both Kali's ecstasy and the colonizing woman's composure become even in their opposition uncanny replications of each other, or mythological and historical repositories of the costs of omnivorous power.

In Kali, Parks confronts an image of all that the picturesque cannot officially know: while the parameters of its understanding can clearly accommodate the goddess, she must remain as a body transcribed but not read. Her clothes are fetching, recalling Parks's early comment on her first encounter with the black population of Nicobar: "Really the dark colour of the people serves very well as dress, if you are determined not to be critical" (WP, vol. 1, p. 16); her adornments turn such bodies into objects of aesthetic and economic value. As woman she represents the dangers of sustenance rather than those of ravishment, but that which she consumes produces further tyranny for her. When Parks observes Kali, she is close to acknowledging what pigmentation signifies to the Anglo-Indian picturesque. In the absence of any sustained regard with which to image alternative cultures, Kali is a reminder to an Anglo-Indian decorum of the wanton embellishment of a culturally gendered skin.

It was in the picturesque mode, however, that Parks began her narrative, and such is the idiom in which she concludes it: "And now the pilgrim resigns her staff and plucks the scallop-shell from her hat,—her wanderings are ended—she has quitted the East, perhaps for ever:—surrounded in her quiet home of her native land by the curiosities, the monsters, and the idols that had accompanied her from India, she looks around and dreams of the days that are gone" (*WP*, vol. 2, p. 496). This farewell synecdochically repeats the entire mood of the text, in which each Indian experience can be objectified and owned until the power of Ganesh or the threat of Kali become as calm as the narrator herself. That such fragility can be epistemologically expensive is acknowledged in the tentativeness of Parks's third person conclusion, which converts the narrator into yet another artifact: having survived the threat of the subcontinent, the Anglo-Indian woman must now face the greater tyranny of her own composure and its crippling will to aestheticize the pilgrim into the picturesque.

THE POST-MUTINY MEMOIR OF HARRIET TYTLER SERVES AS A MILITARISTIC COR-ollary to Fanny Parks's pre-Mutiny picturesque. Born in Oudh in 1828, Tytler exemplifies that Anglo-Indian woman who does not travel eastward into the estrangement of colonization but who is born into it: Parks's romantic journey to India is paralleled by Tytler's more literally recounted first voyage to England, where she herself is perceived as an Anglo-Indian exotic. Like Parks, she is a daughter of an officer in the British army, who further sustains her military rather than civil colonial connection by marrying a captain in the East India Company's forces. Exposed to a less privileged version of Anglo-India, Tytler records the hardships of that life with an equanimity so sustained as to be troubling; she is equally calm when she turns to the heart of her narrative, the Great Rebellion of 1857: "Half a century has passed since the events I would now record took place, and abler pens than mine have written of the Great Sepoy Mutiny. Still, as a survivor of the memorable 11th of May 1857 at Delhi, and as the only lady at the siege of that city, I am led to think a simple narrative by an eyewitness of those thrilling events may interest others."[20]

Aside from being the "only lady" at what is known as the Siege of Delhi, Tytler has the further claim of being the only Anglo-Indian woman to give birth to a son in the midst of the British forces, supplying the troops with an emblem of which could be said, "We shall have victory now that this baby has come to avenge the deaths of the murdered children" (HT, p. 172). Despite the decorum of the picturesque, Tytler's narrative is completely aligned with such an ethos of vengeance and presents her infant as a harbinger of the Raj:

The soldiers wanted him to be called Battlefield Tytler. I
felt that would be a dreadful name to give the poor child, so I com-
promised the matter by naming him "Stanley Delhi-Force." My
husband had been reading to me *Marmion* just before the Mutiny and, recollecting Marmion's last words, "On, Stanley, on," it
struck me as being both pretty and appropriate. (HT, p. 172)

In the midst of the colonial trauma and bloodiness signified by the Great Rebellion, Tytler's picturesque turns with phantasmagoria to Walter Scott; the
first child of the Raj receives the "pretty and appropriate" appellation of
Stanley Delhi-Force; the mother is proud to have him regarded as a military
reinforcement. Rather than as a "simple narrative by an eyewitness," in
other words, Harriet Tytler's memoir demands to be read as a compelling
account of the derangement of maternity in Anglo-India.

In the feminine picturesque, maternity functions as a figure for culturally specific acts of psychic separation. Stereotypically, British women
arrived in India both to protect and to be protected, nurturing colonial gener-
ations who could return to assume the duties of their fathers. The narratives
of such mothers, however, record with ambivalence the familial decentering
of Anglo-Indian domesticity, in which maternity must lease out its progeny
to either one culture or the other: both precursors and successors of Stanley
Delhi-Force would be fed by Indian breasts and hands before being returned
to the educative sustenance of England. Anglo-Indian maternity is therefore
confined to a curious position of psychic and economic barter in which it can
produce the incipient colonial but remain powerless to supply a coherent cultural plot to what will be the narrative of the child's existence. The plotless
memories of both Fanny Parks's and Harriet Tytler's journals are thus figurative replications of the absence of control implied by Anglo-Indian
maternity, causing the women to stand in equal relations of dubiety to both
their narratives and their children. As a child of Anglo-India herself, Tytler's
memoir opens to describe her first formative recollection: "Mother said she
could not understand how it was, but I seemed to have a presentiment of her
leaving me, and nothing would persuade me to go out of her arms . . . only
to awake in the morning to call for mamma. Getting no response I gave way
to bitter tears and cried out, '*Hum janta mamma chulla gai, chulla gai!*' ('I
know Mamma has gone away, has gone away'). I recollect that scene perfectly; no one could comfort me, till I sobbed and sobbed myself to sleep
again. Strange, I have no recollection of their coming back" (HT, pp. 5–6).
Confined in a pidgin Urdu that is the idiom both of the breast and the kitchen,
Tytler as Anglo-Indian child essentializes the cultural costs exacted by colo-

nial domesticity, in which the perpetual leave-taking of maternity obliterates the sequential reassurance that mothers will return.

The physically maiming absence of the maternal creates a curious vacancy in Tytler's discourse that is further accentuated by her unwavering calm, which, despite whatever personal or historical trauma she may be recording, remains consistently even. As in the "dead calm" that oppresses Fanny Parks's narrative, Tytler's equanimity is antithetical to the excessive catalog of deaths that her memoir transcribes, illustrating instead the picturesque's ability to embalm the violence of Anglo-India. Children in particular are eminently killable: "Not many years ago," the second page of Tytler's memoir informs the reader, "I heard of the death of a poor little English baby. The parents had gone out for their evening drive, as is customary in India, leaving the baby with the ayah. . . . The ayah bathed the child and put on its nightdress as usual, when the poor little thing gave a fearful cry. The ayah . . . tried to pacify the child by hugging it closer and closer, but each time she did so, the child gave a fresh scream, until it went into violent convulsions and died. When the parents came home, they would not believe the ayah's story that the child had cried without any fault of hers and then died so quickly. However, when the poor little one was undressed to be laid out in its coffin, they found the scorpion and knew what it all meant. Evidently the ayah disturbed it each time she clasped the child to comfort it, resulting in a fresh sting, till the agony was more than the little life could bear" (HT, pp. 6–7). The tale interrupts Tytler's reminiscences of her own childhood both as a forewarning of the bereavements that are to follow and as a parable for the extreme vulnerability of Anglo-India, in which each home can be infested with deadliness and its children killed by comfort.

While the picturesque is too claustrophobic a narrative space to allow for a reading or a questioning of the sensationalism attendant on such depictions of vulnerability, it provides an epitaphic record of each casualty taken by the threat of India. In Tytler's work, one of the first casualties is the Anglo-Indian child's sense of trust in the idea of maternity: the narrator's mother is described as calm, placid, and absent, or devising duties for her progeny that could only register as punishment: "I don't know whether the little sleep I had did me any harm or not," Harriet remarks with docility, "but I know that my long hair fell off so badly that the doctor advised mother to have my head shaved, which was done and repeated five times. It was dreadfully mortifying" (HT, pp. 21–22). As the picturesque develops, in other words, pilgrim is transformed to penitent.

The fictionality of colonial self-construction that Tytler's memoir embodies is of course highly ambivalent about how much significance a female narrator can claim when she tells an Anglo-Indian story. By presenting herself as a cross between Maggie Tulliver and Esther Summerson, Tytler implies both that she is more psychically self-aware than the constraints of a feminine picturesque license her to admit and that furthermore the Anglo-Indian woman is defined by her digression from a historical into a fictional narrative. The digressiveness of her story as a consequence supplies a crucial strategy through which the woman as colonialist can turn history into tale, reducing its violence into the commiserative idiom of anecdote that recounts the poor little English baby's death without having to examine the symbolic ramifications of such a vignette. An equally disturbing vision of Anglo-Indian fragility is offered by Tytler's next digression, which serves as a paradigm for her ability to raise explosive colonial questions in the guise of narrating pitiable colonial events:

> A very sad tragedy took place [at Agra] when I was there as a child. The Taj gardens used to be a great resort for picnics in those days. On one of these occasions, the whole station was there, when after lunch some of the officers and their wives proposed to run a race to the top of one of the beautiful white marble minarets. There was a poor young English woman, a Mrs. Monkton, a civilian's wife, who won the race and was so excited over it that she fell backwards over the very narrow parapet and was smashed to atoms. It was a terrible shock to all present. Her poor remains were placed in our doctor's palankeen and taken back to cantonments. (HT, pp. 12–13)

However surreal the actual event, Tytler's digression further emblematizes the infantilism of Anglo-India, particularly of its women: the gratuitous levity with which they must function first produces the casualty of Mrs. Monkton and then discursively replicates her scattering in Tytler's narrative. While Tytler can thus embody the violent costs of colonial entertainment, her language may stray into pathos but no deeper into a self-examination of the cultural trauma that is its subject. The incongruity of pathos, however, is striking enough to cause Tytler's reader early to dread her deployment of the epithet "poor," which serves as an unfailing index that its recipient will be a corpse before the end of the next paragraph.

Part 1 of *An Englishwoman in India* is supposedly an account of Anglo-India at peace and functions as a prelude to the second part of the text, in which Tytler recounts her experience during the 1857 Siege of Delhi. In such a binary structure, the woman chronicler first tries out her narrative hand on her natural territory of peaceful domesticity before venturing out onto the historical terrain of the male Anglo-Indian. Despite the text's clear desire to maintain its gendered structural dualism, the psychic derangements manifested by its first part illustrate the obsolescence of a war-and-peace dichotomy to the violence of Anglo-Indian narrative. The opening section of ostensible peace digresses into death too invariably to allow its equanimity to register as anything other than the phantasmagoria of the feminine picturesque, constructing instead an impoverished vision of how both mother and child function as symbolic tokens of colonial loss: disease, absence, and accident create so malevolent a plot that an aura of either bereavement or orphanhood surrounds each representation of maternity and infancy. When part 2 turns to the Great Rebellion, it therefore requires very small adjustments of tone and posture to accommodate the public theater of history, merely suggesting that the deathly equanimity of domesticity can now be translated into a disturbing reading of war's redundancy to an already deeply embattled colonial stage.

Despite her status as eyewitness, Tytler evinces a perfunctory understanding of the historical inevitability of the 1857 war, offering instead a conspiracy plot that locates the reality of a rebellion against colonial practice with imperial machinations by "the conquered but very wily Mohammedans":

> At the time of the Indian Mutiny, the reigning emperor was Bahadur Shah, an old man quite in his dotage, who lived, surrounded by the remembrance of past glory and vast power, on a generous pension provided by the East India Company. His two sons, along with the old man, had evidently but one idea and that was of regaining their power as soon as an opportunity should occur and for which opportunity they had waited over fifty years and had never shown their teeth, until '57. But when the order for the use of the Enfield rifles was issued, they at once set to work to poison the minds of the Hindu soldiery, who thoroughly believed them and nothing could convince that we had no desire to destroy their caste. . . . So all the Mohammedans had to do to drive us out of the country was to poison the minds of the gullible Hindus. Now the time had come to do this and they succeeded to their hearts' content. (HT, pp. 109–10)

Tytler will not venture beyond genealogical stereotypes of the wars of 1857 and offers instead the originary fetish of the Enfield rifle as a prime mover of all mutinous action, the much-touted cartridge of which was greased against

the grain of both colonized forces.[21] In such a trivialized context, the picturesque retains its narrative equanimity by reading colonial history as the
obsolete narrative of Old Testament vengeance: the economy of Anglo-India
is thus replaced with an equally monopolistic interpretation of what blood
must be shed before a colonial parity may be declaimed.

Tytler's account of the Siege of Delhi is paradigmatic of a colonial will
to remain immune to historical action even while it is immersed in history;
she interprets each violent clash of cultural and social code according to the
simple logic of retribution without examining her own implication in the plot
that she constructs. Instead, she collects details of war from the vantage point
of the picturesque, observing casualties in order to comment, "Such handsome, splendid specimens of high casted Hindus. One man had a hole as large
as a billiard ball through his forehead, a perfect giant in death. I could not
help saying, 'Serve you right for killing our poor women and children who
had never injured you.' At any other time my heart would have been full of
pity and sorrow at such awful sights, but after all we had suffered at the hands
of our treacherous sepoys, pity had vanished and thirst for revenge alone remained. Such are the effects of warfare upon the hearts of gentle, tender-
hearted women" (HT, p. 145). They have equally deranging effects on the
limits of maternity, according to Tytler, who tells the following anecdote of
how she entertained her daughter during the siege: "At last a bright idea
entered my head. It was a rather unique one, which was to scratch holes in
my feet and tell her she must be doctor and stop their bleeding. This process
went on daily for hours. No sooner did my wounds heal, when she used to
make them bleed again for the simple pleasure of stopping the blood with my
handkerchief. But it had the desired effect of amusing her for hours" (HT, p.
149). The self-sacrificial virtue that this scene represents to Tytler is more
significantly an enactment of a transgressive need to essentialize maternity
into nothing other than a bodily presence that can entice the child into a bond
of self-mutilation. If the public events of the Siege of Delhi afford Tytler the
pleasures of retribution, the intimate details she records point to the pleasures of self-flagellation: in both cases, an obsession with embodiment
prevents the narrative from recognizing the point at which public and intimate punishment converge in the construction of historical action.

After the fall of Delhi, Tytler's memoir comes to an abrupt and in-
conclusive end. Her narrative impulse has been to aestheticize the Mutiny
into a tale of treachery and revenge, allowing the easy pieties of the picturesque in order to assign guilt or exonerate crime without any awareness of
the narrative's own cultural complicity in the political upheavals it records.

During the months of colonial consolidation that followed the fall of Delhi, Tytler recounts one event alone from her sojourn in that city: "Towards the very end of September my husband came to tell me Government had issued an order to knock down every house inside the fort walls. I exclaimed, 'What a pity no one will know hereafter what the home of the Emperors of Delhi was like. How I would like to paint it!'" (HT, p. 167). The picturesque returns, in other words, to its proper colonial function, making memorabilia out of a culture still alive but one that it must nevertheless takes pains to embalm. "When I undertook the task of painting," Tytler adds, "I thought I might sell it to Barnum the showman, but we did not get home for nearly three years afterwards, when the great interest in the events of the Mutiny were over, and so we thought it was no use trying" (HT, p. 169). The female contribution to the spectacle of colonialism may operate at the level of Barnum and Bailey rather than at Lockwood Kipling's association with the Imperial Assemblage of 1877,[22] but it still repeats in diminution the impulse to aggrandize and avenge.

An Englishwoman in India documents the extent to which the feminine picturesque colludes in the public narrative of the Raj, illustrating thereby the collaboration between violence and sentimentality in the myth-making that attends the events of the Mutiny. To the British, as Bernard Cohn points out, "the Mutiny was seen as a heroic myth embodying and expressing their central values which explained their rule in India to themselves—sacrifice, duty, fortitude; above all it symbolized the ultimate triumph over those Indians who had threatened properly constituted authority and order."[23] Tytler's memoir both celebrates the reconstitution of such authority and unwittingly supplies a map of her own psychic maiming at the hands of Anglo-India: in her narrative, picturesque equanimity transmutes into the discourse of a sentimentality that possesses an inherently violent excess. As the Anglo-Indian repository of sentiment, the colonial mother becomes dangerous in her dead calm; her will to aestheticize turns to a cultural monumentalization in which the child of the Raj can walk upon his newly consolidated empire as an imperial emblem in himself, commemorating the mutinous dead in the violent name of Stanley Delhi-Force.

THE EIGHT VOLUMES OF *THE PEOPLE OF INDIA. A SERIES OF PHOTOGRAPHIC IL-lustrations, with Descriptive Letterpress, of the Races and Tribes of Hin-dustan, Originally Prepared under the Authority of the Government of India, and Reproduced by Order of the Secretary of the State for India in Council* was published during the second decade of the British Raj, from 1868 to 1875. The volumes consist of 468 photographs, each of which is accompanied by a "descriptive letterpress," or texts that veer between excessively unfavorable and favorable racial and cultural commentary. Edited by John Wilson Kaye, Secretary of the Political and Secret Department of the India Office, and John Forbes Watson, reporter for Products of India in the same institution, *The people of India* represents a massive consolidation of the picturesque into the official information with which the India Office supplied its civil servants. It was furthermore what Ray Desmond describes as "the first major ethnographical work to employ photographs on a large scale,"[24] and as such constitutes a document as methodologically progressive as it is ideologically retrograde. The intertwining of these impulses, in which scientism cannot sustain its commitment to catalog without a heavy reliance on a picturesque aesthetic, converts *The people of India* from an official ethnographic record into a text of dizzying colonial ambivalence: which racial type will be selected or censored from its sequence; to which image will the letterpress arbitrarily choose to confer or deny its racial favor, and how is a reader subsequently to cope with the deranging discrepancy between image and text? Each photograph is categorized according to race, religion, caste, geographical region, and traditional occupation, as well as with reference to the represented type's most typical vices and virtues, if there are any of the latter to record. Despite the unrelenting authority that the project exudes, however, implicit in the order of each volume is an acknowledgment of the cultural anarchy that the subcontinent poses to a colonial epistemology, in which the racial and cultural unreadability of India is reified even as it is excessively exposed to the classifications of an imperial camera eye.

As the dead calm of the picturesque transmutes into the demeanor of official authority, the collective zeal of *The people of India* demands to be read as an act of cultural negotiation through which the Raj could symbolically demonstrate its intimate knowledge with the range and diversity of colonized peoples, constructing thereby an ethnographic manifesto of colonial legitimacy. While the commentary is intended to supply an authoritative illustration of such claims, the interplay between image and text creates a confrontational narrative in which commentary cannot finally contain its subject, focusing instead on fixities of racial categories as a means to stave off its hidden admission of cultural ignorance. The ethnographic photography of *The people of India* thus serves a highly fraught interpretative function, in that it culls images that act as self-interpretations and remain insubordinate to the descriptions imposed upon them. In such a schizophrenic division between illustration and explanatory material, the images themselves are of less interest than the descriptive powerlessness exuded by the text: rather than confirm the Raj's intimacy with its Indian subjects, the letterpress secretly admits to a guilty liaison with the attractions and repulsions through which racial difference disturbs the demarcations of colonial power. Ostensibly freezing both race and caste into visually assimilable compendiums of information, *The people of India* exemplifies an English inability to recognize social and cultural hierarchies more dynamic than its own.

Thirty years before the appearance of *The people of India*, Macaulay had similarly frozen the issue of education into a shield against the unknowability of India, arguing in his notorious "Minutes" that the British must "do our best to form a class who may be interpreters between us and the millions whom we govern; a class of persons, Indian in blood and colour, but English in taste, in opinions, in morals, and in intellect."[25] The creation of an alienated subgroup would serve the purpose of the Raj by supplying indigenous populations with exemplary models of what racial and cultural crossbreeding could produce: India would henceforth have a more than ample supply of natives in the guise of Jude the Obscure. In the Kaye and Forbes Watson project, the India Office produced a corollary document that equally aimed at an obsessive subgrouping through which the Indian races could be both contained and objectified within a British system of interpretation. While its record of race calmly implies a familiarity with questions of cultural difference, the actual text mutates into a narrative fearfully conscious of the terrors of colonial categorization; religious, racial, and regional affiliations are conflated to produce a grid into which each Indian type may be potentially slotted, but the completion of such a geometry continues to evade the totality of colonial control. In massively seeking to document an understanding that cannot avoid its own dismantling into ignorance, *The people of India* becomes a record instead of a specifically colonial racial anxiety and a victim of its own picturesque calm.

The imperial stereotyping of the nineteenth century is consistently interested in maintaining a belief in the cultural stasis of the subcontinent: as late as 1850, Robert Knox's troubled and troubling text *The Races of Men: A Fragment* makes the paradigmatic claim, "Little is known of the dark races of Asia, even of those of Indostan. It is a fact worthy of the deepest reflection, that neither Northern India nor Indostan proper have altered since the time of Alexander the Great; that is, for twenty-three or twenty-four centuries of years they have not progressed nor changed. This I am disposed to think decides the character of the race or races; for no doubt there must be many races inhabiting these widely-extended and still, I presume, populous regions.

Their extreme populousness I am disposed to question; their possible improvement is questionable."[26] While *The people of India* approaches the question of Indian stasis with a far greater breadth of information than that possessed by Robert Knox, its ethnography is equally committed to conceiving the races of the subcontinent in terms of immutable categories oblivious to the historical dynamism of the systems it depicts. Here, the deployment of photographs for the classification of ostensibly unchanging racial types poses a peculiar interpretative problem, in that the specificity of each image begs to be read as illustrative only of itself rather than as a representative of an ahistorical racial type. As the people of India stare back at the reader of the volumes to which they supplied both images and title, the question asked by Sayyid Ahmad Khan returns with yet another racial perspective. Examining the volume in 1869, long before the completion of the project, the Muslim educationist wondered of the colonialist, "What can they think, after perusing this book and looking at its pictures?" The temporal specificity of the photographs forces a historical imagination to return to that moment of ethnographic arrest when the subject gazes back into the colonial lens and will not tell what it thinks.[27]

The letterpress commentary to *The people of India* draws from official reports, citations from regional authorities, and readings of the individual images. Throughout the text, the strict binarism between Aryan and aborigine is further complicated by the parallel binarism of Hindu and Muslim, the ineffectual categorization of which is illustrative of the text's failure to recognize that it records less racial reality than historical contingency. Such an acknowledgment could, however, lift the colonial representation of India out of a static and feudal picturesque to privilege instead the dynamism of its social and economic hierarchies, which would signify a discursive impossibility to the idiom of Anglo-India. In order to maintain strict dualities between colonizer and colonized, it is equally necessary that such alteritism is imposed upon the subordinated peoples, who are required to fit within similarly containable structures. Where *The people of India* most clearly reveals its own ambivalence with such oppositions is in its characterization of non-scheduled or casteless tribes that transgress against the project's ideology of racial control. In commentary exemplary of ethnographic uncertainty, the text to plate 232 in volume 5 describes the Changars, a "low caste wandering tribe" at that moment located in Lahore, with a repressed rage more accurately directed against the futility of categorization than against the group itself:

The tribe to which the group depicted in the photograph belongs, has an unenviable character for thieving and general dishonesty, and forms one of the large class of unsettled wanderers, which, inadmissible to Hindooism, and unconverted to the Mahomedan faith, live on in miserable conditions of life as outcasts from the more civilized communities. . . . In appearance, both men and women are repulsively mean and wretched, the features of the women in particular being very ugly. . . . It is a difficult ethnological problem to determine to what class of aborigines these isolated wandering tribes belong. Unlike the Santhals, Gonds, Koles, [the Changars] seem to have clung to the Aryans, and, unaffected by their civilization, to have followed them, feeding, as it were, on the garbage left by them, neverchanging, never improving, never advancing in social rank, scale or utility; outcasts and foul parasites from the earliest ages, they so remain, and probably will continue as long as they are existent. . . . In their clothes and their persons the Changars are decidedly unclean and, indeed, in most respects, the repulsiveness of the tribe can hardly be exceeded.[28]

Historical necessity, in other words, cannot impinge upon the Changars, who according to the text have an innate desire for the part of the pariah: they have not been excluded from the larger hierarchical complex of social acceptance into which the tribe is placed, but instead embody a will to untouchability with which the interpretations of colonial history must not interfere.

The imperial fallacy here at work involves both a repressed attraction to the Indian body and a concomitant misreading of a cultural system in which the economy of alterity is centrally located within social conditions of acceptability. That a tribe like the Changars, however, could be a countenanced component of Indian society is as incomprehensible to the colonizing imagination as was the social acceptability of the courtesan to the Anglo-Indian woman writer. Both represent forms of transgression that, within the hierarchies of the subcontinent, are accorded a public and recognized cultural space: the colonial desire to maintain strict boundaries between public and private or transgressive and decorous ways of life is thus vexed by the bewildering irrelevance of its Western models.

Instead of attempting to read the peoples of India in the absence of such futile tools, however, the ethnography of the text disintegrates into a triangulated interpretation in which aesthetic judgment is transmuted into an

ethical verdict and then yoked with violence into the authority of a sociological pronouncement: "It will be seen at a glance how widely [the
features of the Jokya tribe from Sind] differ from those of real Mahomedan
tribes, how they utterly lack the comeliness and dignity of the Belochees. It
is very probable that the intermarry in their own tribe exclusively, and thus
the ancient Hindoo physiognomy, in this case a remarkably ugly type, has
been preserved" (*PI*, vol. 6, p. 313). The complex economies of race and religion, in other words, are to the imperial eye essentialized into the literalism
of figure and feature; colonized bodies are frozen both as photographs and by
a commentary that hysterically insists on the static readability of physicality. Coming as Childe Roland to the dark tower of the subcontinent, the
Victorian ethnographer cannot avoid repeating the fallacy of Browning's
protagonist; "Seldom went such grotesqueness with such woe; / I never saw
a beast I hated so; / He must be wicked to deserve such pain."

Implicit in such a clash of moral and aesthetic evaluations is a self-
punishment characteristic of the colonial picturesque, in which the obser-
vance of woe generates a dislocated fury attributable only to the abjection of
the colonized. Rather than follow through the ineluctable logic of imperial
interconnectedness, a picturesque discourse provides instead an unhinged
aestheticism that veils and sequesters questions of colonial culpability, but in
so doing, becomes a casualty of its own abstracted guilt. Much as Fanny
Parks's picturesque was deranged by the racial actuality of body and skin and
sought safety instead in series of dress and adornment, so too *The people of
India* locates its peace in descriptions of all that conceals the disturbance of
embodiments of race: "The Rind photographed is a man of no importance,
but is a fine specimen of the warlike Belochees. . . . He wears national arms,
and costume of the Beloch guides and others in the pay of Government on the
northern frontier. . . . Round his waist is tied a handsome silk scarf, which,
with his arms, shield, and voluminous white turban, completes a costume, as
handsome and picturesque, as it is becoming to its wearer" (*PI*, vol. 6, p. 298).
Where the physiognomy of racial difference can evoke only a colonial fear of
the greater cultural alternatives it symbolically represents, costume provides
comfort: it can be regularized and itemized into a sartorial aesthetic that
somehow suggests that the colonized can be completely known. The ethnography of *The people of India* is never on safer ground than when it
confines itself to the comparative refuge of clothes.

If the colonial picturesque is in itself a discourse of dressing and adornment, a mode of perceiving racial bodies as though they were pictures before
the act of representation, then the ethnographic fallacy of *The people of India*

most quickens with overdetermination when it turns to descriptions of the Indian woman's veil. The availability of diverse tribes and social groups to the colonial gaze is most frequently measured in relation to the visual accessibility of their women, while the female dress and its degree of hiding becomes an uncanny surrogate for the cultural and ideological veiling assumed by the project itself. In a paradigmatic comment on a photograph titled "Lambani Woman," the text unwittingly reveals its own obsession with an aesthetic of cultural concealment:

> We present this Photograph as it gives a fuller view of the peculiar costume of the women of this strange and peculiar sect. . . . The scarf thrown over the head, and hanging behind, conceals the high comb which is universally used to confine the hair tied in a knot. The strange long ear rings, intermixed with flowers and knots of hair, which hang down to the chest; the brightly embroidered and quilted bodice, which reaches to the hips . . . all combine to form one of the most graceful of Indian costumes. Like most Lambani women the features of the woman photographed are hard and repulsive; but many of the girls and younger women are very beautiful, with deep Spanish colour, and superb figures. (*PI*, vol. 7, p. 420)

Again, cultural interpretation is confined to the idiom of beauty, but a beauty in which colonial ethnography is strangely torn between recording its attraction to or repulsion from the synecdoche of alternative civilizations represented by the female body. Costume can be described with confidence; physiognomy itself, however, elicits the nervous terror of a possessor unable to record with any psychic stability an understanding of what he may possess: the Lambani woman must necessarily be "hard and repulsive" to the colonial gaze, yet the promise of her physical beauty cannot be withheld from the reader. Her dress is therefore an undress, a curiously revelatory discursive gesture through which the colonial enterprise of *The people of India* betrays its own dependence on systematic cultural and racial veils.

In the context of both the particularities of *The people of India* and the proliferating narrative of the picturesque engendered by the colonization of the Indian subcontinent, the veil is figuratively transferred from the colonized female body to the colonizing discourse itself; rage and hiding become the impulsions of an ethnography that knows it cannot see the full implications of its association in the racial repulsion that it seeks to transcribe. Even as the abundance of a colonized culture cannot be reduced to safe inventories of clothes and caste, so too the vicissitude of a colonial picturesque must beat

its head against the ungendering of imperial complicity, or that secretive aesthetic whose serenity is dangerously dependent on the inapplicability of
gender to the logic of colonialism. The subcontinent will not remain metaphorically female to the invading man, as *The people of India* knows full well
when it turns to the cultural anomaly represented by its interpretation of a
"Sikh Sodhee": "The Sodhees have in general an evil reputation for immorality, intoxication, and infanticide, the latter being justified by them on the
ground that it is impossible to marry their female children into ordinary Sikh
families. . . . The subject of the photograph resides at Lahore. He has lost an
eye, which is covered by an ornament pendant from his turban; and it is a
strange peculiarity of this person, that he dresses himself on all occasions in
female apparel" (*PI*, vol. 5, p. 240). The photograph itself smiles back a cultural mocking at the colonizing camera eye: dragging in his unreadability to
upset an imperial reliance on the gendering and costuming of its empire, the
image confirms what the text has already guiltily acknowledged—to dress
the colonial picturesque in either feminine or masculine garb is tragically to
defer that cultural realization which knows that its official representations
remain psychically skin-deep.

5

The Adolescence of *Kim*

WITH KIPLING, THE STORY OF EMPIRE LEARNS HOW TO ATROPHY IN ITS OWN prematurity. In varying degrees, imperial narratives consistently demonstrate their discomfort with the temporal negotiation that allows stories to represent their situatedness within a chronology that roughly approximates a history. Since empire both arrives too early and leaves too late, however, chronology is always an uneasy issue, implying that the precarious condition of the present tense is the only safe construction in which to articulate its tale. To name the present tense of history is of course to turn to journalism, to its absorption in the moment and the concomitant youthfulness suggested by such exuberance of attention. In the story of journalism, history is perpetually novel and necessarily occurs in the absence of precedent: in place of a more ponderous relation to the necessity of chronology, its narratives are impelled by the novelty of surprise. His literal profession as a journalist notwithstanding, Kipling's ability to supply a proliferation of voices to an imperial astonishment at its temporal and historical location make of him both the most obvious and the most intransigent of Anglo-Indian chroniclers. For in Kipling, empire confronts the necessary perpetuation of its adolescence in relation to its history, and conducts the cultural calibration required to energize repetitions of the tense idiom of dark surprise.

To read Kipling's narratives as representations of an atrophic adolescence, therefore, is less to condemn his imperial ideology than to attempt to comprehend their brilliant literalization of the colonial moment. While the antecedents of his storytelling are most frequently located in the genre of nineteenth-century adventure and detective fiction, they could perhaps be more fruitfully traced back to Burke's excessive anguish over the prematurity of colonial power. In the view of the eighteenth-century parliamentarian, colonial history could arrive at the status of an "age" only if the imperial project learned to tame the novel violence with which it handled a venerable colony. India was aged; its colonizers were young: "Young men (boys almost) govern there. . . . Animated with all the avarice of age and all the impetuosity of youth, they roll in one after another, wave after wave;

and there is nothing before the eyes of the natives but the endless, hopeless prospect of new flights of birds of prey and passage, with appetites continually renewing for a food that is continually wasting" (CW, vol. 2, p. 462). Where Burke implies an organic metaphor through which colonial history could—morally speaking—come of age, Kipling's equally terrified vision of imperial youth responds that the possibility of such an attainment of venerability is a historic fiction. To the nineteenth-century journalist of the Raj, the interest of colonialism inheres in the fact that it is perpetually novel.

If the novelty of Kipling can be located in his ability to bridge the gap between colonial terror and a more popular language of surprised colonial celebration, then his writing serves as a paradigm for a post-Mutiny rewriting of a Burkean indignation. This paradigm represents a cultural shorthand that allows empire to attain its modernity through a constant cutting of discursive corners, through a disinterest either in history's origins or in its chronology. Instead, colonial encounter becomes domesticated into the familiarity of every day facticity, so that terror becomes the norm rather than the exception. While such an illusion of immediacy accounts for much of the surface seduction of Kipling's tales, it simultaneously obscures the enduring disturbance of his narration, the act of which is best characterized figuratively as a cinematic animation of the Indian sublime.

When the appeal of animation is juxtaposed with the enervation of cultural claustrophobia that Raj narratives obsessively represent, then the former's energy demands to be read in contexts other than merely the masculinist or the imperialist. In the wake of 1857, colonial terror could be deemed sufficiently animated in its operation to render Kipling obsolete even before he assumed his heady representations of the British Raj. What redundancy impels his desire to animate imperial horror and its concomitant images while they are still decidedly alive? When, furthermore, can the stasis of novelty proffer itself as the most acute journalistic record of the functioning of colonial time? In what ways can the energy of obsolescence suggest the irrelevance of origins to both the facts of colonial encounter and its ensuing narratives, implying that the immediacy of colonialism can only be recorded secondhand? Where Kipling becomes more problematic than other equally popular writers of his time is precisely in his apprehension of the applicability of journalism to imperial narration, and of the temporal extinction that such narratives signify.

While it may appear unnecessarily arch to characterize Kipling's narratives as cultural acts of animated extinction, such seems to be a provisional method with which to read his narration of colonial chronologies. Kipling engages in the politics of the parochial, situating both categories—like Kim—in the abundance of such ambivalence that it becomes difficult to detect whether empire is an allegory for the history of the colony or whether colony is arrived at only to illustrate that empire has merely perfunctory claims to its own historicity. To a contemporary reader such as Oscar Wilde, such a skewed arena of attention can register only as the amazing flaw of Kipling's talent: "As one turns over the pages [of] *Plain Tales from the Hills,*" appreciates Wilde, "one feels as if one were seated under a palm-tree reading life by superb flashes of vulgarity."[1] With a critical acuity only to be expected, Wilde detects both the stasis and the momentum that Kipling will continue to syncopate: although Wilde's exquisitely Orientalist eye requires a palm tree as a reading aid, as a constant against which to interpret the "vulgarity" of colonial "life," Kipling both corroborates and moves beyond the dictates of such judgment. He will not seek to dignify the act of colonial narration for anything other than what it is, thus making a point that contemporary anthropological discourse is at pains to labor. Cultural description is always vulgar; its most animated moments occur only when "one" is "reading life by superb flashes of vulgarity."

More than an appreciation of the griefs of cultural anthropology, however, Kipling supplies a narrative means to read the implications of imperial time. Here, "imperial time" demands to be interpreted less as a recognizable chronology of historic events than as a contiguous chain of surprise effects: even as empire seeks to occupy a monolithic historic space, its temporality is more accurately characterized as a disruptive sequence of a present tense perpetually surprised, allowing for neither the precedent of the past nor the anticipation of a future. Instead, its grim montage of autonomous moments implies a certain threadbare dynamism in which surface is the only space that legitimizes signification. Kipling's narrative internalization of the superficiality of imperial time engenders both the adolescent energy of his tales and—in a text like *Kim*—the immanence of tragic loss, of an obsessively impelled discourse that lacks any direction in which to go. The "What is Kim?" and "Who is Kim?" questions that haunt the latter half of the text, therefore, are equally queries that the narrative poses about empire's relation to the colonization of its time. For the colonization of temporality is one of the several ill-effects caused by the acquisition of empire, and Kipling is perhaps the most clairvoyant narrator of the temporal derangements dictated by such an abnegation of chronology.

Kipling's embodiment of the peculiarities inherent in colonial dischronology has received curiously scant critical attention, or is somewhat patronizingly judged as a manifestation of imperial propaganda. Edward Said offers an important historicist caveat in his attempt to place Kipling's sense of imperial time in a context other than that of the propagandist or of the Orientalist vision of colonial 'timelessness': "Kipling's admirers and acolytes have often spoken of his representations of India as if the India he wrote about was a timeless, unchanging, and 'essential' locale, as a place almost as much poetical as actual. This, I think, is a radical misreading. . . . If Kipling's India has qualities of the essential and unchanging, it was because . . . he deliberately chose to see India that way. [It must be interpreted] as a territory dominated by Britain for three hundred years, but beginning at that time to exhibit the increasing unrest which would culminate in decolonization and independence."[2] While Said's rereading of Kim helpfully questions the ostensible changelessness of Kipling's India by examining it as a necessary evasion of history, his argument could be extended to suggest how effectively Kipling collapses both categories into a narration of imperial time. In other words, the history of empire is in itself evasive, and a postcolonial readership cannot confine such a strategy of storytelling to the narrator's political and moral relation to his times.

To impute an ethical blindness—or better, a moral vacuity—to the structure of Kim is as a consequence to evade the relentless mimesis with which Kipling attempts to mirror his recollection of colonial India. Here, we must turn back to the wistfulness that enters even such a powerful reading of Kipling as Edmund Wilson's "The Kipling That Nobody Read": "What the reader tends to expect is that Kim will come to realise that he is delivering into bondage to the British invaders those whom he has always considered his own people, and that a struggle between allegiances will result. . . . [But the fiction of Kipling] does not dramatise any fundamental conflict because Kipling would never face one."[3] Much in the Burkean vein, Wilson wishes to see the adolescent ebullience of empire come of age in order that it may tell stories of a less vertiginous and disturbing chronology. Such a disturbance, however, is surely central to Kim's vision of imperial will, the youthfulness of which is always interchangeable with its rapacity.

Despite Wilson's perspicacious longing for a mature narrative of colonial rule, Kipling's engagement in the idiom of imperialism suggests that this desire for happier conclusions is in contravention to the structure of the colonialist project. Here, the questions posed by Wilson concerning the possibility of closure in a post-Mutiny narrative call for a further array of cultural doubt, as raised by Said's critique of the blindness implied in "The Kipling That Nobody Read." For Said, the absence of "conflict" is again located in the repressed intentionality of the author: "There is no resolution to the conflict between Kim's colonial service and loyalty to his Indian companions not because Kipling could not face it, but because for Kipling *there was no conflict*. Indeed, one of the purposes of the novel was to show the absence of conflict. . . . That there might be a conflict had Kipling considered India as unhappily subservient to colonialism, of this we can have no doubt. The fact is that he did not: for him it was India's destiny to be ruled by England. "[4] Such a deranging "absence of conflict," however, could further be imputed to the structure of imperial ideology, which Kipling represents with an irony that both Wilson and Said seem unwilling to address. If one of the manifestations of the anxiety of empire is a repression of the conflictual model even where economic and political conflict is at its most keenly operative, then Kipling's transcriptions of such evasion point to his acute understanding of the ambivalence with which empire declares its unitary powers.

While *Kim* remains Kipling's most subtle study of the delusional "absence of conflict" that fuels colonial energies, his shorter works of fiction are equally engaged in illustrating both the tawdry quality of imperial glamor and its vertiginous alienation from any "rational" system of hierarchy and control. In "The Conversion of Aurelian McGoggin," to turn to an obvious example, the chronology of power and the complete inefficacy of its order are precisely the objects of the mercilessness of Kipling's imperial gaze:

> Life, in India, is not long enough to waste in proving that there is no one in particular at the head of affairs. For this reason. The Deputy is above the Assistant, the Commissioner above the Deputy, the Lieutenant-Governor above the Commissioner, and the Viceroy above all four, under the orders of the Secretary of State, who is responsible to the Empress. If the Empress be not responsible to her Maker—if there is no Maker for her to be responsible to—the entire system of Our administration must be wrong. Which is manifestly impossible.[5]

Here is a manifesto for colonialism's "absence of conflict," the narration of which sharply illustrates the anarchic disempowerment underlying such a system of control.

We turn to *Kim*, then, to reread the consequences of imperial prematurity: rather than merely embody a colonial desire to erase the conflictual paradigm, the text proffers a far more problematic representation of how rarefied may be colonialism's engagement with cultural conflict. Thus Kipling's protagonist is indeed a marvelous boy whose fate is to carry messages to the point where his very body is synonymous with the information of empire. Despite his ostensible mobility and cultural dexterity, however, Kim is an imperial casualty of more tragic proportions than he is usually granted. It is not as though Kim stands outside the colonial system called the Great Game and—as Edmund Wilson implies—has the luxury of choosing whether or not to play it: instead, Kim *is* the Game, and finally is unable to separate it from the parameters of his own history. Kim's collaboration is therefore emblematic of not so much an absence of conflict as the terrifying absence of choice in the operations of colonialism. If the structure of the tale is a relentless mapping of the point where the messenger becomes the message, then the aphasic quality of Kim's penultimate collapse cannot be merely read as a necessary step in his ultimate "recovery." The loss of language and the inability of the message to contain anything worth reading suggests instead how liable an "absence of conflict" is to cave in upon itself, how liable to enter interpretive spaces like the Marabar in order to learn nothing. For the Great Game can certainly be read as a precursor to the Marabar Caves, in that its impact lies in its astonishing availability to unintelligible information.

Kipling's interest in colonial aphasia is frequently linked to his engagement in the representation of imperial adolescence, in which the misplacing of discourse curiously replicates the obsolescence encoded in the brief shelf life of journalistic language. Aphasia not only generates the silent question, "What is Kim?", but furthermore supplies a crucial disruption in the coherence of chronology, so that its occurrence retards the possibility of a colonial "coming of age." In the 1887 "Tract" offered by "The Conversion of Aurelian McGoggin," aphasia seizes the youthful colonial administrator simply because he is too addicted to the logic of a positivistic chronology. McGoggin brings both energy and an earnest positivism to colonial India; both work him into a collapse that the station doctor diagnoses as colonial aphasia. McGoggin's recovery signifies a recognition that colonialism cannot possess the course of its own chronology:

> "But I can't understand it, repeated [McGoggin]. "It was my *own* mind and memory."
> "I can't help it," said the Doctor. "There are a good many things you can't understand; and, by the time you have put in my length of service, you'll know exactly how much a man dare call his own in this world."
> That stroke cowed [McGoggin]. He could not understand it. He went into the Hills in fear and trembling, wondering

whether he would be permitted to reach the end of any sentence he began.

This gave him a *wholesome feeling of mistrust*. The legitimate explanation, that he had been overworking himself, failed to satisfy him. Something had wiped his lips of speech, *as a mother wipes the milky lips of her child, and he was afraid—horribly afraid.*"[6] (Emphasis added)

The parable indicates no possible recuperation of control, but gives a cynical endorsement of the "wholesome" engendering of mistrust and fear. It proceeds to suggest that once colonial adolescence has reached its crisis, there can be no transition into a comforting myth of "growing up" or an attainment of maturity. Instead, there can be only a repetition of the dispossessed panic of youthfulness; there can be only a stale recurrence of the adolescent question, "What is Kim?"

Kim is the colonial voice on the brink of aphasia, so that the abundance of its narrative is perpetually arrested by the potential dischronology embodied in a cessation of cultural reading. As such, it incorporates the terrors of imperialism into the very energy of adventure narratives: something is on the verge of wiping the lips of *Kim*'s speech, of which the Great Game is only the rude literalization. Even as the text renders the transcendentalism of the lama's quest coterminous with Kim's complicity in the literalism of imperial espionage, it articulates the novelty of an imperial narrative astounded at the possibility of its silence. Both the lama and Kim represent two opposite poles of cultural adolescence: Teshoo Lama's naivete suggests an atrophied absence of adulthood that is mirrored by the aggressive exuberance of his ostensible disciple. There is no doubt that their union is as enchanting as it is incongruous, but it can be enacted only on the grim colonial territory that declares that boys will be boys and nothing more.

As a study of cultural possession and dispossession, *Kim* remains one of the most disturbing narrations of nineteenth-century colonial astonishment. Much as its opening pages can make the somewhat unusual claim that "India is the only democratic land in the world,"[7] so too the text distributes cultural surprise equally between colonizer and colonized. The protagonist embodies both aspects of such surprise, in that his status as a dispossessed colonizer is perpetually mediated by his intimacy with and filiation to the cultures of the colonized. While this mobility allows Kim to know the shocks posed by alterities from every angle of the colonial encounter, it nonetheless implies a facility that is ultimately synonymous with his victimization. Kim is either his own victim or that of the Great Game's; he either possesses the lama or is possessed by him: the ambivalence of the narrative allows for no easy resolutions of such questions, but further suggests that the position of dispossession is more primary than secondary, and that each actor on the colonial stage is complicit in it.

From the outset of a story that bases its plot on the continual exchange of misread messages, the possibility of cultural possession implies the most dangerous misreading. In keeping with an imperial intimacy that has surprise, shock, and a "wholesome feeling of mistrust" as its inception, *Kim* opens to manifest the illegitimacy of possession. Rather than representing an archaic or an alteritist civilization to Kim, the lama is desirable because of his novelty: "This man was entirely new to all his experience, and he meant to investigate further: precisely as he would have investigated a new building or a strange festival in Lahore city. The lama was his trove, and he purposed to take possession" (p. 16). The amateur ethnographer, in other words, plans to own the lama's story and to recast its plot in the image of his own excitement. No mere "adventure tale" can ensue from such an encounter, the first misread message of which implies that the novelty of difference can logically lead to possession. In the combination of the charming and the tragic that characterizes the narrative of *Kim*, the price of such a will to possess constitutes what—at the end of the text—can possibly remain of Kim.

If the initial desire for possession is transmuted by the bonds of affection and intimacy generated between this unlikely pair of questers, the novelty of this union never changes character: Kim's capacity to surprise the lama, and the lama's to surprise Kim, remain a self-repeating constant from the opening to the closing pages of the text. And the very prematurity of surprise—or its epistemological inability to process information as it is received—lends a troubling vacuity to what has been called the "wisdom" of the novel. In his generous reading of the "wisdom and humanity" of *Kim*, Mark Kinkead-Weekes argues for the centrality of both literal and figurative representations of vision: "Kim also embodies the urge to obtain a deeper kind of vision, the urge not merely to see and to know from the outside, but to *become* the 'other.' Kim's more-than-chameleon ability to change, not only his clothes, but his voice and mannerisms, his whole identity, represents . . . something far more creative and imaginative in Kipling: not merely the observer's sharp eye, but the dramatist's longing to get into the skin of many 'others.' Kim is an expression of what Keats called 'negative capability.' "[8]

While indeed vision is crucial to the cinematic structure of the narrative, the suggestion of deeper visions of racial and cultural difference perhaps gives colonial history more coherence and depth than it deserves. This is by no means to deny the compassion of the text, but to posit that that colonial compassion may well be predicated on the surprise of its own futility, and that the brilliance of *Kim* lies in its ability to represent cultural multifariousness while at the same time illustrating that its historical context must inevitably lead back to the monolith of the Great Game.

Since surprise and possession are largely both the impetus and the results of the Great Game, the lama's and Kim's complicity in such states of mind causes a shifting in the text's demarcation of the parameters of power. It would be too easy a dualism to read the quest as an enclave of innocence that is somehow detached from, rather than subservient to, the experience of the Game. Whatever ideological commitment Kipling had to the supremacy of the imperial ideal, his apprehension of colonial history is too prescient to allow for such ready distinctions between the "true" and the "real." Here, Edward Said's response to Kinkead-Weekes aptly characterizes the ambivalent historicity of Kipling's narrative: "Yes, the lama is a kind of antiself, and yes, Kipling can get into the skin of others with some sympathy. But no, Kipling never forgets that Kim is an irrefrangible part of British India: the Great Game does go on with Kim a part of it, no matter how many parables the lama fashions. We are naturally entitled to read *Kim* as a novel belonging to the world's great literature. . . . Yet by the same token, we must not unilaterally abrogate connections *in it*, and carefully observed by Kipling, to its contemporary actuality."[9] The historical necessity that forces Kim into the course of the Game must be interpreted; however, the lama's quest needs to be examined in equal detail. What, finally, differentiates his desire from an imperial will to create what Francis Hutchins calls the "illusion of permanence," or a teleology as bound to the economy of possession as it ostensibly seeks to be released from it?[10] The shock of Kipling's historicity implies that on the contrary, the lama is as much part of the Game as is Kim. While his complicity in the demands of empire are unknown to him, he functions as does Kim: both unwittingly endorse a colonial intimacy in which refinements of the modes of acquisition hardly modify the greater acquisitiveness that necessarily defines the quest that they pursue.

As has been frequently noted by readers of *Kim*, the infantilism of the lama exceeds that of his boy guide: his ostensible otherworldliness sheathes him from the routine cartography that constitutes colonial life, in which rivers are named, in which wheels have more to do with agriculture than with

Buddhist mysticism, and in which the "Middle Way" most typically represents the petty ineptitudes of colonial administration. The lama's studied blindness to such detail, however, cannot be taken as an equivalent for Kipling's equal repression of the facticity of colonial existence, for the former's very childishness can be read as a reactive strategy to address the situation of colonialism. In an acute interpretation of the infantile in Kipling's Indian narratives, S. P. Mohanty suggests that "the separate world of childhood registers and refracts crucial political anxieties of imperial Britain";[11] the lama's absence of anxiety must be similarly read as an expression of complicity in a Game that does not signify mere espionage but provides instead a dramatic figure for the imperial enterprise. The childishness of Kim, argues Mohanty, tells "a distinct and specifiable political story in which adventure is indistinguishable from surveillance, pleasure intertwined with power, and the values of childhood a thin allegory for imperial ideology."[12] Such an allegory assumes a greater thickness when it becomes evident that the childhood of the lama—furthermore his concomitant understanding of colonial pragmatics—is a fiction of surprise equally balanced with a fraught economy of the Game.

Here it becomes necessary to reread the lama in terms of his interceptions in colonial reality. He subsists in post-1857 India, dimly recalling the year of the Great Rebellion as a "black year"; he charms the would-be imperialist into a recognition of the seductions represented by a failure to recognize the mapping essential to imperial self-fashioning. While his desire to turn a blind eye to the ways of the "great and terrible" world may be part of the lama's quaint appeal, it calls to be interpreted as a desire rather than as an actuality. Despite his insistence on the "Middle Way," the lama knows how to negotiate within a colonial framework, and further knows that "acquiring merit" can be synonymous with the expedience of "buying education." The scene in which the lama negotiates with Mr. Bennet and Father Victor is consequently crucial to the narrative, in that it dramatically revises the lama's otherworldliness even as it effectively disrupts the texture of the novel. Until chapter 5, *Kim*'s buoyancy promises to unfold into a tale of cross-cultural male bonding: with Kim's captivity and the ensuing barter over his future, however, the narrative shifts radically into a parable of male desire and of male separation.

While it would be unnecessarily reductive to read the desire that obtains between the lama and Kim as a figure for the submerged homoeroticism that attends on colonial encounter, it would be equally injudicious to ignore the passion that describes their connection. The moment of passion, of course, is unleashed by the fact of separation, reminding the reader that for at least two-thirds of the text this connection remains in suspended animation. Once Kim has found the fetish of his father's regimental flag and has immediately toppled from a subaltern world into an imperial world, the immediacy of the lama's grief reveals more than a cursory acquaintance with the cultural and political gulf now opened between them:

> Then the lama raised his head, and looked forth across them into space and emptiness.
>
> "And I am a follower of the Way," he said bitterly. "I made believe to myself . . . that thou wast sent to me to aid in the Search. So my heart went out to thee for thy charity and thy courtesy and the wisdom of thy little years. But those that follow the Way must not permit the fire of any desire or attachment. . . . I stepped aside from the Way, my *chela*. It was no fault of thine. I delighted in the sight of life, the new people upon the roads, and in thy joy at seeing these things. . . . Now I am sorrowful because thou art taken away and my River is far from me. It is the Law which I have broken!"
>
> "Powers of Darkness below!" said Father Victor, who, wise in the confessional, heard the pain in every sentence. (Pp. 94–95)

Here, the jaunty quality of the picaresque is recast into confessions of a far more enduring desire, in which the vicariousness of Kim's cultural position will seduce the lama far more than his quest for the River.

The lama's acquiescence in the face of desire, however, is less remarkable than his ability to move from the idiom of mourning into that of negotiation. As is typical of the text as a whole, the transaction must be carried out through a mediating translator, emphasizing the precarious potential of misreading that dictates the transmittal of colonial messages:

> "Do they give or sell learning among the Sahibs? Ask them," said the lama, and Kim interpreted. . . .
>
> "And— the more money is paid the better the learning is given?" The lama disregarded Kim's plan for an early flight. "It is no wrong to pay for learning; to help the ignorant to wisdom is always a merit." *The rosary clicked furiously as an abacus. Then he turned to face his oppressors.*
>
> "Ask them for how much money do they give a wise and suitable teaching? and in what city is that teaching given?" (P. 96, emphasis added)

The sale of information and the economy of colonial knowledge, in other words, is by no means beyond the ken of the "otherworldly" lama. He not only understands the structure of oppression, but furthermore has an intuitive knowledge of the price that very literally accompanies such a reality. While Kipling allows the lama to confess to human desire and to no other sense of cultural vulnerability, this moment of rupture in *Kim* crucially reveals the old man's implication in the transactive dynamic generated by colonial rule. When he learns that he may purchase education for his "beloved," and when his rosary clicks as "furiously as an abacus," then the simile confirms synechdocically the grim thrust of chapter 5: there are no quests that live a charmed life outside the confines of colonial desire, much as the oppression of amorous loss is inevitably subsumed into the abstract oppressiveness signified by the economy of the Great Game.

That a Tibetan priest can resort to utilitarianism, however, implies the density rather than the limitation of Kipling's colonial vision. On one level, the lama's transgression of his code allows for the child a rite of passage into the adolescence of espionage; on a more disturbing level, it forces upon Kim's cultural mobility the tyrannical status of a Macaulayan "interpreter." In the infamous claims made by the "Minute on Indian Education," Macaulay justifies an Anglicist education policy for the Indian colony by anticipating the creation of a class of native informants: "It is impossible for us, with our limited means, to attempt to educate the body of the people. We must at present do our best to form a class who may be interpreters between us and the millions whom we govern; a class of persons, Indian in blood and colour, but English in taste, in opinions, in morals, and in intellect."[13] While Kim is initially the mirror image of such an interpreter, the pragmatics of his education as a sahib severely unhinge the confidence of his cultural transactions. His race manifests itself as an imprisonment: the lama may believe that he is purchasing the liberation of knowledge, but Kipling clearly indicates that such tutelage is merely preparatory to Kim's participation in the tyranny of the Great Game. He will be taught to interpret according to the monolithic needs of imperial ideology, which substitute the acquisition of information for nuanced readings of culture. Where Kim first looked in order to read, he is now confined to the far more imaginatively stultifying task of locating messages in order to convey them.

It is only after the paternity of race and regiment has been bestowed on Kim that the lama becomes the focus of Kim's desire. The figurative trove that the latter represented is literalized through education, forcing the potential of picaresque bonding into the static actuality of separation. In his status as "Friend of all the World" Kim is most promiscuously sought after for adoption, which suggests that his desire is hardly for a lost parent. Instead, once Kim has been invisibly slotted into a system of message-bearing, the lama becomes the only focus for Kim's intuitive ability to read: he remains the sole territory, as it were, upon which Kim may exercise the diversity of interpretation. After the bereavement of their parting, the mediated and arduous nature of their desire to exchange information provides a brilliant figure for the repetitive intercessions that delay colonial intimacy. Here, the narrative's reliance on the dissemination of information represented by the official "letter-writer" deftly interweaves the spoken with the written, the vernaculars with the imperial language, and the space for misreading which necessarily intrudes between them. In Benares, the lama dictates a letter—presumably in Hindi—to a letter writer with the skills to translate the message into English. Father Victor consequently receives a somewhat tangled message, which simultaneously exemplifies the urgency underlying the communication of cross-cultural desire:

> Sitting on wayside in grave meditation, trusting to be favoured with your Honour's applause of present step, which recommend your Honour to execute for God Almighty's sake. Education is greatest blessing if of best sorts. Otherwise no earthly use. . . . So going to Benares, where will find address and forward rupees for boy who is apple of eye, and for God almighty's sake execute this education, and your petitioner as in duty bound shall ever awfully pray. . . . Please note boy is apple of eye, and rupees shall be sent per hoondie three hundred per annum. For God Almighty's sake. (Pp. 105–6)

Even though the text informs us that the plea to "God Almighty" would have annoyed the lama had "he known how the bazaar letter-writer had translated his phrase 'to acquire merit' " (p. 108), the intrusion of the third voice quickens rather than dulls the immediacy of his desire to be read. If Kim alone can read him, the lama would be freed less of the Wheel than of the burden of cultural description. Both partners in the intimate enterprise, therefore, function as shields against the possibility of each other's misreading within the realities of the colonial framework in which they must operate. Their quest is intimately linked to the exigencies of colonial communication, as the hasty desire of Kim's epistolary response indicates. Again, a letter writer transcribes the space of voice into written discourse: "To Teshoo Lama, the holy one from Bhotiyal seeking for a River. . . . In three days I am to go down to Nucklao to the school in Nucklao. The name of the school is Xavier. I do not know where that school is, but it is at Nucklao. . . . Come to me! Come to me! Come to me!" (pp. 117–18). Much as the letter lacks an accurate map for what will be Kim's actual geographic location, it is equally ignorant of the reasons that impel the urgency of its need. In the case of both the lama's letter to "his oppressors" and of Kim's to the lama, the message is overwhelmed by its own impetus. And now that a mode of colonial possession no longer dictates their idiom of exchange, separation must characterize the vitality of their desire.

In the extraordinary encounter that follows this exchange of letters, the moment of meeting is indeed redefined as a recognition of loss. The lama keeps vigil for Kim outside the gates of St. Xavier's School, but insists that his pilgrimage is motivated by a colonial pragmatic: "A day and a half have I waited—not because I was led by any affection towards thee—that is no part of the Way—but, as they said at the Tirthanker's Temple, because, money having been paid for learning, that I should oversee the end of the matter. . . . I had a fear that, perhaps, I came because I wished to see thee" (p. 123). Rather than function as a guide, in other words, Kim clearly represents to the lama a serious impediment to his desire for the River, or his quest to be desireless. Read as a colonial parable, this necessary denial of intimacy obliquely illustrates Kipling's disturbing vision of the psychic price demanded by a repression of colonial desire. Again, Kim proves to be the better reader of such a cost, in that he will not countenance the lama's fiction of practicality: "But surely, Holy One, thou hast not forgotten the road and all that did befall on it. Surely it was a little to see me that thou didst come? . . . I am all alone in this land; I know not where I go nor what shall befall me. . . . Do not altogether go away" (pp. 123–24). If imperial time has no memory, however, if it can read events only one at a time, then the separation it imposes lacks the luxury of recall, causing the articulation of each loss to be defined by the act of going "altogether away."

Cultural reading muddies single-minded motives. Thus, even as the lama assumes he is purchasing an educational space in which Kim can read, his ostensible pragmatism is shaken by the immediacy of Kim's appeal. Initially, their territories of control are very neatly demarcated, with the River being the lama's province; the Road, Kim's. With the intrusion of an imperial education, such cartography begins to lose its clarity, suggesting instead the overdetermination that underlies each will to classify. To the lama, the quest for the River is the ultimate model of classification, one that cannot readily accommodate the unclassifiability of Kim. Their second parting is as a consequence a keen refiguration of an attitude toward both cartography and classification. "Do not weep," the lama urges Kim, "for, look you, all Desire is an illusion and a new binding on the Wheel. Go up to the Gates of Learning. Let me see thee go. . . . Dost thou love me? Then go, or my heart cracks. . . . I will come again. Surely I will come again" (p. 124). The wheel at hand will come again, for its revolutions are too bound to the functioning of a colonized time to support the lama's myth of autonomy. His need for Kim—and Kim's need for him—suggests an alternative colonial cartography upon which classification cannot occur, for the Road and River can no longer determine those proper distinctions that separate their aims. Instead, land and water meld into a new geography, both more troubling and surprising in their ability to mirror one another.

Kim's youth, of course, is the "gate of learning" that allows for the following betrayal, and for his alacrity in adopting the glamor of the Great Game as an alternative to loving the lama. Adolescence legitimizes misremembrance: it licenses Kim to take on colonial history as though there were only messages to convey, even when they are messages most killing in their bearing. The Great Game that dictates the latter half of the text, however, knows the paucity of such colonial communication well enough to juxtapose motive, plot, and consequence with the sad desire to pose love—specific, individual love—as an alternative to colonial imbrication. His failure must register as an imperial epiphany, whereby reading is no longer a tool useful to the imperial imagination, and thus in Kipling an ineradicable example of the futility represented by empire.

To stress Kipling's intuitive apprehension of the futility of empire is by no means to imply his segregation from the realities and ideologies of imperialism, but to question instead the strange congruences between futility and belief that characterize Kipling's narrative. Much as Burke remains committed to a critique of a particular colonial practice rather than colonialism itself, similarly Kipling is able to read the details of colonial loss without necessarily proceeding to a larger abnegation of the whole. The predicament of *Kim* is precisely its democratic ability to represent a catalog of loss but to swerve into abrupt inconclusion at the very moment when such a list most evidently demands reading, reassessment, revaluation. Here, of course, the text quickens with a more intimate set of congruences, where the reader is forced to examine the replication of the narrative. Both perform necessary acts of misreading that allow them to continue to function as readers within a colonial world, and both are clairvoyantly aware of the price that remains to be exacted. This redoubling, through which character and narrator function as secret sharers in the chronology of the tale, points less to Kipling's ambivalence toward empire than to the inherent limitations that imperialism necessarily imposes on the narratives that seek to represent its chronology.

In David Bromwich's resonant reading of Kipling, these limitations are refigured into a study of what the idiom of the "jest" signifies to Kipling's prose and poetry. Like journalism, a jest as genre accrues a certain colloquial power of contemporaneity; it is not required to resolve the conflictual surprise with which it claims closure. Bromwich plots the "jest" of *Kim* by turning to the concluding third of the text, after Kim has been released from education and made to enter the Great Game: the action is set in the Himalayas, where the lama believes that Kim is merely following his quest for the River, whereas Kim is far more closely involved in the knowledge implied by counterintelligence. The irresolvable jest at hand, according to Bromwich, refers to the futility of any interpretive attempt to determine which belief has precedence: "A jest (the trick that baffles the [Russian] spies by coaxing their wicked designs into the open) leads to a truth (the lama's discovery of the connection between wickedness, self, and the desire for revenge). On this view the jest that gives the story its final turn is a trial of both of the authorities that have set the plot in motion. . . . The result is that both authorities are confirmed. We never learn to which of them Kim owes his first loyalty."[14]

The jest, in other words, confirms the absence of precedence in the narrative, in ways that are illustrative of Kipling's journalistic ability to incorporate colonial dischronology into his tales. This dischronology, however, suggests its own decorum, or a sequence of immediacy that allows Kipling to claim in an 1888 article: "You stand on the threshold of new [imperial] experiences—most of which will distress you and a few amuse. You are at the centre of a gigantic *Practical Joke.* Strive to enter the spirit of it and jest temperately."[15] The temperate jest, or a surprise that recognizes its own mediated nature, allows *Kim* to establish those bonds of love that are not only manifested between the lama and Kim, but are further reduplicated by the peculiar reciprocity between narrative and protagonist. As Bromwich notes on the concluding "adventure" of the novel, "By now, the analogy between Kim and his maker ought to be clear. They are the hidden agents of a legitimate authority. . . . One might variously describe what they achieve by the sum of their inventions. A fair name for it, which Kipling himself was happy with, is empire."[16] That empire may jest, however, cannot minimize its deranging power to limit the powers of reading, and it is only an acknowledgment of jest's curtailment of history that forces a retracing of Kim's trajectory. At what point does the love affair of *Kim* cease to become a colonial joke? When does a reader learn that the tragic erotics of the story have less to do with the lama and Kim than with imperial narrative and an emblem of cultural mobility? Let us return to the passion that informs the separation of the Road from the River; the young from the venerable: "'The Gates of Learning' shut with a clang."

Kipling assiduously omits to describe the education that the lama buys for Kim, and furthermore draws the reader's attention to his omission. In the quick elision of Kim's experiences within the "gates of learning," the narrative makes an unmistakable indication concerning the location of its audience, which by implication is situated far from the "country-born" quality of India and thus requires cultural description in order to understand the machinery of a colonized culture:

> The country-born and bred boy has his own manners and customs, which do not resemble those of any other land; and his teachers approach him by roads which an English master would not understand. Therefore, you would scarcely be interested in Kim's experiences as a St. Xavier's boy. . . . His quickness would have delighted an English master, but at St. Xavier's they know the first rush of minds developed by sun and surroundings, as they know *the half-collapse that sets in at twenty-one or twenty-three*. (Pp. 124–26, emphasis added)

Here, Kipling supplies a casual but crucial anticipation of the collapsibility of Kim: in keeping his institutional education a secret from the reader, moreover, the narrative suggests that Kim's real instruction lies in the hands of Colonel Creighton, Mahbub Ali, Lurgan Sahib, and Hurree Babu, who train their "colt" for the Great Game. The jest at hand, of course, indicates the futility of the lama's intervention, which—far from saving Kim—physically secures him for his role in the Game.

As Kim is inexorably reduced to the sum of his utility, his power as a cultural reader is simultaneously curtailed. The magical quality of his hybridity, of his ability to be one with each disguise that he assumes, is modified by the nature of the disguises that the Game requires he adopt. Much as a Macaulayan interpreter, Kim is trained to gather bureaucratically useful facts: his access to cultural "wisdom" must necessarily be reduced to the acquisition of pragmatic information. In this context, the lama's commitment to "acquiring knowledge" assumes the fatigued irony that is Kim's undoing, for within the parameters of the Game of colonialism, all epistemologies reduce to utilitarianism.

While it would certainly be erroneous to imply that *Kim* is intentionally an allegory of imperial education in the subcontinent, the text indeed lends itself to such an analogy. Kim's tutors fall into Orientalist and Anglicist camps, with the Anglicists clearly winning over the Orientalism that the lama represents. The text thus fictionally embodies the questions raised by Gauri Viswanathan's cogent reading of the interconnectedness between literary study and British rule in India, particularly when she observes, "The fact that English literary study had its beginnings as a strategy of containment raises the question, Why literature? . . . What accounts for the British readiness to turn to a disciplinary branch of knowledge to perform the task of administering their colonial subjects? What was the assurance that a disguised form of authority would be more successful in quelling potential rebellion among the natives than a direct show of force?"[17] *Kim* unwittingly aligns itself to such questions by posing, in the first place, the possibility of disguise as an enchantment of cultural mobility, but then grimly collapsing such youthful fantasy into "a disguised form of authority." The longer Kim serves the needs of the Great Game, the more circumscribed are his abilities to interpret.

The figure of education in *Kim* thus becomes synonymous with the tautology of colonial encounter, in which the child who is already culturally fluent must be caught in order that he may learn the far more alienating idiom of cultural description. Where cultural authority was once disparate and as dialogical as Kim's delight in his various disguises, the very excesses of the Game render it localized within a colonizer's bureaucracy. Here, Edward Said's reading of colonel Creighton as the emblem of the dialogue between anthropology and colonial chronology deserves attention: "Creighton embodies the notion that you cannot govern India unless you know India," claims Said. "And to know India means understanding the way it operates. . . . To the government personality the main consideration is not whether something is good or evil, and therefore must be changed or kept, but whether something works or not, whether it hinders one in ruling what is in effect an alien entity. Thus Creighton satisfies the Kipling who had imagined an ideal India, unchanging and attractive, as an eternally integral part of the Empire."[18] The stasis of such a model of cultural epistemology is in complete contrast with the readership embodied in the preeducated manifestation of Kim, and calls for further attention to his ability to transmogrify from adolescent mobility into the inflexibility represented by colonial knowledge.

What, however, of the anthropologist as journalist, of a mind ravished by the immediacy of all that colonial knowledge may signify? Under such a rubric, are the attractions of empire further reduced to an adolescent intransigence toward education, pointing to Kipling's interest in a discourse of cessation that proleptically images the language of partition at the historical moment of the most established colonial strength? Which is the idiom in which adolescence must die before it is allowed to attain the colonial maturity that Burke devoutedly desired? *Kim* suggests that the anthropology undertaken by the narrative requires even closer scrutiny than does the figure of Colonel Creighton, for Kipling in the guise of anthropologist locates highly novel forms for the moment of cultural extinction that it is his business to record. Once Kim has been released from St. Xavier's, the narrative assumes an oddly deferential tone toward the child who thus far has supplied the tale with an abundance of energy. Even though Kim continues to play the Game, he is increasingly represented in the third person: in the opening chapters of the book, the reader sees the subcontinent through Kim's eyes, but in the concluding sections of the narrative, the reader is forced to cast an anthropologist's eye upon the figure of Kim.

The crucial crossing of the text consists in its swerve from the mode of journalism into anthropology, allowing for the journalistic present tense to assume a more elegiac recognition of its protagonist's unavoidable extinction. If a submerged homoeroticism impelled the initial love of surprise between the lama and Kim the latter sections of the novel redirect that passion to the relation between narrator and protagonist. As Kim learns to play the Great Game, the narrative forces us to conceive of him as a third person: "The pallor of hunger suited Kim very well as he stood, tall and slim, in his sad-coloured, sweeping robes, one hand on his rosary and the other in the attitude of benediction, faithfully copied from the lama. An English observer might have said that he looked rather like the young saint of a stained-glass window, whereas he was but a growing lad faint with emptiness" (p. 196).

In such a visual reconfiguration, Kim has become the image of the colonizer, but one that is elegiacally mourned as passing in its prematurity. Even though the final "adventure" of the novel returns the disciple to the alternative knowledge of his tutelary status with the lama, the passion for Kim is curiously displaced into the narrative's desire to hold him as a nonverbal object that is somewhat exempt from its subjugation to the transmittal of

colonial information. After having established Kim as the inevitable victim
of imperial education, in other words, Kipling seems drawn to an anthropologist's farewell to the emblem that finally reveals the classifiability of
cultural dexterity. The impishness of Kim's ingenuity drops away from the
verbal into the visual, so that the reader is continually reminded of his bodily
presence. Whereas the preeducated Kim was both a voice and a body that
commanded comfort wherever it found itself, the posteducated Kim is suddenly vulnerable to the pains of mind and body. Rather than dictate the
energy of the narrative, posteducated Kim becomes the focus of the narrative's futile compassion. It is no surprise, therefore, when the crucial scene
that allows the Russian spies to destroy the lama's map is envisioned from
perspectives that Kim could not possibly see: "They came across an aged
lama . . . sitting cross-legged above a mysterious chart held down by stones,
which he was explaining to a young man, evidently a neophyte, of singular,
though unwashen, beauty" (pp. 239–40). Until this moment, Kim's beauty
has been manifested by his linguistic range, or his ability to read cultures
rapidly and well. His sudden elevation into an aesthetic icon, therefore, dangerously anticipates the third-person silence imposed by the education that
signifies the playing of the Great Game.

The loneliness of Kim's adolescent question "Who is Kim?" is thus
transferred to the reader, who must now picture the marvelous boy as an
analogy for colonial casualty. Whatever may be the journalistic enthusiasm
for the present tense of colonialism, *Kim* darkly illustrates its epistemological ill-proportion. Nothing indicates its astonishing obfuscation more than
the conclusion of the text, where an Anglicist narrative and an Orientalist
lama collide in vying for the affections of the protagonist. The surprise of
Kim inheres in such a battle, which the text conducts for the fealty of its
protagonist: is Kim loved more by the lama or the narrator, or who more
totally frames him in colonial imprisonment? As an allegory of colonial education, the conclusion of *Kim* extracts significance at the very point where it
appears to confer imperial meaning.

The narrator knows that Kim must be killed. He hands the deed over to
the otherworldly lama, however, with whom he remains in perpetual con-
testation for Kim's love. In the chilling conclusion of the book, Kim's
recuperation is necessarily followed by the lama's claim that he alone constitutes the salvation of the boy: "I meditated a thousand things, passionless,
well aware of the Causes of all Things. Then a voice cried: 'What shall become of the boy if thou art dead?' and I was shaken back and forth in myself
with pity for thee; and I said: 'I will return to my *chela*, lest he miss the

way'" (pp. 287–88). Such intervention, however, is hardly passionless. Neither is the concluding sentence of the text, which once again images Kim in a magnificent moment of uncontrol: "[The lama] crossed his hands on his lap and smiled, as a man may who has won Salvation for himself and his beloved" (p. 288). Here, Kim is envisioned as the absent other that indicates the silence of classical Urdu poetry, in which the beloved has no voice at all. But it is colonial education that has silenced his voice, and demonstrated that in its adolescence is its end.

6

Forster's Imperial Erotic

WHETHER *A PASSAGE TO INDIA* IS READ AS AN ICON OF THE LIBERAL imagination or as an allegory in which the category of "Marabar Cave" roughly translates into the anus of imperialism, the novel remains one of English India's most troubling engagements in the fiction of cultural self-examination. The familiarity of its tropologies is an undiminished embarrassment to postcolonial discourse, in that the text continually prepares to address the latent infantilism within the possibility of cross-cultural friendship. If the question "Why can't we be friends now?" concludes the unanswerability that *A Passage to India* seeks to address, it further reiterates the persistent permutations of adolescence that inform the rhetoric of subcontinental colonialism. Over Forster, the discursive ghosts of Burke and Kipling shake hands; the youthfulness that both locate as the danger of colonial power now learns that its chronology is pitiably dependent upon the mythology of "being friends," or a fiction reliant on the dischronology of "not now", "not yet."

A Passage to India translates the question of cross-cultural friendship into a more vertiginous study of how cultures both issue and misread invitations to one another. As such, Aziz's notorious invitation—"I invite you all to see me in the Marabar Caves"—indicates the incongruity of civility within a colonial context. The oblique violence of the text points both to the fraught ambivalence with which Forster invokes the category of "friendship" and to the absence of civil spaces upon which the possibility of friendship may be discussed. If *A Passage to India* attempts to engender an illusion of cross-cultural conversation, then it is a dialogue that is highly conscious of the limits rather than the expansiveness of cultural sympathy. As Forster himself confessed to Syed Ross Masood, "When I began the book I thought of it as a little bridge of sympathy between East and West, but this conception has had to go, my sense of the truth forbids anything so comfortable. I think that most Indians, like most English people, are shits, and I am not interested whether they sympathize with one another or not."[1] Even as the narrative explores mythologies of colonial friendship, in other words, it is resolutely critical of an "only connect" rhetoric that would allow for the fiction of any transcultural male bonding.

In *Kim*, the protagonist's ability to function as a "Friend of all the World" to the various cultures inhabiting the colonized subcontinent comes dangerously close to a promiscuous liability, and finally culminates in his silenced status as the lama's beloved. *A Passage to India*, on the other hand, disallows any distinction between friend and beloved: both terms are precariously coterminous in a colonial world where cultural reading is predicated on the passionate misinterpretation of the art of invitation. The intimacies of colonialism are thereby translated into the social and political peculiarities represented by the question, how can a people invite another people not into a home, or into a different culture, but into that alternative civil space known as a friendship? Into what caves of disappointed sublimity must such civility collapse, before it can articulate the fact that colonial friendship is never autonomous from the literal presence of the racial body?

While the homoeroticism of *A Passage to India* could be explained away with biographical reference—by reference to Forster's love for Syed Ross Masood, the friend who lent his lineaments to the shaping of Dr. Aziz—it is far more productively disturbing in the context of Forster's revision of an imperial erotic. In place of the Orientalist paradigm in which the colonizing presence is as irredeemably male as the colonized territory is female, *A Passage to India* presents an alternative colonial model: the most urgent cross-cultural invitations occur between male and male, with racial difference serving as a substitute for gender. As race is thus sexualized, the novel draws attention to its relentless questioning of the amorphousness of friendship, in which the visibility of race is rendered synonymous with the invisibility of sexual preference. If Forster's critique of the feminine picturesque is all too overtly available in Adela Quested's search for the "real" India, his more haunting apprehension of a colonial aesthetic of sublimity inheres in the narrative's ability to literalize what homoerotic disappointment has signified to English India.

The erotic of race, and its concomitant cultural complications, is most clearly figured in the narrative's curious relation to the overdetermination that is Aziz. From the opening chapters of the novel, it is evident that Aziz is accorded a certain mobility as a racial body which allows him an exemption from his role as complete participant in the colonial encounter. Aziz has to be punished into history through the route of his pursuit of friendship, which ultimately leads to his espousal of a nationalist rhetoric. Friendship thus functions as the conduit or the Marabar Cave that allows Aziz to transmogrify from a racial into a nationalist entity, but such evolution suggests the limits rather than the attainment of cultural autonomy. We first see Aziz after he has accepted an easy invitation into a home of his own kind, but even in such a setting, Aziz rests on the peripheries of political conversation more as an observing body than as a participant:

> He lay in a trance, sensuous but healthy, through which the talk of the two others did not seem particularly sad—they were discussing as to whether or no it is possible to be friends with an Englishman. Mahmoud Ali argued that it was not, Hamidullah disagreed, but with so many reservations that there was no friction between them. Delicious it was indeed to lie on the broad verandah with the moon rising in front and the servants preparing dinner behind, and no trouble happening. . . . "They all become exactly the same, not worse, not better. I give any Englishman two years, be he Turton or Burton. And I give any Englishwoman six months. All are exactly alike. Do you not agree with me?"
>
> "I do not," replied Mahmoud Ali, entering into the bitter fun, and feeling both pain and amusement at each word that was uttered. "For my own part I find such profound differences among our rulers."[2]

Here, Aziz remains merely an audience to the amorous "pain and amusement" that characterize his host's discourse: the narrative allows him a certain bodily autonomy from the debate on cultural friendship only to render his body the site upon which the exquisite costs of such friendliness shall later be determined.

If Aziz can be read as an emblematic casualty of the colonial homoerotic, then his iconic status must necessarily be released from too literal a correlation with the secrecy that attended Forster's own homosexuality. In this context, Rustom Bharucha's somewhat archly titled essay, "Forster's Friends," is symptomatic of the unhelpful critical urge to link the sexual politics of *A Passage to India* with the idiosyncrasies of preference rather than with the imperatives that subcontinental colonial encounter generated between the cultural distinctiveness of race and gender. "An ethos of masculinity developed during the British Raj of India, first in England, and then later, through a process of imitation, within India itself," claims Bharucha. "Whether a man was serving his country at home or abroad, he was required to be 'manly'—aggressive, competitive, and in control of his emotions and duties. The Empire had no particular use for women or for the values associated with femininity. Homosexuals were tolerated only insofar as they remained discreet about their activities and functioned within the strict confines of marginal societies like Bloomsbury and Oxbridge."[3] Such a dichotomy relies on an almost surgical critical ability to separate masculinity from a more vexed engagement in the discourse of colonial sexuality, which necessarily implies that manliness—like friendship—is not so easily subsumed within the sexual symbolic that impels the narrative of *A Passage to India*.

If Forster's narrative is uninterested in stereotypical imperial masculinity and instead attempts to reconfigurate colonial sexuality into a homoeroticization of race, then the keenly visual aspects of the novel require attentive reading. The discourse of friendship becomes a figure for how the imperial eye perceives race: the literal minutiae of pigmentation and physiognomy serve to rupture a more general vision of an Oriental culture. A crucial illustration of the rupturing power of the racial body occurs during the court scene, where Adela's attention is caught less by Aziz than by "the man who pulled the punkah":

> Almost naked, and splendidly formed, he sat on a raised platform near the back . . . and he seemed to control the proceedings. He had the strength and beauty that sometimes comes to flower in Indians of low birth. When that strange race nears the dust and is condemned as untouchable, then nature remembers the physical perfection that she accomplished elsewhere, and throws out a god—not many, but one here and there, to prove to society how little its categories impress her. This man would have been notable anywhere: among the thin-hammed, flat-chested mediocrities of Chandrapore he stood out as divine, yet he was of the city, its garbage had nourished him, he would end on its rubbish heaps. (P. 217)

This culturally troubled passage exemplifies the colonial eye's ability to see the racial body as a specimen whose sexual aesthetics contravene principles of imperial classification. Its ostensibly casual invocation of caste further complicates the muddied gender boundaries of the text, in that the untouchability of the godlike body of the fan-puller is homoeroticized: in Forster's narrative, the untouchable no longer refers to caste alone, but is extended to include an embodiment of homosexual desire.

While the anonymity of the fan-puller can serve as a synecdoche for the troubling aesthetic posed by the colonized male racial body, the beauty that Aziz represents is touched upon far more obliquely. The second chapter of the novel describes him as "an athletic little man, daintily put together, but really very strong" (p. 18); similarly, Mrs. Moore later describes him as "rather small, with a little moustache and quick eyes" (p. 30). In the courtroom, Aziz appears to Adela as a "strong, neat little Indian with very black hair and pliant hands" (p. 220). His physical diminution serves as a distraction from the untouchable beauty that the text gestures toward but will not put into language: having granted Aziz a brain and a partial cultural autonomy, Forster cannot afford to linger on the articulation of attraction that Aziz represents. Here, *A Passage to India* reifies a hidden tradition of imperial looking in which the disempowerment of a homoerotic gaze is as damaging to the colonizing psyche as to that of the colonized, and questions the cultural dichotomies through which both are realized.

Even though the homoerotic strategy of *A Passage to India* cannot be explained away with reference to Forster's own curiously class-conscious and cross-cultural homosexual experiences, it would be a theoretical error to ignore their relevance to the text's embodiment of the situation of alternative desire in the construction of colonial encounters. Aziz is thus both a tribute to Syed Ross Masood and a memorial to Forster's Egyptian lover, Mohommed el Edl, who died while *A Passage to India* was still being written. After the lover's death in 1922, Forster's diary records obsessively his dreams of Mohommed: "I passed a young man in black with a slight but a well defined moustache. He was and was not Mohommed—not he outwardly but he in his intensity, the quality of emotion caused in my heart . . . [then] he lent against the edge of [my] bath, half sitting, half standing, entirely naked, his dark bush distinct, and he smiled. The effect was not physical nor was my awakening ghastly except that I awoke."[4] In the context of the phantasmagoric quality of Forster's diaries, the simultaneous production of *A Passage to India* instantiates a relation of acute strain to figurative uses of the subject of homoeroticism. As a consequence, Aziz represents a belittled racial body whose attractions can never be literalized, and the space upon which Forster can enact the unavoidable partition that the longing of class creates within the context of colonial knowledge.

The death of Mohommed shapes Aziz. Aziz has hands rather than genitalia; he is too tiny to assume the status of a godlike body. But he is still urgently implicated in the cultural crossing represented by the many repetitions of the trope of the Bridge Party, which remains the central figure upon which the possibility of friendship is enacted. While the cultural invitations generated by such encounters are too dangerous to ignore, their inevitable misreadings signify an acute evasion of what the anxiety of masculinity represents to the discourse of colonialism. The phantasmagoria of cultural bonding certainly dictates Forster's diaristic comments on colonial homoeroticism, allowing him to sustain an idealized belief in the availability of racial as well as erotic intermingling. Once Mohommed dies, Forster can write, "You are dead, Mohommed, and Morgan is still alive and thinks more of himself and less of you with every word he writes. You [once] called my name . . . it was dark and I heard an Egyptian shouting who had lost his friend: Margan, Margan—you calling me and I felt we belonged to each other now, you had made me an Egyptian."[5] An extraordinarily complicated Orientalism accompanies this claim, which implies that "friendship" can make an Egyptian of E. M. Forster, so that the imperial rather than the Oriental body can also be textualized. A Passage to India, however, functions as a wry reminder of the impossibility of such cultural and ethnic relocations: even when dead, Mohommed cannot provide an option for Forster's cultural belonging. His death signifies only a moment in the imperial erotic that converts absence into an illusion of cultural transference. In contravention of the work of mourning and optimism that Forster's diary performs, however, A Passage to India works resolutely against those commitments to transcendence that allow Egypt to enter England.

It is hardly irrelevant that the composition of A Passage to India caused Forster to burn what P. N. Furbank somewhat quaintly calls his "indecent short stories": "The burning took place early in April [1922] and was done, he told himself, not as a moral repentance but out of a feeling that the stories 'clogged' him artistically. They were a 'wrong channel' for his pen."[6] Whether or not such a ritual of erotic immolation is indeed an autonomously aesthetic gesture, it surely informs the excisions of intimacy that cause the subsequent text to claim: "We must exclude someone from our gathering, or we shall be left with nothing" (p. 38). To turn to the cross-cultural friendship that subsists between Aziz and Fielding, therefore, is in its most overdetermined sense of the term to approach a cultural "nothing."

THE DISEMBODIMENT AND CONCOMITANT EMBODIMENT OF AZIZ IS RARELY AS starkly choreographed as in chapter 7 of the opening section of A Passage to India, "Mosque." In the first physical encounter between Fielding and Aziz, the narrative informs the reader that the latter knows the former by sight; the former knows the latter "very well by name" (p. 64). Between these discrepancies of sight and name, Aziz and Fielding attempt to articulate an alternative colonial intimacy that can escape the predictability of empowered and disempowered discourses, but is still predicated upon the license of mis-reading. Neither man is in direct vision of the other: Fielding is both naked and concealed when Aziz arrives at his home. "He was dressing after a bath when Dr. Aziz was announced . . . he shouted from the bedroom, 'Please make yourself at home.' The remark was unpremeditated, like most of his actions; it was what he felt inclined to say. To Aziz it had a very definite meaning. 'May I really, Mr. Fielding? . . . I like unconventional behaviour so extremely' " (p. 63). The formalism of informality is immediately at play in their attempt to conduct conversation in an environment alternative to that of colonial communication.

What follows is perhaps the most notoriously oblique homoerotic ex-change in the literature of English India. The scene is so familiar that its erotic as opposed to its cultural and colonial sartorial implications seem too obvious to read. The disastrous Bridge Party held by Chandrapore's collector has already occurred; Fielding's version of an alternative Bridge Party is de-signed to let the Anglo-Indian woman in search of the "real India" literally see what Indians may be. Before the women can enter to dilute the sin-gularity of gender, however, Fielding and Aziz have already conducted a secret gesture of intimacy that barely needs decoding. The exchange involves a transfer of an object as domestically ludicrous as a collar stud: Aziz not only wrenches his own off his collar in order to supply Fielding with what he may be missing, but further proceeds to assist Fielding in the insertion of the stud. Apart from the concluding paragraph of the novel, and the "half-kissing" gesture with which the two protagonists part, the collar stud is the only cru-cially disruptive signifier through which—in a colonial configuration—men are allowed to touch men.

The exchange of the stud—in itself nothing more than a moment of irreversible cultural embarrassment—suggests an erotic interaction that de-mands attention to its own cultural outrage. While the counterimperialist Western gentleman is in the act of dressing, he requires the aid of the "little" Indian who can both charm and complicate the dialogue that follows between them. The great erotic tenderness that attends the first encounter between Aziz and Fielding is made visual only through the transfer of a stud. Aziz wrenches his own property from his body, and proffers those signs to Field-ing: "I say, Mr. Fielding, is the stud going to go in?" (p. 65). What follows is an elaborate acknowledgment of what sartorial necessity may have to say to the invisibility of colonial friendship. For of course the stud will go in the collar of the Englishman, who stands, neck bowed, accepting the assistance of his new Indian friend. "Let me put in your stud," exclaims Aziz; "I see . . . the shirt back's hole is rather small and to rip it is a pity" (p. 65). It is through the paraphernalia of dressing with decorum, in other words, that erotic trust can establish its tenuous parameters: the immediate lovemaking that transpires between Fielding and Aziz suggests the prevailing cultural sadness that inhabits utopian narratives of the possibility of friendship across cultures. Aziz's domestic prophesy dangerously redounds of what political ramifications lie behind the assumption of international friendliness—the hole is indeed rather small, and to rip it is a pity.

In *A Passage to India*, however, nothing can be whole or sole that has not been rent. The novel intimacy between the two men is soon interrupted by the intrusion of Mrs. Moore and Adela Quested: Aziz "was disappointed that other guests were coming, for he preferred to be alone with his new friend" (p. 66). With the entry of the women, Aziz is rapidly Orientalized, in that he is read through the lens of the feminine picturesque—for Adela, he becomes the key through which the secrets of the real India may possibly be read. This colonial expectation is sufficient to induce a strained falsity in Aziz's discourse, causing the invitation into friendship to assume more and more phantasmagoric proportions. By reading Aziz's invitation to visit his home too literally, Adela unwittingly renders Aziz homeless:

> "I don't know why you say [that you can give us nothing], when you have so kindly invited us to your house."
> He thought again of his bungalow with horror. Good heavens, the stupid girl had taken him at his word! What was he to do? "Yes, all that is settled," he cried. "I invite you all to see me in the Marabar Caves." (P. 74)

Here, Aziz chooses the cultural anonymity of geography in order to keep concealed the privacy of his home, and the moment is illustrative of Forster's meticulous revision of a colonialist-as-heterosexual paradigm. Rather than the male seeking to possess a feminized territory, the female seeks to enter the habitat of colonized domesticity, thereby forcing the "little Indian" to retreat into the exotic but empty space of an unvisited cave.

Fielding's tea party thus represents a dispersal of sexual promise, or an emptying of intimacy into unintelligibility. A scene that opens with the anticipation of new modes of cultural contact is evacuated into an emblem of erotic isolation, converting each of the assembled bodies into stereotypes of colonial embarrassment. Invitation has occurred and has failed, as the song sung by Professor Godbole exemplifies. His sudden flight into song at the end of the tea party translates the submerged desire of colonial encounter into a new mode of incomprehensibility: "His thin voice rose, and gave out one sound after another. At times there seemed rhythm, at times there was an illusion of a Western melody. But the ear, baffled repeatedly, soon lost any clue, and wandered in a maze of noises, none harsh or unpleasant, none intelligible. Only the servants understood it. They began to whisper to one another. *The man who was gathering water chestnut came naked out of the tank, his lips parted with delight, disclosing his scarlet tongue*" (p. 79, emphasis added). While Godbole proceeds to translate his song, this arresting and momentary intrusion of the male nude requires some decoding in itself. Since the scene opened with Fielding's invisible nudity, this evocation of a literal Indian nudity takes on a curious parallelism. In a colonial configuration, is a colonized body the only one that can be represented as stripping into cultural secrecy? Like the fan-puller in the later court scene, this nude embodies an act of aesthetic rupture: his appearance is singularly nonphallic, with Forster focusing instead on the mouth as an aperture that can disclose a scarlet tongue. In an encounter fraught with imperial displeasure, the nude presents an alternative if untouchable pleasure that the narrative can almost anthropologically record but into which it has no entry.

The pleasure generated by Godbole's song, of course, is further ironized by the fact that its literal subject concerns the absence of pleasure. It supplies the text with a crucial figure both for imperial longing and for the gender-crossing that gestures toward the possibility of cultural crossing. In order to sing this particular song, Godbole must ventriloquize a woman's voice:

> "I will explain in detail. It was a religious song. I placed myself in the position of a milkmaiden. I say to Shri Krishna, 'Come! come to me only. The god refuses to come. I grow humble and say: 'Do not come to me only. Multiply yourself into a hundred Krishnas, and let one go to each of my hundred companions, but one, O Lord of the Universe, come to me.' He refuses to come . . ."
>
> "But he comes in some other song, I hope?" said Mrs. Moore gently.
>
> "Oh no, he refuses to come," repeated Godbole, perhaps not understanding her question. "I say to Him, come, come, come, come, come, come. He neglects to come." (P. 80)

While a critic such as Benita Parry attempts to read both this passage and the novel as a whole as illustrative of Forster's engagement in the dialogue between Islam and Hinduism in the Indian subcontinent, it is perhaps more productive to consider Godbole's song as a figure for the erotic and colonial disappointment that permeates *A Passage to India*.[7] Much as the actors on the colonial stage exchange veiled invitations to future intimacies, Krishna will decline to be invited into the sexually explicit longing of the milk-maiden. Rather than representing the alterity of polytheistic culture, Godbole's song is synecdochical of the tautological desire that vexes imperial narrative. It encompasses all the permutations of what friendship may be within the context of empire, and further anticipates the necessary deferral of desire that impels the text's conclusion.

The song that serves as the punctuation mark to Fielding's tea party suggests that imperial pleasure invariably occurs elsewhere; not yet, not here. As a consequence, the trajectory of the friendship between Fielding and Aziz is quickened by the necessary disappointment that it must continually generate. These disappointments are not necessarily the results of cultural misreadings, but indicate instead the limits of homoerotic knowledge in English Indian narrative. According to Benita Parry, the failure of friendship in *A Passage to India* can in large measure be ascribed to the barriers created by the problematic category of differences in "national character": "Ultimately their relationship is tainted by the context of their encounter. Fielding is instinctively patronizing, as befits an Englishman in India . . . and Aziz, who craves an intimacy which Fielding is temperamentally incapable of meeting, is in turn importunate and easily offended, the occupational hazards of those obliged to be clients of a master-race."[8] While characters in the text obsessively talk about what it means to be English as opposed to Indian, their discourse suggests an anxious artifice behind the desire to keep these categories intact. If both serve as accomplices in each other's alterities, then the inevitability of colonial disempowerment is equally meted out to Fielding and Aziz.

Here, it may be productive to read the friendship of the two men less as an aborted exchange between colonizer and colonized and more as an instantiation of what Kaja Silverman calls the "double mimesis" of colonial encounter. In her perceptive reading of T. E. Lawrence's *Seven Pillars of Wisdom*, Silverman presents an alternative model for the construction of colonial identification: "Lawrence clearly projects his homosexuality and masochism onto the Arabs he fights with, so that the sexuality he finds within them, and with which he identifies, represents a mirror image of his own. . . . The passing of the 'self' through the medium of the 'other'—or,

even more radically, through the medium of what has been culturally desig-
nated as 'Other'—effects more than an alienation: it also holds open the
possibility for a significant shift in the terms of the subject's sexuality, and
hence of his or her identity."[9] Even though Lawrence's Orientalist Arab
identification was far more obsessional than Forster's with India, the comparison allows for a greater apprehension of how a homoerotic dynamic
complicates the empowerment of colonialism. If Forster's diary can represent the writer as "becoming Egypt" through his love for Mohommed,
then *A Passage to India* can be read as a partial Indianization of Fielding.
More precisely, his availability to cultural intimacy problematizes the interpretive usefulness of such static categories as the "English" versus the
"Indian."

While the exchange between Fielding and Aziz is represented in resolutely heterosexual terms—Aziz plans to visit brothels in Calcutta; Fielding
marries Stella—their friendship plays out a subterranean homoeroticism
that functions as a figure for the limits of colonial epistemology. After the
gift-giving of the collar stud and the ominous invitation to the Marabar
Caves, their next conversation takes place as a mirror image of the first.
Fielding invites himself to visit Aziz's sickbed, thus transgressing the cultural privacy that the invitation to the caves had been designed to protect.
The visit is a humiliation for Aziz, and as Fielding is about to leave, "rather
disappointed with his call" (p. 113), Aziz confesses the real reason of his prior
coldness: "'Here is your home,' he said sardonically. 'Here's the celebrated
hospitality of the East. Look at the flies. . . . Isn't it jolly? Now I suppose
you want to be off, having seen an Oriental interior'" (P. 115). Fielding's desire for intimacy, in other words, can register only as a violation of Aziz's
space within the colonial world: rather than heighten the cultural trust between the two, the visit initially serves to exacerbate the distance between
them.

In keeping with the logic of an imperial erotic, in which intimacy is
always too excessive or too scant, Aziz proceeds to shift the emotional register of their encounter by suddenly evoking an image of his dead wife. By
inviting Fielding to look at her photograph, Aziz inverts the traditional colonial paradigm in which the colonizer seeks to penetrate the secrets of the
zenana. As the woman's veil is temporarily lifted, Fielding is forced into the
position of a cultural voyeur: "She was my wife. You are the first
Englishman she has ever come before. Now put her photograph away" (p.
116). While the oblique tenderness implicit in the symbolic exchange of the

woman may serve as the next link in the construction of friendship, it further confines Fielding to the illiteracy of his gaze. He is left in a position similar to the photographers of *The people of India*, who could collect but could not read representations of gender and race. Aziz's gesture both feminizes the domestic space into which Fielding has intruded and inevitably engenders an anthropological anxiety in his friend: "'Put her away, she is of no importance, she is dead,' said Aziz gently. 'I showed her to you because I have nothing else to show. You may look around the whole bungalow now, and empty everything'" (p. 117).

Where Fielding seeks the specificity of a localized intimacy, he meets an imperial double bind that constrains him into an acknowledgment of his status as a colonial observer. He may have escaped the world of Anglo-India and the ideology of the collector, but he cannot fail to recognize that he functions as a figurative collector in his own right. Even though the photograph has been imposed upon him, it cannot but underscore the implicitly anthropological interest that he takes in Aziz: "Fielding sat down by the bed, flattered at the trust reposed in him, yet rather sad. He felt old. . . . Kindness, kindness, and more kindness—yes, that he might supply, but was that really all that the queer nation needed? Did it not also demand an occasional intoxication of the blood? What had he done to deserve this outburst of confidence, and what hostage could he give in exchange?" (p. 117). As in *Kim*, this enactment of the imperial erotic serves to illustrate the futility of compassion in colonial encounters. The kindness with which Fielding agrees to conduct his reading of the subcontinent cannot claim exemption from the violence of cultural intrusiveness, and the intoxication that he imagines demanded of him points less to the exoticism of the "Orient" than to a more rarefied and internalized exoticism of cultural disappointment.

The second encounter between Fielding and Aziz closes *A Passage to India*'s opening section, "Mosque." Functioning as a prelude to the overdetermined representations of emptiness that dominate the second section, "Caves," "Mosque" constructs an exquisitely hollowed-out figure for the fragility of cross-cultural friendship. For Aziz, the promising mutuality of the second encounter suggests a more long-lasting intimacy: "But they were friends, brothers. That part was settled, their compact had been subscribed by the photograph, they trusted one another, affection had triumphed for once in a way" (p. 122). In a colonial chronology, however, such bonding cannot be settled without simultaneously implying how it can be unsettled and displaced. The compact of sexual friendship is too tenuous to sustain a dialogical discourse across the divisiveness of colonial cultures; it will be both reopened and resealed in the symbolic geography that constitutes a Marabar Cave.

A PASSAGE TO INDIA OPENS AND ENDS WITH EVOCATIONS OF GEOGRAPHY. THE geographic, however, does not suggest a "natural" landscape that lies beyond the parameters of a colonial economy: it no more represents a "real" India than do either its inhabitants or its religious and cultural mythologies. Instead, Forster turns to visualizing landscape as though to an act of cultural description that is relentlessly antiexotic in its intent. If the narratives of English India can roughly be said to have veered between sublime and picturesque representations of the colonial encounter, then *A Passage to India* collapses both modes into a reconfiguration of what disappointment may signify to divergent apprehensions of colonialism. In such a revision, geography assumes the characteristics of a hollow symbolic space upon which the limits of imperial intimacy can both be identified and articulated.

Where Forster's text most distinctly locates itself on the cusp between colonial and postcolonial narrative is in its ability to demystify the mundanities attendant on colonial exchange. *A Passage to India* opens with the productive negative that claims, "Except for the Marabar Caves—and they are twenty miles off—the city of Chandrapore presents nothing extraordinary" (p. 7). What follows is an act of imperial cartography that adopts a curiously dispossessed and dispossessing tone toward the relationship between town and landscape, or a mapping of all the ways that both Chandrapore and its surrounding environs seem to bespeak no inherent interest. In place of the exotic, the ordinary is privileged, so that the narrative need express no desire for either overt possession or a concomitant repulsion. The brief opening chapter melds city and geography, sky and land, to conclude in a startling metaphor of embodiment: "No mountains infringe on the curve. League after league the earth lies flat, heaves a little, is flat again. Only in the south, where a group of fists and fingers are thrust up through the soil, is the endless expanse interrupted. These fists and fingers are the Marabar Hills, containing the extraordinary caves" (p. 9). Not only is the landscape anthropomorphized, but the image of the clenched hand is further hollowed out and emptied into caves, so that the realm of the imperial extraordinary is rendered coterminous with empty space.

The emptiness of geography—or the very structure of the Marabar Caves—functions as the conduit through which each participant in the colo-

nial encounter can come to some troubled terms with the question of historical location. In part 2 of *A Passage to India*, therefore, the symbolic geography of "Caves" becomes the territory upon which both a colonial rape fails to
occur and homoerotic desire must recognize its segregation from the story of
imperial friendship. The delusional rape imagined by Adela Quested, in
other words, makes of her body a further Marabar Cave through which Fielding and Aziz must delimit the historical and ethical possibilities of colonial
intimacy. As in the opening chapter of the novel, "Caves" opens with the
ostensible neutrality of cultural description:

> The caves are readily described. A tunnel eight feet long,
> five feet high, three feet wide, leads to a circular chamber about
> twenty feet in diameter. This arrangement occurs again and
> again throughout the group of hills, and this is all, this is a
> Marabar Cave. Having seen one such cave, having seen two, hav-
> ing seen three, four, fourteen, twenty-four, the visitor returns to
> Chandrapore uncertain whether he has had an interesting expe-
> rience or a dull one or any experience at all. (p. 124)

Such a geography denies both connection and chronology, in that it forces
cultural description into a recognition of its own vacuity. The touristic experience of colonialism is deglamorized into mathematical computations of
how literally banal the exotic may be.

The ready availability of the caves, however, should not lead to the conclusion that geography has no secrets: instead, it suggests that such secrecy is
a further confirmation of a productive emptiness in the reading of cultures.
Thus even as the narrative assumes descriptive power over the symbolic geography that it maps out, it equally questions the limits of its own claims to
comprehensiveness: "But elsewhere, deeper in the granite, are there certain
chambers that have no entrances? Chambers never unsealed since the arrival
of the gods. Local report declares that these exceed in number those that can
be visited, as the dead exceed the living—four hundred of them, four thousand or million. Nothing is inside them, they were sealed up before the
creation of pestilence or treasure; if mankind grew curious and excavated,
nothing, nothing would be added to the sum of good or evil" (p. 125). Those
caves that are untouchable, in other words, transmogrify into the dwelling
spaces of "chambers"; the evacuation represented by their lack of habitation
accords a certain homogeneity to cultural knowledge and cultural secrecy.
Once both visible and invisible caves in the hills of Marabar are rendered
equally empty, then the supposed dichotomy between heterosexual and homosexual desire assumes a similarly interchangeable quality.

Aziz invites his incongruous company to visit with him in the Marabar Caves: in the course of this exposure to an unknown but erotic geography, he further invites upon himself the imperial accusation of rape and a subsequent realization of how impossible it is to maintain the brotherhood of cross-colonial intimacy. Geography thus functions as a cultural determinant that delimits too promiscuous a traversal of its inherent boredom, and as a consequence becomes a figure for the inefficacy of colonial travel, whether it be across acceptable cultural or sexual borders. Such a symbolic topography, of course, is remarkable in its revision of received figurations of the function of landscape in colonial narrative: rather than landscape serving as the female context upon which an imperial man can arrive at storytelling, geography in *A Passage to India* assumes the significance of that presexual space upon which the participants in the great game of colonial intimacy can recognize their postsexuality.

In order to recollect what a radical shift the novel represents in the Anglo-Indian ethos, it is perhaps helpful to juxtapose Forster's symbolic geography with that of a contemporaneous text by Richard Sencourt, *India in English Literature*. This study, published in 1923, reads into the geography of India little other than the tradition of romance. The landscape is invariably feminized and exoticized; it lies in mysterious passivity at the feet of the colonizing sensibility. In place of the meticulous emptiness of the Marabar Cave, subcontinental geography is imaged in all the fullsomeness of exoticism: "If India is stored with such a power of fascination, why is it that so many have turned from her in listlessness or disgust? As she has charmed, so has she repelled. . . . Dusty and hideous India has often seemed. Melancholy is her garment. She offers no home to the Northerner: on the European she must always exert her repulsion as well as her charm."[10] The stale dichotomy between repulsion and attraction is precisely that which *A Passage to India* seeks to dismantle, in order to vitalize a sense of geography that can circumnavigate traditional devices of colonial travel narrative. To Sencourt, Indian terrain is inviting precisely because it is female, and can be attributed to all the predictable lures of a family romance between mystery and repulsion. Forster's geography, on the other hand, articulates itself on the novel ground of disappointment, or a space that accommodates desire but need not necessarily posit cultural disgust as the inevitable corollary to the lure of romance. It is worth noting in passing that Sencourt's preface thanks among others who facilitated his trip to English India one "Mr. E. M. Forster, who read me the M.S. of a delightful novel on India on which he is engaged and his papers on Eliza Fay which appeared in an Egyptian newspaper."[11] Given the secure exoticist Orientalism that impels Sencourt's reading of literature and geography, it remains only an academic wonder as to which sections of *A Passage to India* Sencourt found "delightful."

For there is little delight in the longest journey of the novel, or the section that Forster titles "Caves." In part 2, the romance of invitation sensationally creates the delusion of accusation, allowing geography to extend its parameters in order to include within its purview the theatrical space of the court. The Marabar Caves are allowed no containment, but instead spill over their disappointment to the equal hollows represented by colonial accusations and acquittals. An imperial eye cannot confine the caves to the twenty-mile distance to which they belong from Chandrapore, but instead must watch their dangerous intrusion into the laws of the colony. Adela Quested's accusation of assault by the hands of Aziz merely converts invitation into a possible synonym for the absence of erotic exchange in the high drama of colonial metaphoricity.

The disaster of the Marabar outing has less to do with a condemnation of colonial rape than with a study of the profound fragility of colonial intimacy. After Aziz is arrested on the charge of his violation of Adela, Fielding's defense of the former must face Anglo-India's profound objection to his countenance of imperial friendship: "I have had twenty-five years' experience of this country," the collector informs Fielding, "and during those twenty-five years I have never known anything but disaster result when English people and Indian people attempt to be intimate socially. Intercourse, yes. Courtesy, by all means. Intimacy—never, never" (p. 164). Any alternative geography described by Aziz and Fielding's intimacy in thus circumscribed by the deadening cultural perceptions that lie between Godbole's "Come, come," and the collector's "Never, never."

IN JANUARY OF 1925, FORSTER RECORDS IN HIS DIARY A SUMMATION OF WHAT he appears to be: "Famous, wealthy, miserable, physically ugly. . . . [I] am surprised I don't repel more generally: I can still get to know any one I want and have the illusion that I am charming and beautiful. Take no bother over nails or teeth but would powder my nose if I wasn't found out. Stomach increases, but not yet visible under waistcoat. The anus is clotted with hairs, and there is a great loss of sexual power—it was very violent 1921–22."[12] The violence of sexual power that Forster associates with the composition of *A Passage to India* manifests itself in the text as both an engagement with and a denial of a colonial homoerotic imperative. Increasingly, the women play a subservient role to the friendship that barely subsists between Fielding and Aziz. They remain the peripheries upon which male discourse locates constraints upon the operation of autonomous desires.

If the concluding section of *A Passage to India*, "Temple," sets up any dialogue with an exchange between "Mosque" and "Cave," it is only to reiterate the absence of a continued friendship within the parameters of colonial exchange. Forster's vision of the imperial erotic finally confines itself to the nationalism over which the two men cannot meet. Neither can claim legitimacy over the urge to disempower: "India a nation!" jokes Fielding; "What an apotheosis! Last comer to the drab nineteenth-century sisterhood! She, whose only peer was the Holy Roman Empire, shall rank with Guatemala and Belgium perhaps!" (p. 322). Here, the difficulty of nation is transcribed upon the possibility of sexual friendship, and allows *A Passage to India* to choose instead a geographic location of sexual belonging. The calibration of erotic exchange between cultures is elaborately articulated as a social impossibility, letting both Aziz and Fielding function as signifiers of the abortiveness of colonial exchange:

> "Why can't we be friends now?" said the other, holding him affectionately. "It's what I want. It's what you want."
> But the horses didn't want it—they swerved apart; the earth didn't want it, sending up rocks through which the riders must pass single file; the temples, the tank, the jail, the palace, the birds, the carrion, the Guest House, that came to view as they issued from the gap and saw the Mau beneath: they didn't want it, they said in their hundred voices, "No, not yet," and the sky said, "No, not there." (P. 322)

The longing imposed by geography cannot comply to its own complications of where the hollowness of colonial desire may end. In Forster's representation of an imperial erotic, both race and body are subjected to an awareness of colonial chronology that allows for the signification of love even when it is at its most productively dismal depths.

7

Naipaul's Arrival

MY TITLE REFERS BOTH TO THE EVOCATIVE ANNOUNCEMENT REPRESENTED BY
The Enigma of Arrival, and to an earlier Naipaul essay that anticipates, performs in advance, the burden of Naipaul's later work: published in *The
Return of Eva Peron,* the essay is titled "Conrad's Darkness."[1] Its tentative
idiom seeks to establish a literary vocabulary for a peculiarly postcolonial
problem, which Naipaul has also addressed in fictional and nonfictional narratives, most particularly in the open-ended memorialization that attends
The Enigma of Arrival.[2] "Conrad's Darkness" abbreviates in a canonical context questions of cultural equilibrium that continue to obsess Naipaul's
career: what uneasy commerce can be established between the postcolonial
and the writer? Which imperial gestures must such a writer perform before
he can delineate the relation of his language to the canon of fiction written in
English? Such anguish of affiliation dictates the grimly perfect grammar of a
novel like *A Bend in the River,* which is perhaps the most relentless
postcolonial mapping of how burdensome the novelty of its history can be.
The secret sharer of this novelty, however, is an essay like "Conrad's
Darkness," in that Naipaul continually veers between mooring his writing in
a cultural reality and a canonical one, equally convinced of the limitations
implicit in both modes. Caught between the excessive novelty of postcolonial
history and the excessive anachronism of the canon, Naipaul's language
functions as a fascinating paradigm for one of the several difficulties at work
in the definition of a colonial discourse. Its temporal location is curiously
threatening; its safety is aligned to the ritual of arrival; its fascination with
disparate systems of classification obviates the necessity of facing the question of whether it is possible for a postcolonial writer to exist in the absence of
the imperial theme.

Since readers of Naipaul frequently neglect to recollect the obvious, or
the extreme particularity of his historical position, I must begin by suggesting that Naipaul's career represents a localized and singular moment in the
multifariousness of postcolonial narrative: it can by no means serve as a synecdochical emblem of the whole. Instead, his writing lends expression to a

dying generation, whose linguistic and cultural crises will not again be duplicated in the engaged violence of a given "third-world" history. In an arena of such frenetic change, Naipaul records a perspective that knows its time is done even before it has had the chance to be fully articulated. This perspective has no choice but to register its own bewilderment at the relation between education and empire, seduced as it was into the quaint belief that literature could somehow provide a respite from what it means to gain consciousness in a colonial world. The English language represents a betrayal to V. S. Naipaul that cannot be historically replicated in a second generation of West Indian writers, whose idiom is molded out of the area's independence in the early 1960s, but the circuit of betrayal provides Naipaul with the only energy out of which he can write. His nervously intelligent anticipation of the obsolescence of his discourse, however, causes his narratives to function as those peculiar paradigms that proffer themselves to the world as though they must be paradigmatic, begging an urgent reading before the context of that urgency has been elaborated.

Such haste suggests a profound ideological ambivalence, usually misread as pronouncements of authority abut any country and any historical poignancy on which Naipaul chooses to write. His career, however, is pitted against such static models of authority, since it is so meticulously engaged in undoing the authorial miseries embodied in each of the genres it spans. Coming into its own with the Dickensian verve of *A House for Mr. Biswas*, moving through and recasting the idiom of travelogue and biography,[3] Naipaul's most significant work has little to do with definitive statements about postcolonial history, and more with a perception of the writer's guilty involvement in the construction of his own plots. *The Enigma of Arrival* recapitulates this long dismantling, in that it removes Naipaul from the defensive posture of being both interlocutor and spokesman for the proliferation of non-Western histories that even his meticulous grammar cannot possibly contain. It places him back where he began, at the dark heart of the comic novel.

"It has taken me a long time to come round to Conrad," Naipaul winningly asserts in "Conrad's Darkness," "and if I begin with an account of his difficulty, it is because I have to be true to my experience of him. I would find it hard to be detached about Conrad. He was, I suppose, the first modern writer I was introduced to" (*REP*, p. 223). Modernity, however, is the least significant component of Naipaul's overdetermined relation with Conrad, who signifies not only a powerful precursor but a crucial demonstration of the contiguity between the empire and the canon. If Naipaul's early engagement in Western literature suggests a somewhat naive need to believe that literary discourse exists in a serene segregation from the institutions that surround it, then Conrad functions as a potent reminder that the literary is in fact extraimperial. To write in the language of the other is not to mitigate but to embody the "political panic" (*REP*, p. 233) that the writer must endure as he moves from a colonial to a postcolonial world. "Conrad's Darkness" confesses after the fact to such a reality: "To be a colonial was to know a kind of security; it was to inhabit a fixed world. . . . But in the new world I felt that ground move below me. The new politics, the curious reliance of men on institutions they were working yet to undermine, the simplicity of beliefs and the hideous simplicity of actions . . . these were the things that began to preoccupy me. They were not the things from which I could detach myself. And I found that Conrad—sixty years before, in the time of great peace— had been everywhere before me" (*REP*, p. 233). This passage is emblematic of the complexities of Naipaul's tone, and his nervous will to demystify at the same moment, which is often most provoking to a postcolonial readership that cannot comprehend how a writer from Trinidad can calmly claim that the colonial outrages performed at the turn of the century suggest a time of "great peace." Naipaul's invocation of peace, however, is designed to be outrageous, suggesting both a nostalgic will to conceive of the past in purely literary terms and furthermore, to stake out the idea of unramified time: only in relation to such a canonical clock can Naipaul then map out his idiom of perpetual arrival.

Conrad's danger, therefore, lies in the fact that his language cannot function outside notions of ramification, that he disrupts the young colonial's desire to posit an integrity against which the latter can function as ramified other. "Conrad's Darkness" records, with a mocking affection, the futility of such a misreading, but the ghost the essay addresses is by no means laid. In a curiously revelatory passage, Naipaul describes the one scene that most haunted him from *Heart of Darkness*: the moment when Marlow, traveling up the river toward his encounter with Kurtz, finds in one of the abandoned posts along the river a volume titled *An Inquiry into Some Points of Seamanship*. The moment is indeed one of the few respites of tenderness that Conrad's allegory allows, invoking in Marlow the vision of an unknown but loving reader for whom *An Inquiry* lends structure to the surrounding darkness and the hideous commerce that it conceals. Naipaul extrapolates this encounter between the narrator and his appreciation of the act of reading to comment ruefully on its significance to his youth: "I suppose that in my fantasy I had seen myself coming to England as to some purely literary region, where, untrammeled by the accidents of history or background, I could make a romantic career for myself as a writer" (*REP*, p. 233). This ironic deflation of an early innocence, however, is more guiltily fraught than it first appears, for Naipaul resolutely refuses to remember the crucial turn in *Heart of Darkness* where Marlow actually meets the reader of *An Inquiry*, who turns out to be the harlequin devotee at Kurtz's Inner Post. With the mordant precision that characterizes the narrator's apprehension of his encounters, the Harlequin makes Marlow muse: "I was seduced into something like admiration—like envy. Glamour urged him on, glamour kept him unscathed. He surely wanted nothing from the wilderness but space to breathe in and to push through. His need was to exist, and to move onwards at the greatest possible risk, and with the maximum of privation."[4] At first, a reader of "Conrad's Darkness" is with justification perplexed at Naipaul's repression of Marlow's grim appreciation of the guilty single-mindedness that attends on reading. At a second glance, however, the intentionality of the essay is equally arresting: with a layering of irony almost on a par with Conrad's, Naipaul invites his readers to conceive of him as the Harlequin. He chooses to become that comic figure of incessant arrival, and in so doing inscribes himself as strongly on *Heart of Darkness* as in that tale the Harlequin makes *An Inquiry* serve as the occasion for his own ciphered marginalia.

Thus "Conrad's Darkness" hides in its oblique prose an astonished awareness of the rhetoric of reading that indicates a far more impacted understanding of imperialism than the one to which Naipaul overtly admits. Canonicity functions as a trope through which the writer can delineate the strange interaction of power and debasement that constitutes colonial history. Despite the ironized and exquisite posture of experience that Naipaul adopts, his writing cannot but exude an amazement that a second generation of West Indian writers could not possibly share: located as they are at the intersection of the colonial and postcolonial worlds, Naipaul's narratives are forced to record the astonishment of the initiate. They cannot believe that there are no sacred texts—not even the vestigial grace of a canon—in a postcolonial context. "Conrad's Darkness" reiterates this reluctance on a thematic level, and further serves as a structural example of how frequently Naipaul's narratives develop in order to undo their ostensible subjects: the writer invokes the authority of a prior text, be it Conrad or colonial history; in the posture of a respectful reader, however, he manages to recast himself as a character in the former tale in such a way that it becomes a frame, a preparation for his continuing plot. By deliberately fashioning himself as the Harlequin, the borderer on someone else's story, Naipaul is then enabled to dismantle the trope of arrival, exhibiting its haphazard uneasiness as opposed to its possible romance. Instead, arrival and disappointment are represented as crucially synonymous terms, their literary location suggesting a historical correlative at which Naipaul will only hint. If he wishes to address the terrible incompletion that accompanies schemes of national independence, he chooses to write about Conrad. The darkness of Conrad, therefore, becomes a moment of examination for Naipaul that far exceeds a simple admission of what an introjection of the English canon signifies to a postcolonial writer, particularly when that writer can assess the proliferating disappointment of history only in the language of another's literature.

It is then hardly surprising that Naipaul's version of Conrad is deeply invested in a reading of ideas of disappointment, so that finally, the figure of darkness is indistinguishable from the idiom of emptying: "Mystery—it is the Conradian word," Naipaul claims, "but there is no mystery in the work itself, the things imagined; mystery remains a concept of the writer's. . . . Mysterious words are repeated . . . 'enigma,' 'Certitude, immaterial and precious.' But there is no narrative and no real mystery" (*REP*, pp. 241–43). This statement of necessary misreading is of course more closely linked to the writer's recognition of his own literary predicament than it is to Conrad, but Naipaul's strength as a writer is such that his language can be elated only by moments of recognition, even when they seem to beckon an apprehension of failure. "Conrad's Darkness" admits to its own failure at arriving at an idiom in which to address adequately both literary and historical modes of classification; the essay concludes to invoke its own confusion: "Conrad died fifty years ago. In those fifty years his work has penetrated to many corners of the world which he saw as dark. It is a subject for Conradian meditation; it tells us something about our new world. Perhaps it doesn't matter what we say about Conrad; it is enough that he is discussed. You will remember that for Marlow in *Heart of Darkness*, 'the meaning of an episode was not inside like a kernel but outside, enveloping the tale which brought it out only as a glow brings out a haze' " (*REP*, p. 245). This recognition of the ambivalence of reading is a necessary moment in postcolonial self-definition, a gesture both more tentative and more courageous than the emphatic political rectitude that, for example, Chinua Achebe exhibits when he demands the complete censorship of *Heart of Darkness* in independent Africa.[5] For Naipaul, Conrad uncannily suggests the adulterated nature of historical plot, the fact that arrival is always the scene of prior disappointment.

In *The Enigma of Arrival*, Naipaul reiterates with a lucid reluctance concepts that "Conrad's Darkness" describes as "Conradian words": "mystery," "enigma," "arrival." This idiom most frequently leads readers of Naipaul to criticize what is perceived as his anglicized romanticism of postcolonial history, or his inability to come to terms with the stringent economy of empire.[6] On this score, however, Naipaul becomes too readily available as a whipping boy, a readiness in which he is indeed complicit. The flagellatory implications in the postcolonial dynamic between writer and reader, however, demand a scope far beyond the possibility of the present chapter, which can only suggest that the model of nineteenth-century imperialism has never been so well replicated as it has in the relation between writers and critics of the postcolonial academy.[7] Naipaul's career, and the stubborn reception that his writing has received from readers most interested in defining a postcolonial discourse, provide a dismaying example of such intransigence. He is assigned an ideological whiteness with an emphasis that lacks the admitted miscomprehension of his own apprehension of Conrad's darkness; his study of mystery as a synonym for disappointment is completely denied its context of a highly sophisticated ironizing of imperial mythmaking. Thus the brilliance of *A Bend in the River*—Naipaul's previous novel, and his most sustained revision of the passage represented by *Heart of Darkness*—must be dismissed as conservative, as merely a novel, simply because it makes the canon of Western literature the occasion for its engagement in the history of the other to which his language belongs.[8]

Since *A Bend in the River* is a text that arrives both at Conrad and at a meticulously specific postcolonial encounter, that of the East African Asian's migration to a newly independent central African state, its idiom deserves a more comprehensive reading than it routinely receives from the most advanced critics of postcolonial literature. When Edward Said, for example, contemplates the situation of the postcolonial intellectual, he resolutely ignores the possibility that *A Bend in the River* may address fictionally the issues that Said addresses critically: "The irony . . . is that people like us are in fact at even greater risk [than] in the formerly colonized world, where in many places critical ideas are considered a menace. . . . The most attractive and immoral move, however, has been Naipaul's, who has allowed himself quite consciously to be turned into a witness for the Western prosecution [of the third world]."[9] The unsettling seduction of *A Bend in the River*, however, suggests that such a prosecution is double-edged, for the writer is never exempted from the text's graphic indictment of the postcolonial world. Its indictment, furthermore, cannot be read literally: it represents the convolutions of tone through which Naipaul recasts and syncopates his tenderness for his subject into a grim rarification of a comic idiom. The novel opens to repeat the journey of *Heart of Darkness*, substituting the mythic quality of travel by water with the resistant and somehow more historical quality of travel by land: "As I got deeper into Africa . . . I thought: But this is madness. I am going in the wrong direction. There can't be a new life at the end of this. But I drove on. . . . And I couldn't help thinking that that was how it was in the old days for the slaves. They had made the same journey, but of course on foot and in the opposite direction, from the centre of the continent to the east coast . . . like the slaves far from home, I became anxious only to arrive" (*Bend*, p. 4). The arrival toward which this journey moves must be understood beyond overly defensive anticipations of "Western prosecution"; it instead seeks to articulate both the precision and the amorphousness that attend historical definition in a postcolonial context.

Naipaul makes the canon of Western literature an implicated witness to his mapping of the moment of postcolonial arrival. The imperial irony of *Heart of Darkness* serves as a lackey to the astoundingly noncommittal narrative voice of *A Bend in the River*, recasting Conrad into the audience for a tale as interested in the shared responsibility of storyteller and audience as is its Western precursor. For Naipaul's mature writing no longer conceives of the literary as a recourse from the political, but instead internalizes the imperial tradition represented by both modes into a dazzling idiom that no longer needs to indicate the referents of its discourse. As a consequence of this condensation, such a language will never clearly identify the object of its indictment. Its burden is, of course, to demonstrate the objectlessness of postcolonial indignation, as that discourse seeks to establish the parameters of its suffering. For the narrator of *A Bend in the River* suffers the literary to become an equal participant in the outrage of colonial history, and allows neither authority nor amelioration to the canon that threatens to envelop him. A crucial moment that illustrates Naipaul's ability to do away with simple constructs of authority occurs when his narrator muses why the town at which he has arrived should choose a Latin motto as its announcement of municipal identity. Like Marlow's mythic stations, the city remains unnamed, the anonymous Congo now being repeated by the anonymous Zaire, its ideological referents emerging out of the ghostly mobility with which a postcolonial narrative acknowledged the irony that its history cannot but suggest:

> [The priest] explained the second motto of the town for me—the Latin words carved on the ruined monument near the dock gates: *Miscerique probat populos et foedera jungi.* 'He approves of the mingling of the peoples and their bonds of union': that was what

the words meant, and again they were very old words, from the
days of ancient Rome. They came from a poem about the founding of Rome. The very first Roman hero, travelling to Italy to
found his city, lands on the coast of Africa. The local queen falls
in love with him, and it seems that the journey to Italy might be
called off. But then the watching gods take a hand; and one of
them says that the great Roman god might not approve of a settlement in Africa, of a mingling of people there, of treaties
between the Africans and Romans. That was how the words occurred in the old Latin poem. In the motto, though, three words
were altered to reverse the meaning. According to the motto . . . a settlement in Africa raises no doubts: the great Roman
god approves of the mingling of peoples and the making of treaties in Africa. . . . I was staggered. Twisting two-thousand-year-
old words to celebrate sixty years of the steamer service to the
capital! Rome was Rome. What was this place? To carve the
words on a monument beside an African river was surely to
invite the destruction of the town. *Wasn't there some little anxiety, as in the original line of the poem?* (*Bend*, pp. 62–63;
emphasis added)

While such passages are usually read in the context of what Anthony
Appiah terms the "Naipaul fallacy," or a perspective that forces the reader
"to understand Africa by embedding it in European culture,"[10] this criticism
fails to address Naipaul's uncanny ability to map the complicity between
postcolonial history and its imperial past. Allusions to Virgil and Conrad
hardly serve to create a Eurocentric aura in the novel, but instead—emptied
of their literariness—work as perfunctory witnesses to the anxiety of empire
that is Naipaul's subject. *A Bend in the River* suggests that such anxiety is
the scene of postcolonialism: old models of authority, whether aesthetic or
political, all fall short of apprehending the nature of this anxiety, in which
historical discourse is represented as both radically obsolete and radically
novel at the same time. In this discourse, the idiom of indictment is curiously
dislocated, so that the reader can never clearly identify what its object may
be, or whether indeed the narrative ever develops beyond the self-accusa-
tory. Here, Naipaul's indictment of his own narrative voice and his
willingness to proffer it as a postcolonial case history needs to be examined as
a political gesture rather than simply as an impulse to autobiography. Its necessary narcissism converts geographic space into theatrical space, allowing
Naipaul's narratives to move with a bewildering mobility from Trinidad to
East Africa; from India to Zaire. As in *A Bend in the River*, historical location

alone is never the point: literary location is equally crucial to the writer's anxious embodiment of the politics of postcolonial arrival.

THE SUBJECT OF INDIA FUNCTIONS AS A CONTINENTAL DIVIDE IN NAIPAUL'S career providing the space on which he first articulated his ostensibly auto-biographical narrative. *An Area of Darkness* extends and elaborates the idiom of travel broached in the earlier text *The Middle Passage* to suggest disturbingly that the genre of the travelogue launches a writer into the lan-guage of ignorance rather than that of experience. This language is so troubling that it almost begs rejection as a gratuitously remorseless attack on the inevitable political and cultural crisis that marks the first two decades of India's independence; its gloom is further exacerbated by Naipaul's failure to contextualize his reading of contemporary India by any reference to the highly engaging struggle for political independence that characterized the last century of British rule over the subcontinent. Instead, *An Area of Darkness* constructs a triangulated idea of India, in which an ancient India of prehistory confronts an English India of the Raj, which in turn dissolves into the phantasmagoria of the post-history that Naipaul reads into the India of today. With some justification, this reading has received its fair share of in-dignant responses,[11] many of which rightly point out that the subject of *An Area of Darkness* is not India at all but instead is V. S. Naipaul. Given Naipaul's self-consciousness as a writer, however, it then becomes necessary to examine why he should deliberately choose the idiom of self-punishment; why need he so deeply implicate the writer in his construct of historic dis-array?

According to Edward Said, the answer suggests simple professional ex-pedience: "Two things need to be said about the small band whose standard bearer Naipaul has become. . . . One is that in presenting themselves as members of courageous minorities in the Third World, they are in fact not interested at all in the Third World—which they never address—but in the metropolitan intellectuals whose twists and turns have gone on despite the Third World, and whose approval they seem quite desperate to have. . . . [Second,] what is seen as crucially informative and telling about their work—their accounts of the Indian darkness or the Arab predicament—is precisely what is weakest about it: with reference to the actualities it is ignorant, illite-rate, and cliché-ridden."[12] While such an argument needs to be made, particularly for the benefit of a Western audience prepared to credit Naipaul with more authority than he asks for, it will not admit to the possibility that perhaps the "actualities" of the third world are never intentionally Naipaul's subject. Instead, his fascination with the cliché and the readily available colonial myth may be his only means to arrive at an idiom in which to address his perception of himself as a postcolonial cliché. Even if this perception is deemed ideologically reprehensible, it has already been too influential to be dismissed out of hand, particularly since a closer reading of its project suggests that Naipaul's writing is perhaps more revisionary than it first appears. The need for angry critiques of his work is now obsolete, or such critiques must be prepared to admit to what each successive text, from *An Area of Darkness* to *The Enigma of Arrival*, makes increasingly clear: Naipaul has already been there before them, and has been exquisitely angry at himself.

"The past for me—as colonial and writer—was full of shame and mortifications," *The Enigma of Arrival* quietly announces, "yet as a writer I could train myself to face them. Indeed, they became my subjects" (p. 245). The wry equanimity of this tone is anchored in the difficulty of what has been previously written, in the deeply unsettling narrative of *An Area of Darkness*. For the latter text has not yet arrived at the luxury of the past tense, enacting instead striking parallels between the nature of colonial shame and that of literary mortification. Both become instances in a failure in language, so that the syntax of *An Area of Darkness* is always on the verge of fracturing into hysteria: its subject is too disabling for the text to recuperate a steady belief in its own viability. And its subject, of course, is the idea of the foreign. For a second-generation displaced Trinidadian Indian, the journey to India should represent a return, a mythic if nostalgic reconstruction of historical location. Rather than serve such a function of cultural and political replenishment, however, the journey deconstructs, leaving the narrator with a fearful apprehension of how foreign he is to his own history and to the language in which he writes. As a consequence, the narrative can only enact a moment of postcolonial panic, in which inchoate impressions of place only barely intrude on the text's relentless mapping of its own absence of location. Naipaul nowhere implies that he intends to give an untrammeled sociological account of a writer's journeying through India in its second decade of independence: his tropological relation to India is established from its title on, and his defensively literary approach to the subcontinent is tellingly described as an arrival at "a resting-place for the imagination" (*Area*, p. 29). *The Enigma of Arrival* clearly delineates the literary quality of Naipaul's Indian arrival: "India was special to England; for two hundred years there had been any number of English travelers' accounts and, latterly, novels. I could not be that kind of traveler. In traveling to India I was traveling to an

un-English fantasy, and a fantasy unknown to Indians of India. . . . There
was no model for me here, in this exploration; neither Forster nor Ackerley
nor Kipling could help. To get anywhere in the writing, I had first of all to
define myself very clearly to myself" (pp. 153–54).

An Area of Darkness thus becomes a compelling record of delusion,
where neither the genealogy of body nor the genealogy of language can function as a cultural plot. Naipaul's ancestry proves insufficient to allow him to
intuit an Indian narrative; his affiliation with Western literature does not automatically align him to a colonialist narrative. Although the desire to
embody both is strongly present throughout An Area of Darkness, finally
Naipaul's obsessive need to apprehend his own hybridity becomes the central
force of his narrative. As Homi K. Bhabha's powerful and impacted reading
of the colonial hybrid suggests, "Hybridity is the revaluation of the assumption of colonial identity through the repetition of discriminatory identity
effects. It displays the necessary deformation and displacement of all sites of
discrimination and domination. It unsettles the mimetic or narcissistic demands of colonial power but reimplicates its identifications in strategies of
subversion that turn the gaze of the discriminated back upon the eye of
power."[13] An Area of Darkness precisely addresses the psychic terror implicit in such a sense of cultural malformation: its lack of alignment to the
worlds that surround it ultimately force the narrative to locate itself in representations of a wasted postcolonial body. These representations are perhaps
the most disturbing and uncivil revisions of what narrative location may
mean in a postcolonial context, yet they are curiously overlooked in current
assessments of what is seen as Naipaul's dangerously anachronistic literariness. According to Bhabha, "It is to preserve the peculiar sensibility of
what he understands as a tradition of civility that Naipaul 'translates' Conrad, from Africa to the Caribbean, in order to transform the despair of
postcolonial history into an appeal for the autonomy of art. . . . Naipaul
turns his back on the hybrid half-made colonial world to fix his eye on the
universal domain of English literature."[14] Universals, however, are very
much lacking from the atmosphere of An Area in Darkness; instead, with
exact awareness of the postcolonial irony implicit in such a reference, its
hybridity allows all of its voices to clamor at the same time, "This thing of
darkness I acknowledge mine."[15]

The literary indeed serves as a crucial system of classification in all of
Naipaul's writing, but it functions as a category in which the trauma of
postcolonial culture can be enacted and can locate its plot, and thus cannot be
read merely as the writer's retrenchment into the civil or universal. Instead,

literariness becomes an idiosyncratic idiom in which Naipaul powerfully and self-consciously indicates the limitations of his relation to imperialism. *An Area in Darkness* records the failure of literary classification as an available grid on which to trace the anxiety of cultural location, while at the same time it demonstrates that since Naipaul's language is so deeply invested in its ability to make narrative, his discourse can approach the historical only as though it were a literary genre. The frightening category of history confronts the archaic category of romance, and out of the violence of this generic collision emerges a self-punishing narrative voice that is still unsure whether it has earned the right to be historical. Its uncertainty becomes its hysterical subject. While it is possible to read the crucial narcissism of this enactment as a gesture of facile extraterritorialism, such readings pay insufficient attention to why Naipaul as a postcolonial writer should find it necessary to enact so publicly a sense of colonial shame from the points of view both of the possessor and of the possessed. If *An Area of Darkness* misreads colonial history simply to make an easy identification with postimperial nostalgia for the Raj, then indeed a reinterpretation of its discourse would be redundant. Its obsessive narrative, however, with its acute focus on relics—both historical and human—must be fully understood before it can be left behind. For its language embodies two vital junctures in a consciousness peculiarly situated between colonial and postcolonial worlds: on the one hand, its revision of the literary represents a defetishization of the canonical authority of the British; on the other, it is prepared to address the possibility that the only alternative location left to its narrative is the obsolete fetish of the colonial body.

The landscape of *An Area of Darkness* is littered with bodies. On first reading, Naipaul's obsession with the population and poverty of India seems quite in keeping with established traditions of Orientalist narrative, in which hysteric descriptions of an engulfing Eastern physicality serve as buttresses to uphold the isolated sanity of the Western eye. In the typical travel narrative of the nineteenth century, the imperialist's gaze draws its sense of significance from a committed reading of the colonial body as a figure of complete literalism: the undecipherable cultural codes represented by such bodies is quickly reread as a certain absence of metaphoricity.[16] The colonial body thus functions in the narrative as a node of meaninglessness, and is described as an object so seeable that it immediately becomes unseen. When *An Area of Darkness* opens with all too familiar accounts of the docks of Bombay or the crowds of Calcutta, it appears simply to repeat the great divide that colonialist narrative constructs between comprehending eye and uncomprehending bodily clutter. But Naipaul's project blurs such lines of demarcation, since—almost against its will—the text begins to acknowledge the narrator's bodily availability to interpretation, making it increasingly unclear whether the perceived or perceiving body is the greater redundancy on the narrative scene. This conflation first occurs in a questioning of the authoritative frame of the Orientalist eye: "India is the poorest country in the world. Therefore, to see its poverty is to make an observation of no value. . . . Do not think that your anger and contempt are marks of your sensitivity. You might have seen more: the smiles on the faces of the begging children, that domestic group among the pavement sleepers waking in the cool Bombay morning . . . it is your gaze that violates them, your sense of outrage that outrages them. You might have seen the boy sweeping his area of pavement, spreading his mat, lying down . . . it is your surprise, your anger, that denies him humanity" (Area, pp. 47–48). Each time the narrative eye stops to acknowledge its possible limitations, a vestigial sense of metaphor is returned to the sleeping bodies on the docks of Bombay.

Thus even at those points where An Area of Darkness seems most invested in maintaining a canonical reality, or a discourse aligned to Orientalist narrative and the stereotypes that it engenders, the narrator's perception of a shared incomprehension between the observed and the observing body muddies his own stereotypical allusions. As Naipaul's reading of his precursors would have surely made evident, the colonial voice is fundamentally disembodied ("That was exactly what I had been looking forward to—a talk with Kurtz. I made the strange discovery that I had never imagined him as doing, you know, but as discoursing. I didn't say to myself, 'Now I will never see him,' or 'Now I will never shake him by the hand,' but 'Now I will never hear him.' The man presented himself as a voice").[17] By attempting to give the postcolonial version of that voice a bodily location, An Area of Darkness suggests crucial revisions in the extensive literature of what it means to see racially: its confusions and its hysteria continually return to painstaking accounts of the act of racial seeing, and the peculiar segregation between literal and figural seeing that records of such acts have traditionally generated. The narrative, of course, remains ignorant of its own revisionary impetus, in that it consists of a montage of anecdotes that begs the luxury of a metonymic accretion; its structure insists that no one anecdote can assert significance over another. In the process of such a telling, An Area of Darkness structurally replicates the crowds of Bombay, allowing tale to lie next to autonomous tale in an indiscriminate chain that will not acknowledge its obsession with racial seeing, needing instead a reader to blame: "It is your surprise, your anger, that denies [these tales] humanity."

A reader who does not share in the narrator's anxieties, however, will indeed discriminate, and accord significance to those anecdotal moments in *An Area if Darkness* where the narrative reneges control of meaning, and can no longer distinguish its function as a body. The most striking instance of such a narrative collision occurs when Naipaul attempts to image himself as a bodily presence in India: "For the first time in my life I was one of the crowd. There was nothing in my appearance or dress to distinguish me from the crowd. . . . In Trinidad to be an Indian was distinctive. To be anything there was to be distinctive; difference was each man's attribute. To be an Indian in England was distinctive. . . . Now in Bombay I entered a shop or a restaurant and awaited a special quality of response. And there was nothing. It was like being denied part of my reality. Again and again I was caught. I had been made by Trinidad and England; recognition of my difference was necessary to me. I felt the need to impose myself, and didn't know how" (*Area*, pp. 45–46). This passage dramatizes the obliterating impulse of racial seeing, in which to be seen is immediately to be unseen, but crucially revises the norms of colonial narrative to make the narrator equally the object of such obliteration. That both the narrator and the crowds of Bombay share in the discomfort of being bodies seen to the point of invisibility, however, does not automatically construct an alternative plot: instead, *An Area of Darkness* veers between anecdotes that seem uncertain whether greater invisibility should be accorded to the India that is "an area of the imagination" or to the narrator's perception of his own phantasmagoric voice. As a result of this irresolution, the narrative powerfully enacts central problems for any discourse that attempts to address what it means to live in a racial body.

Its basic question is quite simple: how should a human body bear itself, when it is required to be seen as a completely figural representation of race? If pigmentation is indeed so figurative, why is the racial body subject to such a literal gaze that meaning will always run off it like water? For a racial body is read in the absence of cultural and social indexes, those codes that mitigate the physicality of human presence. The language of racial self-consciousness cannot but address this splitting, in which the body is first synecdochical of a huge abstraction, and then synecdochical of nothing but itself. These two parallel readings are perhaps more readily imaged in the famous moment from *Black Skin, White Masks* where Fanon relentlessly maps out the consequences of the degraded discourse that greeted him with the perpetual refrain, "Look, a Negro!"[18] Out of a language so low-grade that it allows for only a shattering literalism, Fanon laboriously reconstitutes the possibilities of discourse, so that "Look, a Negro!" can be reformulated as negritude.

With great rhetorical tenderness, he attempts to rethink his own skin as concept and constructs a narrative space in which race can proclaim its outrage at colonialism's literal reading of racial difference, asserting instead its reentry into historical discourse as a conceptualized body. The split, however, remains: the cry of "Look!" suggests the injunction "Do not look!" and each narrative that seeks to make sense of such conflicting commands must necessarily founder under the weight of its own visibility. *An Area of Darkness* attempts to address this visibility and fails: too frightened by its own implications, it posits and then retrieves the narrator's body as an object available for inspection, thereby replicating the great contradiction of the excessive literalism or the excessive metaphoricity of the racial body. In either case, it draws on the idiom of excess.

Each time *An Area of Darkness* approaches an overt recognition of the bodily and consequently racial quality of its own narrative, its storytelling quickly veers away into the safety of some third-person tale, in which the body at issue becomes a representative of Indian otherness to Naipaul. But the narrative's need to create such pockets of disembodiment for its own voice is finally as revealing as those confessional sequences that present the narrator as a racial body. A significant example of the former mode occurs when Naipaul predictably moves from looking at crowds to looking at squalor, offering a curiously literal and pre-Freudian reading of filth: "Indians defecate everywhere. They defecate, mostly, beside the railway tracks. But they also defecate on the river beaches; They defecate on the hills; They defecate on the banks; they defecate on the streets; they never look for cover. . . . These squatting figures—to the visitor, after a time, as eternal and emblematic as Rodin's Thinker—are never spoken of; they are never written about. . . . *Indians do not see these squatters* and might even, with complete sincerity, deny that they exist" (*Area*, pp. 74–75). While the narrator seeks to draw a distinct physical boundary between himself as "thinker" and such images of unthinking evacuation, his idiom simultaneously expresses a fascination with the exposure of the racial body and its ability to be both unseen and too much seen at the same time. As a consequence, the hysteria of Naipaul's catalog provides a rhetorical replay of the excessive defecation that it records: the narrative's blindness to its own tautology suggests that both image and idiom are equally committed to believing in their necessary invisibility. In attempting to expose bodies already too exposed, *An Area of Darkness* is forced to contemplate its own extraneousness as a narrative, and its secret arrival at an image of race as the evacuated body.

The idea of evacuation is crucial to the method through which *An Area of Darkness* constructs narrative sense. Its language is deeply invested in representing the literary as an evacuated site, so that Orientalist narrative is already a ruin before Naipaul as tourist arrives at it. A cultural evacuation is of equal importance to Naipaul's sense of his own emptied alienation, a sense that is usually read in the unhelpfully vague context of postcolonial exile,[19] but which needs to be recontextualized into the specificity of the evacuated system embodied by a text like *An Area of Darkness*. This system is, of course, the structure of caste, the disturbing classification of which precludes the necessity of positing otherness outside its own social and cultural purview. That such classification is deeply embarrassing to read is evidenced by how untouchable the subject of caste has become to most readers of Naipaul: at best, caste is translated into an economic grid only relevant as an illustration of the fact that a middle-class Trinidadian Brahmin cannot possibly know what he is talking about when he turns to the social system of India.[20] *An Area of Darkness*, however, is disturbing precisely because it privileges such narrative ignorance, and approaches the classification of caste as though it too could function as an evacuated genre, or another obsolescence through which the narrative could attempt to understand the tropological nature of race.

Naipaul's relation to caste begins with the castelessness of Trinidad, where the Hindu population as he describes it can no longer legitimately function within its hierarchy: "In Trinidad caste had no meaning in our day-to-day life; the caste we occasionally played at was no more than an acknowledgement of latent qualities; the reassurance it offered was such as might have been offered by a palmist or a reader of handwriting" (*Area*, p. 36). Such a disclaimer is necessarily misleading, for *An Area of Darkness* clearly demonstrates that the idea of caste is in fact more threatening when it has lost the pragmatism of its function in India, where racial and economic difference has been historically accorded a ritual and tragic space. In Naipaul's discourse, caste functions as a tropology that allows him to obsess on dislocated untouchability: just as the racial body causes his language to veer between images that are extremely visible and invisible at the same time, his sense of caste focuses on the mobility that can belong to the category of the untouchable. Here, the "touch me not" aura that *An Area of Darkness* exudes in its judgments of contemporary India takes on a very complicated responsibility, in that the narrative—with painstaking literalism—attempts to apprehend racial reality through a description of what can and cannot be touched. "I had seen the starved child defecating at the roadside while the mangy dog waited to eat the excrement," Naipaul's catalog wearily declares; "I had seen the physique of the people of Andhra, which had suggested the possibility of an evolution downwards, wasted body to wasted body, Nature mocking herself, incapable of remission. Compassion and pity did not answer; they were refinements of hope. Fear is what I felt. Contempt is what I had to fight against . . . in the end it was fatigue that overcame me." (*Area*, p. 48).

Accompanied by its own absence of remission, this fatigue dictates the dismantling structure of *An Area of Darkness*, in which the narrator moves from a perception of himself as a Trinidadian Brahmin in quest of the grail of mythic India into an acknowledgment of his own historical redundancy and his function as the new untouchable on the scene of Indian history. Despite the fact that India is the space on which Naipaul arrives at such a formulation, India proper is indeed extraneous to the narrative. Instead, it serves as the occasion for a further refinement of the language of arrival, which now takes on the more elliptical connotations of evacuation. In the ellipses of this idiom, *An Area of Darkness* grimly suggests that the trope of travel, of incessant movement, can function as a deferral for postcolonial narrative: it deflects attention from the writer's complicated relation to a racial body, a steady apprehension of which Naipaul has yet to reach.

MUCH AS *AN AREA OF DARKNESS* NEEDS TO POSIT THE FICTION OF INDIA IN order that Naipaul may find a language for his own darkness, so *The Enigma of Arrival* posits the fictiveness of autobiography in order that he may write about the act of making fiction. Thus far, his essay into the fiction of autobiography has been received with both acclaim and puzzlement: from the point of view of an already irritated postcolonial perspective, the book represents a final admission of Naipaul's real subject, or his narcissistic engagement with an individual writer's relation to England. From an Anglo-American and somewhat more canonical point of view, however, the work is welcomed as a meditation by a writer whose language is powerful and lucid enough to have earned the right to be meditative. At least in their initial reviews, both perspectives seem unwilling to address Naipaul's revision of his vocabulary of "enigma" and "arrival": the terms function as ideologically suspect signposts in one critical discourse; as comforting referents to the tropes of romanticism in the other.[21] Instead, reviewers focus on questions of genre and classification, puzzling over why Naipaul subtitles *The Enigma of Arrival* "A Novel" when it reads suspiciously like an autobiographical narrative. In Naipaul's career, however, autobiography is a highly overdetermined category: *An Area of Darkness* clearly demonstrates the degree of narrative concealment represented by the ostensibly autobiographical mode.

Just as *An Area of Darkness* structured its narrative on an apprehension of how secretive the act of confession can be, so *The Enigma of Arrival* suggests postautobiography: no longer defensive about its own ellipses, the book is a remarkable compendium of all the subjects about which Naipaul found it impossible to write, and skirts those areas of darkness that must still be submitted to his taut internal censor.

A key example of such self-conscious censorship is provided by the title, *The Enigma of Arrival*, itself. The phrase is not Naipaul's, but the title of a Chirico painting; the title of the painting is not Chirico's, but Apollinaire's, who gave the name to the painting that so haunted Naipaul. The narrative deliberately leaves vague whether the title or the picture has the greater capacity to haunt: this conflation of image and idiom allows Naipaul then to describe a story he wished to write at one point in his career. It was to be called "The Enigma of Arrival," and it was never written. This unwritten tale is invoked as a frame for the enigma of writing that is his current subject: "My story was to be set in classical times, in the Mediterranean. My narrator would write plainly, without any attempt at period style or historical explanation of his period. He would arrive—for a reason that I had yet to work out—at that classical port. . . . He would enter there and be swallowed by the life and noise of a crowded city (I imagined something like an Indian bazaar scene). . . . Gradually there would come to him a feeling that he was getting nowhere; he would lose his sense of mission; he would only know that he was lost. . . . At the moment of crisis he would come upon a door, open it, and find himself back on the quayside of arrival. . . . Only one thing is missing now. . . . The traveller has lived out his life" (pp. 98–99). In the unwritten "Enigma of Arrival," then, a return to the "quayside of arrival" serves as a confirmation of how much the idiom of arrival is involved in both identifying and covering over its necessary obsolescence; the written *Enigma of Arrival* charts, with wryness and wonder, a dependence on the obsolete that allowed so many of Naipaul's narratives to take shape, and prohibited the formulation of so many others.

The joke of the unwritten "Enigma" is its impossible need to juxtapose a classic distance with "something like an Indian bazaar scene," and to allow the literary to function as a vessel for psychic responses to specific enactments of political panic. The written *Enigma*, however, acknowledges this joke, in that it draws attention to the fact that the germinating story haunted Naipaul during the months that he was writing *In a Free State* (1971), a collection of stories set in Africa that *Enigma* now describes as "a book about fear." "It did not occur to me," Naipaul adds, "that the story of *The Enigma of Arrival*—a sunlit sea journey ending in a dangerous classical city—which had come to me as a kind of release from the creative rigors and darkness of my own African story, it did not occur to me that that Mediterranean story was really no more than a version of the story I was already writing" (pp. 99–100). Much as the Mediterranean and African tales converge into the same narrative, *The Enigma of Arrival* makes clear that the history of Naipaul's life as a writer is unable to represent disparate cultural postures at one time, but can only write about one of these peculiar positions while seeming to write about another. Even though such open admissions suggest that Naipaul's narrative is at last less defensively at odds with the shape that it must take, *The Enigma of Arrival* by no means eliminates the writer's prior reliance on self-censorship: in the telling of this tale, the body lends itself to further permutations of untouchability, becoming a point of available reference only after it is dead.

The Enigma of Arrival consists of five autonomous essays arranged in roughly chronological order, set in the Wiltshire valley that was Naipaul's home during his second sojourn in England. Detailed descriptions of this landscape give an oddly bucolic tone to the narrative, particularly since each of the five chapters records a death, sometimes of a person peripheral, sometimes most intimate, to the writer's life; each chapter also addresses pieces of writing that Naipaul did or did not complete during that period of time. In the course of the chapters—from the opening "Jack's Garden" to the closing "The Ceremony of Farewell"—Jack dies, Jack's father dies, a hare dies, Naipaul's friend Alan dies, Mr. Phillips the caretaker dies, and finally, Naipaul's younger sister Sati dies. At the same time, Naipaul writes *In a Free State*, *An Area of Darkness*, and *Guerrillas*, conceives the early version of "Enigma," and then, in the closing pages of the book, begins to write the present *Enigma:* "Faced with a real death, and with this new wonder about men, I laid aside my drafts and hesitations and began to write very fast about Jack and his garden" (p. 345). While death is not presented as an enabling event to the writer, it is certainly placed in an uncanny contiguity to the arrival of writing, making the quietude of the narrative seem eerily serene. Its tone is further complicated by the fact that Naipaul needs to catalog these deaths in a novelistic fashion in order to defer writing about the one real death that frames *The Enigma of Arrival*, but which is kept resolutely absent from the interior of the narrative: the book is dedicated "in loving memory of my brother, Shiva Naipaul, 25 February 1945, Port of Spain, 13 August 1985, London: and its concluding sentence is followed by the dates, "October 1984–April 1986." While the narrative makes no overt mention of this death, those two paired dates in the opening and closing pages of the "novel" ask to be read as signs for what still cannot be written, or for the grave guilt with which Naipaul can approach his brother's body only by according it a complete invisibility.

As *An Area of Darkness* set up the structure of an imaginary India in order that Naipaul could see himself racially, so the censored memorial of *The Enigma of Arrival* requires overloaded descriptions of English countryside as preludes for its attempt to see the body both familially and historically. The familial body is most clearly conceived in Naipaul's account of his sister's death: "For more than thirty years, since the death of my father in 1953, I had lived without grief. I took the news coldly, therefore; then I had hiccups; then I became concerned" (p. 345). The coldness here suggests the panic that attends the discourse of grieving, a language secretly frightened of falling short of its proper object, translating the death lament into the nearly parodic hiccup of the comic writer. It further exemplifies Naipaul's continued need to obliterate the domestic body, as though writing can happen only in the complete absence of intimate presence, even when he is at that point in his career when he is prepared to discuss this strange contingency that language forces upon him. The act of unseeing the intimate body certainly complicates most of Naipaul's novels, which tend to represent intimacy in the context of publicly racial spectacles, but the issue of invisibility is somehow a more painstakingly literal one than the distant and ironized men and women of Naipaul's narratives suggest. The only piece of writing that takes on the plangency of such literalism is the chapter titled "Prologue to an Autobiography," published in *Finding the Centre,* the book that immediately precedes *The Enigma of Arrival* and is in many ways a preparation for the latter. "Prologue to an Autobiography" faces the literal without Naipaul's usual recourse to oblique and elliptical representations: the piece is about what Naipaul can afford to remember about his father.[22]

The Brahminical elitism often credited to Naipaul's perspective is curiously reversed in this account of his father's life, a poignant story of a Trinidadian journalist who essentially saw himself as a failed writer, and whose life reeks of professional and personal humiliations. The first indignity is intimate: the father is dependent on his wife's more established family; Naipaul gains consciousness in a world of such extended relations that they obviously indicate his father's marginality to the authority of that social system. "There were desperate quarrels," Naipaul writes, "animosities and alliances shifted all the time; people had constantly to be looked at in new ways. . . . I didn't see my father for days. His nerves deteriorated . . . one Sunday evening, in a great rage, he threw a glass of hot milk. It cut me above the right eye; my eyebrow still shows the scar" ("Prologue," p. 27). No other sentence, perhaps, so clearly maps out Naipaul's censored relation to bodily authority. Given the precisions of his language, a reader must stop over the repression of grammar in Naipaul's sentence: "he threw a glass of hot milk"—at what? at me? The intention, however, and the circuit of bodily communication it suggests, are rendered invisible, registering only as a memory, a scar that suggests recognition to the writer alone.

"Prologue to an Autobiography" unwillingly records that which continues to be Indian in a non-Indian world. It licenses the writer to touch on the idea of obsolescence in a peculiarly overloaded fashion, for the essay must find an idiom in which to put together the castelessness of caste in Trinidad, the uncannily literal significance of the body of a dead father, and a language that is itself obsessed with the grammar of an outlived hierarchy. Not only must Naipaul confront the fact of that body's death, but he must further revise its relation to Hinduism and to ritual ways of situating bodies into cultural and historical localities—always a problematic issue in Naipaul's writing. He approaches such an act of framing when the crisis of the essay occurs, which describes the son's discovery, years after his father's death, of a 1933 *New York Herald-Tribune* clipping: "Threatened by death by the Hindu goddess Kali, Seepersad Naipaul, native writer [of Port of Spain], today offered a goat as sacrifice to appease the anger of the goddess. Naipaul wrote newspaper articles revealing that native farmers of Hindu origin had defied government regulations for combating cattle diseases and had been substituting ancient rites of the goddess Kali to drive away the illness attacking their livestock. The writer was told he would develop poisoning tomorrow, die on Sunday, and be buried on Monday unless he offered a goat sacrifice. Today he yielded to the entreaty of friends and relatives and made the demanded sacrifice" ("Prologue," p. 61).

For Naipaul, the clipping represents another moment of postcolonial panic, since it robs the image of the writer of its accoutrements of modernity and neutrality, forcing him instead to acknowledge connections between the memory of writing and an archaic penitence that he would sooner forget. Along with the glass of hot milk, the sacrificial goat serves as a painfully ludicrous reminder of how the act of writing accentuates rather than mitigates the fear of bodily harm. The image of the father thus becomes dangerously linked to the vulnerability of the writer's body when it is reflected on the mirror of caste; it must consequently be repressed in order to allow the son to function in a casteless world. Literal sacrifice is replicated on a figural level, but in an uncanny twist, the narrative allows the sacrificial father to oblite-rate himself: "I said to my mother . . . 'Why didn't you tell me about the sacrifice?' She said simply, 'I didn't remember.' She added, 'Some things you will yourself forget.' 'What form did my father's madness take?' 'He looked in the mirror one day and couldn't see himself. And he began to scream' " ("Prologue," p. 70).

"Prologue to an Autobiography" can do no more than record this cru-cial moment of bodily unseeing in the protective hieroglyphics of quotation marks: it cannot afford to linger on the relation between the racially public event of the sacrifice and the racially private moment of specular opacity, where the reality of one leads to the unreality of the other. The event lends a retroactive power to Naipaul's prior visions of racial invisibility, particularly to his hysterical fear that he could not "be seen" in India. The father must be erased from the narrative in a manner that anticipates Shiva Naipaul's era-sure from *The Enigma of Arrival:* both visibly signify the writer's fear of the racial gaze and its potential for obliteration. At the same time, however, the subject gains a powerful attraction, simply because it suggests another story that cannot as yet be written.

The Enigma of Arrival attempts to write out this story in a minor key. It refocuses the racial gaze onto the historical body, and constructs a comic postimperial parable out of the relationship, or lack thereof, between Naipaul the Trinidadian tenant and his English landlord, a hypochondriacal remnant of an almost obsolescent gentry. The grimness of such a postcolonial alle-gory as *A Bend in the River* is translated into a more relaxed and ostensibly humdrum idiom, although *The Enigma of Arrival* startlingly repeats the structural principle of the previous text by revising *Heart of Darkness* into a comic tale. Naipaul as narrator is both Marlow and the Harlequin; Kurtz is inverted into the powerless landlord; the wilderness is recast as England at the end of empire, whose entropic impulse Naipaul maps with a quiet but exquisite pleasure. The relation between colony and empire is cinematically represented in Naipaul's excessively detailed descriptions of the cottage he rents on the periphery of his landlord's estate, and of the manor itself, now in a state of disrepair and decay. Naipaul never actually meets his landlord, but much as Marlow is obsessed with reading Kurtz as a principle of understand-ing that makes empire explicable, Naipaul is obsessed with reading the landlord—particularly his decrepit body—as the legacy of empire: "After [a] pampered, protected childhood, a young manhood of artistic talent and promise and of social frivolity. . . . Then in early middle age, after the par-ties, after the second war, a disturbance of some sort, a morbid, lasting depression, almost an illness, resulting in withdrawal, hiding, a retreat to the manor, complicated after a while by physical disorders and—finally—age" (pp. 190–91). This reading is impelled by the ingrown imperialism that the landlord represents, which makes him a casualty of pathos rather than horror, of the petering out of power rather than the swell of power unchecked.

Each time the narrative focuses on the physical helplessness of the landlord as a synecdoche for imperial devolution, the narrator is somehow enabled to situate his own body as a racial presence in the text. This presence becomes increasingly strong in a directly oppositional relation to the landlord's disablement, and the postimperial narrator learns to acknowledge that his imperial counterpart is a secret sharer in his own progress toward bodily stability: "Twenty years before . . . residence in the grounds of the manor would have seemed suitable 'material.' But the imperial link would then have been burdensome. It would have tormented me as a man (or boy) to be a racial oddity in the valley. And I would have been able as a writer (at that time) to deal with the material only by suppressing certain aspects of myself—the very kind of suppression and concealment that narrative of a certain sort encouraged and which have led me . . . to miss much" (p. 191). Such a narrative of concealment is evidenced in books like *An Area of Darkness* and *A Bend in the River*, where the narrator's body is acutely important as a locus of racial invisibility, but at the same time, *The Enigma of Arrival* is not quite prepared to see how much it predicates its own narrative security on the dismemberment of its subject. The text is too committed to maintaining its tone of equanimity, its new arrival at generosity, to notice the exact economy of its drawing of strength from the other's weakness: "I felt an immense sympathy for my landlord, who, starting at the other end of the world, now wished to hide, like me. . . . Privilege lay between us. But I had an intimation that it worked against him. Whatever my spiritual state at the moment of arrival, I knew I would have to save myself and look for health; I knew I would have to act at some time. His privilege . . . could press him down into himself, into non-doing and nullity. So though we had started at opposite ends of empire and privilege, and in different cultures, it was easy for me, as his tenant now, to feel goodwill in my heart for him" (p. 192).

Naipaul's goodwill, however, is a somewhat dangerous thing. The decay both of the grounds and of the landlord's body serve as a necessary compost to *The Enigma of Arrival*, suggesting that its central enigma concerns how many points of departure the narrative has to cover in order to frame its idea of arrival. The narrator's sense of his own historicity gains in

power each time he recounts an episode of imperial evacuation: the ivy killing the trees, the grounds running to decay, the successive deaths of English
bodies that surround the writer. The text's irony saves it from evincing any
simplistic glee at this postimperial inversion, but not from representing the
gesture of inversion as a fundamentally comic act. Finally, its arrival at historical narrative is presented in terms of literary accomplishment: in two key
passages, Naipaul describes his landlord's forays into literature. The first is a
series of poems about Krishna and Shiva: "Krishna and Shiva! There, beside
that river (Constable and Shepard), in those grounds! There was nothing of
contemporary cult or fashion in my landlord's use of these divinities. His
Indian romance was in fact older, even antiquated, something he had inherited, like his house, something from the days of imperial glory, when—out
of material satiety and the expectation of the world's continuing to be ordered as it had been ordered for a whole century or more—power and glory
had begun to undo themselves from within" (p. 212). The imperial body, in
other words, is reduced to effete mimicry of cultural emblems that it continues to misread, thereby unwittingly emphasizing those emblems' physical dignity in their other context of an explosive hierarchy. And the landlord's second book is even more telling: "The story was simple. A young
woman gets tired of the English social round. . . . She decides to become a
missionary in Africa. . . . A ship; the ocean; the African coast; a forest
river. The young missionary is captured by Africans, natives. She has
fantasies of sexual assault by the African chief to whose compound she is
taken; fantasies as well of the harem and of black eunuchs. Instead, she is
cooked in a cannibal pot and eaten. . . . This was the joke knowledge of the
world. . . . And perhaps later knowledge had not gone beyond the joke: outside England and Europe, a fantasy Africa, a fantasy Peru or India or Malaya"
(pp. 281–82).

　　Whose revision of *Heart of Darkness* is better, Naipaul's or the landlord's? Or does the syncopation of racial authority and canonical authority
even need to be framed into an obvious question? To have a "joke knowledge"
of the world is of course a double-edged issue, for if Naipaul obtains a certain
quiet satisfaction about witnessing the imperial body place itself in a can-
nibalistic pot and stew in its own juices, he omits to take note of the fact that
his postcolonial critics are quite willing to let him enter the canonical pot, and
watch what happens to his body. But if Naipaul has arrived at a discourse of
historical simplicity, then perhaps it is time for a different generation of
postcolonial writers—one that does not need to share in his need to spell out
the connection between literary reality and racial invisibility—to arrive at a

recognition that his language too could function as an event of evocative decay. As the imperial enabled the postimperial, so the postcolonial body could indeed assume similar ironies of enablement, saying, "Alright, V. S. Naipaul, I have disliked you long enough"; "Let there be commerce between us."

8

Salman Rushdie: Embodiments of Blasphemy, Censorships of Shame

THE COMPRESSED AND OFTEN SELF-DISLIKING ALLEGORY OF SALMAN RUSHDIE'S *Shame* seeks to represent what was until recently a contraband segment of history in Pakistan—the 1978 execution of its former president, Zulfikar Ali Bhutto.[1] Given the topicality of this particular subject, Rushdie's narrative faces complicated and ambivalent problems of representation: on the one hand, it must write out of the uneasiness that besets postcolonial fiction, as it confronts the discursive difficulty of containing the referents of novelty and of history within a recognizable grammar. On the other, it must take on as its fictional provenance a series of events so sensational, so violent in its currency as gossip, that the text is impelled to construct elaborate defenses against the lure of melodrama by focusing obsessively on its own literariness and its status as a formal artifact. Its narrative self-consciousness suggests a deep embarrassment at the idea of political discourse, a nostalgic will to create apolitical pockets in the garments of such language. As a consequence, *Shame* turns to narcissism as a ploy of evasion, enacting rather than addressing the curious posture of what it means to be ashamed.

Since the book attempts to house idioms of the political and the newsworthy, and finally can only draw attention to its own language in a gesture of defeated surrogacy, *Shame*'s narrative peculiarities become paradigmatic of the casualties frequently accrued by contemporary postcolonial writing. These mutilations are most readily apprehended through a reading of the strangely shrugging course of Rushdie's narrative, which implies that because it cannot possibly do justice to its history, it can at least do violence to itself. Violence, the book hopes, is that which must be censored, both from the point of view of its ostensible historical location, an arena weary of being other, and from the point of its audience, which is—for a novel in English—largely the West. This violence serves as a reminder that the price a postcolonial writer pays for political discourse is linked in a most literal fashion to the economy of audience: the more such a text as *Shame* represses and censors its own ambivalence toward the location of its audience, the more likely it will be to seclude itself in a nervous advertisement of self-conscious ideological rectitude. To write from the pale of oppression becomes necessary solace for a writing that is made jumpy by its own relation to oppressiveness: hence the neurasthenic idiom of novels like *Shame*. They suggest a strategy which seeks relief from such ambivalence by perpetually positing the idea of a censor, located outside the parameters of the text's discourse. In *Shame*, the threat of censorship licenses the book's peculiar structure, its simultaneous denial and recuperation of divergent genres. For a reader, however, its internal censor, or the deletions around which Rushdie's narrative gathers an idea of coherence, provides a compelling opportunity to reconsider the question of why postcolonial narrative should be so amenable to shame.

The aura of shamefulness that Rushdie's text exudes is intimately linked to its representation of censorship on both cultural and canonical levels. As a scarcely veiled allegory of the symbolic violence of historical process, *Shame* is from its inception a text that knows it will be banished from the culture that it represents. It thus accrues a freedom from facticity, an ability to allegorize and fantasize a sequence of events for the benefit of an uninformed audience. This ostensible flexibility, however, functions as a derangement in a narrative that frequently founders in the excessive fictionality that it has won from the hands of historical discourse. As a consequence, Rushdie uses the expectation of censorship as a fetish, drawing on its danger in order that the text can indeed be written in serene anticipation of its own repression. Yet the glamor of censorship—the uneasiness of placing so much malignancy outside the parameters of narrative—begs a series of questions. What must the text omit, in order that it may represent omission? What is the peculiar complicity between a recognizably radical ideology and a startlingly conservative need to take refuge in formalism? *Shame* usefully raises such questions, for its desire to hide in allegory and magic realism is emblematic of the alliance between explosiveness and nostalgia, two imperatives in a postcolonial discourse that maps, with haste and peril, an aesthetic of novelty.

This aesthetic is unavoidably linked to shame, in that its articulation relies on a Western context, the only arena in which such a syncopated category as "third-world history" can have any currency. A writer like V. S. Naipaul powerfully internalizes this shame until it becomes the exquisite idiom in which he can elaborate on Zaire's novelty in *A Bend in the River*, or his own newness in *The Enigma of Arrival*. A writer like Salman Rushdie, however, attempts to construct a different relation to shamefulness, by addressing the issue of how the category of third-world history is continually jostled by its ready availability as "the news." Rushdie's uneasiness suggests that postcolonial narratives are forced to engage in a dismayed revaluation of their status as fiction, or the conjunction between narrative and newsprint that creates a context in which the news behaves like history, and does not happen in order that it may disappear. While novels such as *Shame* may seek to undo the imperial scheme of journalism, an attentive reader must further address the narrative's unstated collusion with a journalistic impulse, which obliterates its sense of audience into the banality of a force-fed public that cannot acknowledge the cultural and ethnic proscriptions underlying a reading of "the news." In a 1987 interview, Rushdie described the ironies of audience by suggesting that his works are read as fantasy in the West and as totally realistic narratives in India and Pakistan.[2] The implication that his subcontinental readership is more literal than its Western counterpart evades a recognition of the fact that such a schizophrenic anticipation of audience is already built into the text. Its reinvention of history is thus shamefully fraught with the fear that finally, postcolonial narrative can only replicate the will to power that impelled colonial historical texts. In its attempt to re-imagine Pakistani history, *Shame* seems guiltily aware that its lineage leads back in the direction of such influential texts as James Mill's *The History of British India*, the first philosophical history of India written by an author who had never visited the subcontinent.

Mill's *History*, a textbook for British administrators in the nineteenth century, is a dangerous precursor for twentieth-century narrative. Its preface ponderously delineates an awareness of the textuality of historical writing: "Whatever is worth seeing or hearing in India," Mill claims, "can be expressed in writing. As soon as everything of importance is expressed in writing, a man who is duly qualified may obtain more knowledge of India in one year, in his closet in England, than he could obtain during the course of the longest life, by the use of his eyes and ears in India." (p. 13) An equivalent awareness of the textuality of third-world history troubles the narrative of *Shame*, even though the novel tries obsessively to evade Mill's ideological logic: "He who, without having been a percipient witness in India, undertakes, in Europe, to digest the materials of Indian history, is placed, with regard to the numerous individuals who have been in India . . . in a situation very analogous to that of the Judge, in regard to the witnesses who give their evidence before him" (*History*, pp. 15–16). Mill's lack of irony allows him to occupy the position of narrator as judge without much ado; Salman Rushdie's narrator is urgently invested in repressing an acknowledgment of this potential posture from the course of the narrative. As a result, the novel seems impelled to keep constructing and dismantling the paraphernalia of legality, in order that the narrator does not need to function as the final court of appeal. In its invocation of censorship, however, *Shame* obliquely acknowledges a complicity in the structure of a cultural judgment that takes the form of a muffled or a silenced voice.

The judgment that it must continually evade makes *Shame* lend a crazy narrative logic to a most sensational event. It tells lurid family tales with the zeal of a distant relative, who seeks an explanation for everything in other people's secrets. Here, of course, the psychic event of the 1947 partition of India functions as an intimacy that no reader of Rushdie can afford to ignore: born in Bombay to a Muslim family, part of which later migrated to Pakistan, Rushdie cannot but be compelled to conceive of the latter country as a trope for betrayal: its betrayal, to him, of the idea of a home, and his betrayal of it, in his need to have none of it. In the story of Bhutto's hanging, therefore, he collapses so many tales that the novel seems distraught at its own inability to draw the line between the idioms that feel most betrayed. Is the narrative most at home with betrayal when it feels intimate with what it represents, or when it feels most alien, visiting a formerly familiar culture almost as a guest? Rushdie packs these potentially embittering questions into a sporadic retelling of Bhutto's political career, which functions as a figure for the elitist struggle that Rushdie sees as the theater of history in Pakistan. In a gesture of defensive withdrawal, Rushdie rehearses the Bhutto story with civilized outrage, which licenses his narrator to maintain a highly scandalized relation to his subject without stopping to consider the obvious costs of his position: the narrative's degree of implication in the structure of scandal. Despite its waves of self-repeating irony, *Shame* is unable to address the issue of complicity, or the narrative's responsibility to the story it must tell. The novel thus enacts a difficulty endemic to postcolonial fiction in English, in that it is finally less shocked by its subject than by its own inability to represent how political information gets transmitted once it has been let loose, as it were, from the decorum of oppression.

This decorum has been the subject of considerable critical attention, generating a discourse that seeks to redress a prior tendency, as Abdul R. JanMohamed phrases it, to "restrict itself by severely bracketing the political context of culture and history. This typical facet of humanistic closure requires the critic systematically to avoid analysis of the domination, manipulation, exploitation, and disenfranchisement that are inevitably involved in the construction of any cultural artifact or relationship."[3] *Shame*, however, demands a more involuted reading, in that the narrative does not merely record what once has been done: instead, it is horrified at its own powers of

replication, its knowledge that it also can oppress. This horror is best addressed by breaking down the great divide that critical discourse sets up
between colonial and postcolonial fiction, in order to determine how the
ghosts of writers like Kipling and Forster still haunt the contemporary Indian
novel in English. Thus Rushdie's complications of tone would become somewhat more accessible if his books were contextualized not merely by a
reading of postcolonial history, but furthermore by some apprehension of
the great embarrassment of what it must mean to be fathered by *Kim*. For
Kipling's powerful transcultural fetish plays a secret role in the energies of
Rushdie's abundant idiom, suggesting an ironic relation that deserves more
careful reading. In place of the remorseless postcolonial paradigm of Prospero and Caliban, a new equation suggests itself: the complicity of comedy
and shame that the postcolonial narrative must experience, when it acknowledges that it indeed descends from the jaunty adolescence of *Kim*.

To readers familiar with the rambunctiousness of Rushdie's first novel
about the Indian subcontinent, *Midnight's Children,* a book that unfolds with
the disarming quality of a joke that knows it is a little too long, the first peculiarity of *Shame* is how ill at ease the narrative seems with its own sense of
fabrication. The hesitancies of its discourse imply that to say what has been
censored is too simple an impossibility, too easy a response to the highly spe-
cialized nature of censorship and to the complicity engendered by that
psychically dexterous system of control. Even though Rushdie ostensibly
disavows the dynamic, self-censoring organization of the story he chooses to
tell, such disavowals merely force his narrative to become guiltily attentive
to that very mobility. As a consequence, the novel opens to defend its claims
to authority, anticipating potential accusations of intrusiveness:

> *Outsider! Trespasser! You have no right to this subject! . . . I
> know: nobody ever arrested me. Nor are they ever likely to.
> Poacher! Pirate! We reject your authority. We know you, with
> your foreign language wrapped around you like a flag: speaking
> about us in your forked tongue, what can you tell but lies?* I reply
> with more questions: is history to be considered the property of
> the participants solely? In what courts are such claims staked,
> what boundary commissions map out the territories? (*Shame,*
> p. 28).

The bravado of this tone only barely obscures the narrator's anxious need to
assert legitimacy by formalizing his apprehension of historical process into
the legality of property rights, invoking the figure of the court in order that

the text may exist outside it, secure in the knowledge of its own illegality. Such gestures of self-exile dictate the structure of the narrative, but each successive pose implicates rather than liberates the tale from the structure of censorship. For an effective system of censorship—of the kind that Rushdie wishes to dismantle in order to write his book—is not interested in the proprietary but in the extraordinary talent with which information can forget to be informative. Rushdie reluctantly collaborates in this forgetfulness, by assuming that the Bhutto story can be easily fictionalized and contained in an idiom other than the seductive sufficiency of fact.

But fact, and the novel's unhappy relation to the molecular profusion of fact that constitutes political discourse, is *Shame's* undoing. A text of such nervous self-consciousness is of course aware of this undoing, and attempts to collaborate in its own unraveling in a series of complicated disclaimers. "The country in this story is not Pakistan," Rushdie writes, "or not quite. There are two countries, real and fictional, occupying the same space, or almost the same space. My story, my fictional country exist, like myself, at a slight angle to reality. I have found this off-centering to be necessary; but its value is, of course, open to debate. My view is that I am not writing only about Pakistan" (*Shame*, p. 29). This evasiveness, however, is more troubling than convincing: in terms of the text's audience, the facticity of this relatively unknown country seems to pose an incomprehensible threat to the narrative, whose arch veerings toward fantasy place unnecessary strain on a reader's credulity. Its somewhat unfinished generic shifts suggest that Rushdie is attempting to accommodate two monolithic audiences at the same time, anxiously misreading their skills as readers. The genre of fantasy gestures toward a Western audience, long since sophisticated at reading the language of the surreal. At the same time, however, Rushdie cannot help but be seduced by the facticity of the sorry tale he chooses to tell, by its gossip value to a more informed audience. As a result, his narrative is forced to gather power from a commitment to the incredulous, or to a language that knows how to retrieve immediately what it has to give. In one such moment of retrieval, the narrator exclaims: "But suppose this were a realistic novel! Just think what else I might have to put in." He then proceeds to construct a comically breathless catalog of all the facts he would have to represent, concluding, "By now, if I had been writing a book of that nature, it would have done me no good to protest that I was writing universally, not only about Pakistan. The book would have been banned, dumped in the rubbish bin, burned. All that effort for nothing! Realism can break a writer's heart. Fortunately, however, I am only telling a sort of modern fairy-tale, so that's all right; nobody need get upset, or take anything I say too seriously. No drastic action need be taken, either. What a relief!" (*Shame*, pp. 69–70).

This self-punishing invocation of censorship indicates how deeply the novel needs to hide behind the idea of formalism that in fact is rendered obsolete by its own narrative structure. Its reference to a "realistic novel," a term that can hardly be taken seriously, suggests a nostalgia for some easy anachronism—a literal reading of realism—beneath which lurks a more difficult anachronism, the ethical responsibility inevitably engendered in the relation between narrative and that which it seeks to contain. It would be far too embarrassing, of course, to talk openly about the ethical, and the compelling erotic discourse to which it inevitably leads. The rawness of postcolonial narrative, however, of which *Shame* is exemplary, presents itself as a peculiarly resonant site for the reading of the erotic structure of morality. In *Shame*, this conjunction is represented by the central female character, an allegorical figure who embodies both what Rushdie sees as the feminine discourse of shame and also its capacity to exceed the limits of censorship in order to articulate the indictment of a culture. With the text's characteristic swerve toward violence, this figure is in addition an imbecile, signifying an ethical inchoateness that is uncannily similar in tone to the sexual terror that marks the novel's disturbingly apocalyptic conclusion. "Realism," therefore, functions in the narrative as a trope for the punishability of discourse, of its curious ability to exude a fear of bodily harm.

In what context, however, can *Shame* describe itself as a "modern fairy-tale"? Its reference is to the obsessive fastidiousness with which the narrative unfolds into two disjunctive modes, veering between documentary fragments on the one hand and an allegorized, third-person tale on the other. The documentary interruptions call attention to the writer as writer, to his ironic sense of the helplessness of storytelling: "And now I must stop saying what I am not writing about, because there's nothing so special about that; every story one chooses to tell is a kind of censorship, it prevents the telling of other tales. . . . I must get back to my fairy-story, because things have been happening while I've been talking too much" (*Shame*, p. 71). In the mode of magic realism, this fairy story relates how its protagonist, Omar Khayyaam,—named after the translated poet—was conceived by three mothers at a moment in time very close to the 1947 partition of India in a town very similar to the border city of Quetta in Pakistan. This overloaded detail warns the reader away from the obviousness of decoding, of falling into the simplicity of assuming that Omar Khayyaam, born out of a trinity of mothers, signifies that fresh arrival of the Pakistani citizen, born neither of Britain, nor of India, nor of Pakistan, which is still too new to be true. Thus allegory itself is subjected to an internal censor, constructing a symbolic structure that is somehow emptied of symbol. It lends the text a certain journalistic evanescence, a charm based on its capacity to disappear. *Shame's* strategic collapsibility can be read as an enactment of what Homi K. Bhabha describes as the workings of the "colonial subject": "In order to understand the productivity of colonial power," writes Bhabha, "it is crucial to construct its regime of 'truth,' not to subject its representations to a normalizing judgment. Only then does it become possible to understand the *productive* ambivalence of the object of colonial discourse—that 'otherness' which is at once an object of desire and derision, an articulation of difference contained within the fantasy of origin and identity."[4] The divisiveness of Rushdie's narrative, however, suggests that perhaps a complete repression of "normalizing judgment" is not possible: when postcolonial discourse confines itself to the vocabulary of otherness, the idea of judgment resurfaces in the figure of the censor.

While the text's structural dependence of censored origins is most frequently discussed in the context of magic realism, Rushdie himself objects to the convenience with which this critical term is appended to postcolonial literature.[5] In attempting to locate a more allusive context, it again becomes helpful to revise the traditional disjunction between British colonial fiction and Indian postcolonial fiction, for the earlier narratives are equally obsessed with magic realism, except that in them, of course, it takes on the structure of romance. From Kipling's marvelous questing boy to Forster's uncanny emptying of absence into disappointment, India has been perpetually figured as an arena for romance. Thus the 1923 Sencourt text, *India in English Literature*, bears repetition: "Literature shuns the obvious: but she has found in India something that provokes those elusive qualities of the mind which give writing its distinction, which by its choice of sounds and suggestions makes life more mysterious, more poignant, vaster and more real . . . [its] essence has given satisfaction to an instinctive appetite of mind and heart which is more than a mere craving for the exotic. And without that hunger for the rich and strange, it is impossible for the west to assimilate India. . . . Its very name echoes the name, as it suggests the power, of earth's Eternal City. We know it as Romance." If the burden of postcolonial writing has been to invert the terms of such Orientalist mythmaking, then one of its most obvious strategies has been to write in a context of a romance gone wrong, a context that does not lead to the evocative absence of romance, but to the horror of

Conrad's imperial parable. *Shame* emerges out of a long tradition of violent refigurings of romance, compelled to make its generic disembodiment literally fleshly as possible. Its ostensible protagonist is named after a poet who turns out to be a fat, voyeuristic doctor; its idealized woman becomes an imbecile who begins her career by tearing heads off chickens and ends it by dismembering human bodies, including the doctor's; its evocation of martyrdom consists of the sensational rise to power and eventual execution of a character called Iskander Harappa, playboy of the Pakistani political world.

Rushdie reads Zulfikar Ali Bhutto's career as a trope for Pakistani history, which is represented as an elitist and familial power struggle between the flamboyant and Westernized Harappa and the militaristic and Islamic Gen. Raza Hyder. While it is certainly possible to so schematize the multifariousness of political life in Pakistan, *Shame*'s self-punishing romance seems at this point its most journalistic; it seeks to rob its plot of any dignity, in a twist that finally makes its narrator appear to be a trivializing reader of historical process. The narrative draws on a post-Khomeini idiom that has done irreparable damage to the Western apprehension of the possible modernity of Muslim national movements, making the disastrous Irani revolution serve as a metaphor for all politicization in the Islamic world. Rushdie's reading extends this idiom by emblematizing the involutions of one peculiar version of postcolonial history into two simple drives: on the one hand, he sets up the urge to Westernization; on the other a will to fundamentalism. Such a mapping, however, is nervously conscious of its own omissions, of its unwillingness to address the most intriguing plot of all, which are the flabbergasting incongruities that surround the inception of Pakistan. Here is where the text exudes its strongest sense of shame, necessitating both its generic veerings and its reliance on the structure of contiguous plots, so that stories keep unfolding in succession to displace one another. Its cumulative effect is less comic than unnerving, in that Rushdie seems impelled to approach the subject of public spectacle and then hastily to retreat into acts of evasive embellishment. The Bhutto story is emptied of all resonance to become instead a squalid and predictable miniseries, for *Shame* is perhaps best described as a televised narrative, fully equipped with commercial interruption and a will to remote control. Such a structure cannot afford to represent historical fact in any other terms than of a readily available nightmare, drawing on an established idiom that David Rubin has described as a major mode of Indian romance, that of India as destroyer.[6]

This zeal for doom has no desire to notice any of the nuances in the

Bhutto plot, nor to recognize how such a story colorfully represents a revision of the greatest peculiarity of mythmaking in Pakistani history: the myth of its founding father, Muhammad Ali Jinnah. As Stanley Wolpert's biography demonstrates,[7] the sheer unlikeliness of Jinnah's rise to power in the Muslim League suggests such an overdetermined relation between national movements and religion that Rushdie cannot afford to iron its complexities out into a simply oppositional structure. His narrative, however, is unprepared to work out the curious filiation with the Jinnah myth, or even to ask the obvious question: why did two such powerfully secular figures exert considerable influence over their Muslim constituencies? In the context of political mythmaking in Pakistan, Bhutto's need to serve as a truant to that country's originary myth—to play mischievous son to Jinnah's stern father—is a compelling narrative that no novel about the latter ruler can afford to ignore. But *Shame* censors the curiosities of its own story, relying instead on the more lurid language of feud and vendetta. Rushdie is somewhat defensive about the idiom, and in an interview given shortly after the book was published, claims that "*Shame* is comic in its mode, because it seemed to me that what you had in Pakistan was a tragedy enacted by people who were not tragic figures. The Zia-Bhutto relationship is tragic—the protege becomes the executioner—but the figures haven't the stature you can associate with high tragedy. These are people who don't deserve tragedy."[8] As with the novel's play on realism, this startlingly literal dependence on formal categories of high and low tragedy requires some decoding. Is it really the business of narrative to confer tragedy on historical event, or is Rushdie obliquely referring to his own desire to gothicize a structure already hopelessly lost in its own ornamentation? What filial anxieties is the writer himself manifesting, when he seeks to deny all dignity to a history that is indirectly his?

"I tell myself that this will be a novel of leavetaking," writes Rushdie in *Shame*. "My last words on the East from which, many years ago, I began to come loose. I do not always believe myself when I say this. It is a part of the world to which, whether I like it or not, I am still joined, if only by elastic bands" (*Shame*, p. 28). Such nostalgic evocations of exile recast the postcolonial writer as Peter Pan, who, after he has learned to fly, returns home to find that his parents have put bars on his bedroom window and a new baby in his bed. This reference is not intended to be facetious: J. M. Barrie's powerful allegory of perpetual adolescence does indeed lend itself to the scene of postcolonial writing. After self-exile, the writer must come to terms with the literalizing urge to return, simply in order to examine a prior history as a prison house, but a prison from which the writer is excluded. At best, he or she can adopt the posture of the voyeur, entranced by the babies in every bed. The connection between the idioms of exile and adolescence has long haunted the literature of empire—the classic text in this mode is *Lord Jim*—but perhaps it is time for critical discourse to examine more rigorously the idiom of exile, in order to determine how inevitably its language must accrue a vertiginous absence of responsibility. *Shame* attempts to write itself out of the absence in a complicated swerve that seeks to project the burden of adolescence onto the story it must tell. The novel thus borrows the Bhutto story in order to empty it of its extenuation, which rests in the wrenching timeliness of its sequence, of how it walked into the world like high fashion, upright with obsolescence. After twelve years of military rule, Pakistan was hungry for a flamboyant, civil ruler; Bhutto was both fetish and scapegoat for this desire.

Shame, however, is not prepared to contextualize this tale, representing it instead as though it were folklore, a constant in the atmospherics over the Pakistani landscape. Here, the narrative demonstrates a will to inscribe the writer's own idiom of contextless exile on its subject matter, so that the need to take on a historical plot becomes curiously synonymous with an impulse to dehistoricize. This impulse surfaces in *Shame*'s reliance on the discourse of gossip as its ordering principle: the Bhutto story is structured in a series of disjunctive and scandalous vignettes, making the reader complicit in the narrative's uneasy relation to the discourse of gossip. The reader of *Shame* is deeply embedded in such ambivalence, for the text's compacted reading of history draws obsessively on the idea of hearsay without any reference to the comforting recirculation of the oral: instead, we are forced to read again and again a discourse that can take shape only behind its subject's back. Part of the disturbance of *Shame* is that it makes its reader feel as guilty as its narrator, as complicit in the redundancy of stabbing a historical body already hanged. Acting against its grain, the novel thus cannot help but collaborate in the structure of the banality of censorship, or the specific rewriting of information which separated Bhutto's name from the pragmatics of political power and hastily mythologized it into a synonym for treachery.

The Iskander Harappa of Rushdie's narrative is indeed treacherous, a figure disquietingly seamless in its available glamor. He is rarely allowed to leave the bedroom or the dinner table, where he is invariably accompanied by lovers, insults, and a daughter known as Virgin Iron-Pants. His story, in fact, is made explicable through the discourse of insult, and Rushdie seems precariously concerned with examining how long that language can sustain itself without accruing retaliation. "Ambassadors," the narrator muses:

> He got through nine of them in his six years. Also five English and three Russian heads of mission. . . . He made them wait weeks for audiences, interrupted their sentences, denied them hunting licences. . . . With the British Ambassador he would pretend to be a hick just down from the villages, and speak only in an obscure regional dialect; in the case of the United States, however, he took the opposite tack and addressed their legate in incomprehensibly florid French. Embassies would be constantly subjected to power-cuts. Isky would open their diplomatic bags and personally add outrageous remarks to the Ambassador's reports, so that one Russian was summoned home to explain certain unusual theories of his about the parentage of various leading Politburo chiefs; he never returned . . . [later], when Virgin Iron-Pants visited her father in his hell-hole of a jail, Iskander, bruised, wasted, sick with dysentery, forced a grin to his lips. "This tenth [ambassador] sounds like a real shit," he said painfully. "I wish I could have made it into double figures." (*Shame*, pp. 185–86).

Bhutto is thus translated into a sequence of dizzying animation that appears astounded by its own ability to bully its audience into comedy, even though the audience—familiar with the structure of cautionary tales—is forced into waiting for the moment when the bully will get it, in the end.

He does. Rushdie's anxiety to tell untold stories leads him to overcomplete and overexplain, so that by the end of the novel, Bhutto's hanging has been rehearsed several times over, his corpse dangling in painful fashion over the ostensible comedy of the narrative. In one such moment of repetition, Iskander Harappa's widow is allowed to look briefly at the body of her husband: "'When you hang a man,'" she murmurs, "'the eyes bulge. The face turns blue. The tongue sticks out. . . . But one thing remains. On a hanged man's neck the rope leaves its mark. Iskander's neck was clean.' 'This is disgusting,' [Virgin Iron-Pants] said, 'I'll be sick.' 'Don't you understand?' [her mother] shouted at her. 'If the rope did not mark him, it must be because he was already dead. Are you too stupid to see? *They hanged a corpse*'" (*Shame*, pp. 187–88). Even execution, *Shame* suggests, is subject to some grotesquely farcical repetition, history behaving then as some enactment of the literal nature of redundancy. This obsessiveness does not quite know what to do with its own corpses, for the narrative's memory works to unbury

the dead: it constructs painstaking scenes of recognition in which death, or
the narrator's absence from his own history, is refigured as a catalog of the
ways in which a human body can die.

In Rushdie's scheme, such violence is necessitated by the narrative's
will to represent the battle between two opposing codes: the masculine code
of honor, as it is manifested in the political world; and the feminine code of
shame, which fights against its confinement within the domestic world.
Shame makes continual references to the split between two languages that
these codes generate: "I had thought, before I began, that what I had on my
hands was an almost excessively masculine tale, a saga of sexual rivalry, am-
bition, power, patronage, betrayal, death, revenge. But the women seem to
have taken over; they marched in from the peripheries of the story to demand the inclusion of their own tragedies, histories and comedies, obliging
me to couch my narrative in all manner of sinuous complexities, to see my
'male' plot refracted, so to speak, through the prisms of its reverse and
'female' side" (*Shame*, p. 173). If female shame becomes the displaced center
of the narrative, then it becomes incumbent on the reader to pay close attention to how Rushdie embeds his rereading of history into a revision of the
psychic structure of shame. The narrator urgently insists that this structure
signifies a cultural imperative which is inherently untranslatable: "This
word: shame. No, I must write it in its original form, not in this peculiar
language tainted by wrong concepts and the accumulated detritus of its
owners' unrepented past, this Angrezi [English] in which I am forced to
write, and so forever alter what is written . . . *Sharam*, that's the word. For
which this paltry 'shame' is a wholly inadequate translation" (*Shame*,
pp. 38–39). The curiosity of shame thus becomes a figure for censorship, an
area of repressed significance that represents the untranslatability of an Eastern culture into a Western context. Even though the involutions of this
courtesy culture have often been the object of historical study—David
Lelyveld eloquently maps out the features of "sharif culture" in nineteenth-
century India[9]—Rushdie needs the mystification of untranslatability in
order that his reading of shame can accommodate not merely secrecy, but the
loaded secrecy of the female body in an Eastern culture.

Here, *Shame* recuperates its structure of a censored and maimed romance: if nineteenth-century romance obsessively imaged the East as a
seductive but violated woman, Rushdie turns this trope inside out, until the
burden of internalized violation transforms the woman into the violator,
the destructive power that wreaks vengeance on the text. The novel self-
consciously tries to place itself beyond the discourse of the rape of imperi-

alism, or the language that allowed Nehru to describe the relationship between England and India as one of fundamental sexual aggression: "They seized her body and possessed her, but it was a possession of violence. . . . They never looked into her eyes, for theirs were averted and hers downcast through shame and humiliation." Rushdie picks up on the downcast gaze of shame and attempts to reconceive it as an act of empowerment, a gathering of strength that finally breaks down the male code of history. To this end, he invents the figure of Sufiya Zenobia, imbecile daughter of Gen. Raza Hyder, who embodies both shame and its potential violence: beauty and the beast. Sufiya grows progressively more deranged through the course of the novel, accumulating all the violence of Pakistani history until she literally becomes that violence. In one of the plot's more unlikely twists, she is married off to Omar Khayyaam, the shadowy protagonist who serves fundamentally as a witness to the Bhutto story, and who is dismembered by his wife in the text's disturbing conclusion. Like an empowered Bertha Mason, Sufiya breaks out of captivity to ravage the Pakistani landscape until she finally confronts her husband: "He stood by the bed and waited for her like a bridegroom on his wedding night, as she climbed towards him . . . he in the darkness, erect, watching the approaching glow, and then she was there, on all fours, naked, coated in mud and blood and shit, with twigs sticking to her back, and beetles in her hair. She saw him and shuddered; then she rose up on her hind legs with her forepaws outstretched and he had just enough time to say, 'Well, wife, so here you are at last,' before her eyes forced him to look" (*Shame*, p. 286).

In the cinematic detail of this scene, the eye of the narrative is completely handed over to the male, so that the reader too is forced to read the text's vision of apocalypse from the point of view of a male terror as it watches the bestiality of the approaching female. In stripping shame, in attempting to represent it in an aspect most raw, the text teeters on the brink of an acknowledgment of its final failure to find an idiom for shame. If shame can be described as a gesture of psychic retreat that calls attention to the body at the moment when the body least wishes to be itself, then Rushdie's vision of the debased female shape replicates that which is inarticulate about the structure of shame. It breaks down the distinctions that Rushdie attempted to maintain between male and female narratives by accentuating instead the novel's hidden fascination with violence, so that finally it too is complicit in the terrible aggressions that thus far it has sought to make solely the provenance of Pakistani history. Rushdie's complicity is perhaps inevitable, given the painfully murderous narrative he has been forced to construct: it suggests that any polarity between violence and civilization is bound to soil itself in the text's enactment. Rushdie invests a great deal of psychic energy in maintaining his narrator's civilization in opposition to the violence of his subject, but ultimately such strategies of distancing expose the curious bonds between author and subject. *Shame* goes to elaborate lengths to repress its awareness that it is indeed an exercise of authority, that its narrator does not have the luxury of standing outside the parameters of the story it unfolds.

Here, of course, is the locus of censorship in *Shame*. It dictates the evasive narcissism of the narrative, a narcissism that needs the figure of authorial intrusion to serve as a red herring. This ploy documents the writer as writer in order to erase his sense of connectedness to the plot itself: the writer is invoked to enable him to disappear. Such tricks of evasion, however, allow Rushdie to construct more complicated tropes of connectedness, as though he were revising Conrad's parable in order to collapse Marlow and Kurtz into the same figure. Rushdie draws on the intricacy of this configuration and so rarifies his sense of audience that he can actually invent the outrageous figure of a guiltless narrator. This narrator merely visits the history of Pakistan; he can firmly refuse to be part of that peculiar fabric of inadequacy and betrayal; he is far more at home in India, a place more in keeping with the proliferation of plot. On a submerged level, however, he is a secret sharer of the horror of this history, who is inscribed in the plot through a most peculiar surrogate, the triple-mothered, fatherless Omar Khayyaam.

After having named his protagonist Omar Khayyaam, Rushdie muses: "Omar Khayyaam's position as a poet is curious. He was never very popular in his native Persia; and he exists in the West in a translation that is really a complete reworking of his verses, in many cases very different from the spirit (to say nothing of the content) of the original. I, too, am a translated man. I have been *borne across*. It is generally believed that something is always lost in translation; I cling to the notion—and use, in evidence, the success of Fitzgerald-Khayyaam—that something can also be gained" (*Shame*, p. 29). Ungainly and unlikable, Omar Khayyaam serves very little function in the plot of *Shame*, other than to represent the narrator's more self-punishing impulses, his sense of being an inept body in a discourse of history. He covers up the narrator's sense of shame by being an embodiment of shamelessness, a "peripheral hero" who can do nothing to alter the course of history but whose body becomes its sacrificial victim in the end. In Omar Khayyaam's dismemberment at the hands of shame, Rushdie compacts explosively troubled reaction to the erotics of narrative responsibility; in a hidden gesture of reparation, he substitutes the body of the writer for the body of history, allowing the death of Omar Khayyaam to cover up for the death of Zulfikar Ali Bhutto. That such substitution cannot work constitutes the poignancy of the narrative, which disintegrates into the immensity of its own effort. It has envisaged history as the failed phallic emblem of a hanged corpse: its terror at its own representation forces the narrative to turn its violence on itself. "And then the explosion comes . . . rolling outwards to the horizon like a sea, and last of all the cloud, which rises and spreads and hangs over the noth- ingness of the scene, until I can no longer see what is no longer there; the silent cloud, in the shape of a giant, grey and headless man, a figure of dreams, a phantom with one arm lifted in a gesture of farewell" (*Shame*, p. 286). A text that calls itself a fiction of leave-taking is entitled to thus end with a gesture of farewell, except that this concluding figure blurs the bound- aries between what is leaving and what is being left. Like Pentheus, postcolonial narrative excises in order to be excised, entranced by the dan- gerous luxury of being carried home in its mother's arms.

THE MURDEROUS INTENSITY THAT IS STILL ATTENDANT ON THE PUBLICATION OF *The Satanic Verses* retards the closely cultural reading that such a text de- mands, distracting its reader into a nervous literalism constrained to inquire, "What will happen to the body that wrote this book? What price will con- tinue to be exacted by its discourse?" For—in the context of academic truism—discourse does nothing, we tacitly agree, but supply the academy with a convenient economy of self-perpetuation. As collaborators in such a system of intellectual limitation, we assert discursive significance even as we remain secretly aligned to alternative models of empowerment, which point to the shattering inefficacy of our own utterance. How then are we to read a cultural crisis that sets forth an undeniable chronology, in which the power of discourse is followed by the threat of death? What complicities between writing, reading, and a concomitant self-censorship are embodied in the ter- rifying efficacy with which Salman Rushdie is held responsible for his commitment to the right to blaspheme? In order to formulate even the most provisional response, the Anglo-American academy must now come to terms with the radical inseparability of the political, legal, and religious questions that surround both the writing and the reception of *The Satanic Verses*. In recent years, this academy has expended much intellectual energy into a the- oretical apprehension of differing configurations of alterity, but the futility of such attention to concept will rarely be more sharply demonstrated than in its current inability to read beyond an immediate fear of cultural ignorance.

In merely translating whatever is vexing about the Rushdie affair into pieties concerning aesthetic freedom of expression, we reveal ourselves to be at the limit of our own ideas of otherness: furthermore, it such pieties are available to us, we must then confront the disturbing logic that suggests—even within our own discourse—that it is indeed possible to be impious.

The alterity at hand, of course, is that difficult word "Islam." Among the many dismaying revelations that have been generated by the Rushdie debate, perhaps one peculiarly burdensome to a postcolonial reader is the alacrity with which certain Western intellectuals transmute the grave dangers that surround *The Satanic Verses* into a *Lord Jim* paradigm, translating cultural complexities into patterns of literary hegemony. That Rushdie is "one of us" implicitly informs even the most well-meaning of the defenses published thus far, which suggest that even though the writer may have been cast beyond the pale of retrievable life, his recuperation inheres in the fact that he will always be read as a secular voice speaking against the impingement of a monolithic fundamentalism. The internal dangers of the text are thus externalized, or rendered unto Iran, a gesture that leaves unread the strong possibility that Rushdie's novel epitomizes the urgent cultural fidelity represented by specific acts of religious betrayal. Here, the imbrication of fidelity and betrayal is surely too demanding of interpretation to be so easily subsumed into the terms of "us" and "them." If Rushdie has indeed been rescued from his own cultural context by the codes of *Lord Jim,* then the archaic paradox that we must now read has less to do with journalistic oppositions between fundamentalism and secularism than it has with the resonances of Stein's verdict on that literary figure of self-victimization: "'He is romantic—romantic,' he repeated. 'And that is very bad—very bad. . . . Very good, too,' he added." In order to comprehend the romance of *The Satanic Verses* in all its postmodern detail, the idea of Islamic secularism must be allowed to complicate the text's ideological self-positioning, which in turn suggests that the desacralizing of religion can simultaneously constitute a resacralizing of history.

How long Rushdie will remain newsworthy is disquietingly uncertain, placing on the academy an even greater responsibility to read the text and the dilemmas its represents in terms that are as culturally specific as possible. Here, the crucial context of Islamic secularism requires close attention, particularly in the light of the powerful questioning dialogues generated by subcontinental Muslim literatures. When, in the furor that surrounded *The Satanic Verses,* legal and religious questions achieve a simultaneity of a peculiar Muslim character, they underscore a fact too frequently ignored in the hysteria of current debate: Rushdie has written a deeply Islamic book. Rather than confine a reading of the text to the somewhat unhelpful oppositions between fundamentalism and secularism, therefore, I propose to move beyond the obvious good and evil implicit in such easy binarism to suggest instead that *The Satanic Verses* is, from a cultural point of view, a work of meticulous religious attentiveness. The idiom at hand is of course legitimated by the aesthetics of a postmodern and postcolonial mobility, but the imperative of its narrative simultaneously allows for a devotional return to the structure of anachronism, enabling Rushdie to extend—with urgency and fidelity—his engagement with both cultural self-definition and Islamic historiography.

While the multifarious abundance that characterizes *The Satanic Verses* can by no means be exclusively confined to a single literary model, either subcontinental or postmodern, its Western readers will doubtless be struck by Rushdie's ability to stand canonicity on its head, and similarly skew narrative's relation to the chronology of history. A text that begins as Joyce ends as Dickens, melding linguistic and cultural mayhem with the problematic excesses of sentimental resolution. Much as its narratological referents imply a historical regression, so too its engagement in the cultural reality of religion assumes a similarly quaint sweetness, positing denial in order that a new strategy of acceptance may then ensue. As a consequence, for readers both familiar and unfamiliar with Islamic culture, one of the most seductive imperatives that *The Satanic Verses* exudes is an acute consciousness of its status as blasphemy. Even before the fundamentalists descend to burn the published text, the book itself inflames, unfolding as an act of archaic devotion to the cultural system that it must both desecrate and renew. The desire to desecrate must here be disaligned from a more simplistic perspective that ponders over whether or not Rushdie has been "offensive to Islam"; instead, it perversely demands to be read as a gesture of wrenching loyalty, suggesting that blasphemy can be articulated only within the compass of belief. In the context of such ambivalence, Rushdie performs an act of curious faith: his text chooses disloyalty in order to dramatize its continuing obsession with the metaphors Islam makes available to a postcolonial sensibility.

On such a score, *The Satanic Verses* is more outrageous to itself than offensive to the most conservative Muslim. The book well knows that faith is obsolete to its discourse, but it must further struggle to comprehend why the betrayal of faith should be so necessary to an unbelieving, postmodern narrative. Such self-questioning makes Rushdie's work far more entangled than is implied by a simple gesture of self-banishment and mockery, illustrating instead its centrality to the contemporary unfolding of postcolonial self-fashioning. Blasphemy thus assumes the intimacy of a novel mode of historical introspection; it translates into a language of cultural questioning that allows the narrative to throw up a pair of Muslim hands at the incongruities that impel its discourse, and to manifest the similitudes between the idioms of betrayal and loyalty that history has imposed upon a postcolonial world. In the second chapter of *The Satanic Verses*, "Mahound," Rushdie's prophet muses on the nature of his God to query, *"What kind of idea is he? What kind am I?"*[10] This prophetic questioning resonates throughout the text with an equal poignancy, posing a similar urgency to disparate centuries of the Islamic calendar, and reformulating in contemporary terms into "What kind of idea is Islamic culture? What historical kind am I?"

If one of the integral concerns of the text is the question of how blasphemy can be articulated in a secular world, then the term "blasphemy" itself must be reread as a gesture of recuperative devotion toward the idea of belief rather than as the insult that it is commonly deemed to be. The interpretative problem that *The Satanic Verses* poses to its readership involves, as a consequence, attention to the forms of veering narrative into which contemporary blasphemy can transmogrify. What kinds of stories, the narrative most self-consciously asks itself, will emerge out of a fidelity to disbelieving? While to a particular audience of *The Satanic Verses* such a recourse to blasphemy operates on the most literal level alone—only Allah can put sentences into Muhammad's head, not Salman Rushdie—such literalism is indeed encoded in the parallel figuration of a text that knows the cultural risks it takes when it seeks to locate, at the present time, naked representations of the archaic narrative of belief. The figure of desecration is thus rendered coterminous with a desire to embody the continuing attractions of Islam in history, so that the narrative can represent cultural leave-taking and homecoming as mutually interchangeable terms.

When the nine sections of the text move in phantasmagoria among a plethora of highly novel and highly archaic tales, it becomes immediately evident that the question of blasphemy is by no means confined to the overtly Islamic chapters. The Thatcherism of contemporary London takes on the features of a mutant blasphemy, while a postcolonial desire for deracination, emblematized by the protagonist, Saladin Chamcha, is equally represented as cultural heresy. Acts of historical or cultural severance become those blasphemous moments that proliferate in the narrative, culminating most significantly in the seductive allegory titled "The Parting of the Arabian Sea," one of the more moving partings in this book of several leave-takings. Finally, in the closing of the narrative, the blasphemy that had been previously embodied is allowed to die, producing a curious textual atmosphere in which the narrative appears to be forgiving itself for its own transgressions, even as it reconfirms the inevitability of their utterance. The somewhat surprising stress of the tropes of forgiveness and reconciliation with which the narrative ends again emphasizes its religious impetus, exuding a nostalgia for the unitary—the Islamic—that it had earlier sought to banish.

Given the prevalence of anti-Arab racism and a concomitant misreading of political expediency as a wholesale expression of Islamic fundamentalism, I must pause to make an obvious point explicit: it is difficult to renounce the elegance of Islam. *The Satanic Verses* evokes that elegance in the syntactical simplicity of its final chapter; it pays earlier compliments to a Muslim aesthetic in the ambiance of gravity that surrounds the text's representation of a mythical Mecca. At such moments in the novel, Rushdie presents a conceit through which a renunciation of religion becomes at the same time a recommitment to the cultural materiality of religion, or a displacement of concept by metaphor. While Rushdie certainly attempts to revise a unitary metaphor and render it plural, such a literary gesture demands to be contextualized by culturally specific traditions, suggesting that *The Satanic Verses* is equally aligned to Western and Eastern aesthetic forms. The narrative's structural reliance on the excessive self-parody of Indian cinema may be a subcontinental precursor most readily discerned by a Western readership; a more ghostly but equally significant subtext is that supplied by the genre of Urdu *ghazal* poetry, one of the more ravishing of Muslim India's cultural productions. In contrast to the tautological abundance of the Indian film, the Urdu *ghazal* haunts *The Satanic Verses* with a narratological desire for the precisions of limitation. Furthermore, it links Rushdie to a highly wrought tradition in which a recurrent trope is the rejection of Islam for some novel object of epistemological and erotic devotion: from Mir to Ghalib, from Iqbal to the Faiz quoted in *The Satanic Verses*, each of the major poets of the Urdu *ghazal* has worked with a similar tropology, in which religious renunciation is figured as a taut and ironized submission to the alterities represented by an Islamic culture in a colonial world. *The Satanic Verses* is both cognizant and admiring of this tradition, which is encoded in the text as one of the multiple cultural compliments that its narrative generously pays.[11]

While neither Indian film nor the Urdu *ghazal* can explain away the urgent self-contradictions with which Rushdie represents the postcolonial subcontinent, their ghostly choric presence serves as a structural reminder of the fact that *The Satanic Verses* engages in the articulation of a proliferating abundance of alterities rather than in obvious declarations of simple binarisms between East and West. They further suggest how much Rushdie's work demands to be contextualized within his prior writing, so that *The Satanic Verses* functions as a necessary supplement to the precarious trajectory of *Midnight's Children* and *Shame*. In those earlier texts, it is Rushdie's great finesse to place in contiguity the excessive novelty of the postcolonial condition with the excessive archaism of the idea of nationality and then allow the encounter to generate a narrative of comedy. If *Midnight's Children* is taken as the starting point of Rushdie's elaboration of postcolonial comedy, the variety of its cultural specificities points to the overdetermination of his localized apprehension of where the boundaries between nationalism and religion may possibly be drawn. Is Bombay a nation-state in its own right? Does the film industry constitute a phantasmic nationalism of its own, supplying an official plot for the manner in which disparate Indian classes and castes love, sing, dance, and die? Could Pakistan be simply a predication of the elegant self-censorship that quickens post-Moghal subcontinental Islam?

Opening in the politically untouchable territory of Kashmir, *Midnight's Children* takes as its shaping narrative premise the centrifugal divisibility that the idea of nationalism produces in the Indian subcontinent. Once the anachronistic idiom of religious difference is rendered coterminous with the rhetoric of independence, the narrative emerging from the curiosities of such historic conflation must pursue its most brilliantly literal query: what does it mean, for a populace to be born at the degree zero of its national history? In both *Midnight's Children* and *Shame*, such oddities of national chronology translate into infinite possibilities for further partition, so that the eros of nation cannot but represent, for the subcontinental psyche, a somewhat titillating induction into the idiom of perpetual separations, or the perpetual repetition of loss.

To read *The Satanic Verses* is therefore to resume the narrative of Rushdie's flabbergasted relation to the divisibility of subcontinental narrative. As a structural principle, such divisibility translates into the convolutions of telling several autonomous stories at the same time: the "Mahound" chapter, or the episode of the satanic verses itself, by no means functions as a focal point in the text, but is instead so allegorical of contemporary subcontinental history as to cease to be allegorical, much as the alternative tales told by the novel are equally informative and obfuscating of the peculiarities of Islam in India. Before it is possible to read Rushdie's representation of Muhammad, therefore, it becomes necessary to question the cultural configuration implied by the text's tautological insistence on at least two central protagonists, at least two nations on the verge of crisis, at least two prophets to embody the centrality of doubt to the structure of religious discourse. Here, what Kipling would call the Great Game of imperial and postimperial history allows Rushdie to extend the inherent tropology of confrontation that informs Anglo-Indian narrative into its postcolonial context. By linking his narrative to the structure of a necessary tautology, Rushdie both crucially revises the unitary myth of Islamic culture and continues that obsessive tale of Anglo-India, which can only sexualize colonial exchange in terms of an aborted homoeroticism. With deference to Fielding and Aziz, to Kim's lama and his beloved, *The Satanic Verses* gives its readership a postcolonial rereading of the homoerotic anxiety that attends narratives embodying a cross-cultural desire, supplying us with the greatly comic interchange between Gibreel Farishta and Saladin Chamcha.

The two figures are most commonly interpreted as embodiments of two opposing Indian desires, with the film star Gibreel Farishta representing the deranged language of a postcolonial visionary and Saladin Chamcha, the clipped and censored discourse of an Anglicized Indian.[12] Such a strict division, however, is muddied from the inception of the narrative, which resolutely opens with the apocalyptic, if accidental, embrace of the two men: a highjacked airplane is blown out of existence over the English Channel and, as the two survivors miraculously hurtle toward land, the narrative pointedly comments that "for whatever reason, the two men, Gibreelsaladin Farishtachamcha, condemned to endless but also ending angelicdevilish fall, did not become aware of the moment at which the processes of their transmutation began" (*SV*, p. 5). Where *A Passage to India* ends ("'Why can't we be friends now?' said the other, holding him affectionately. 'It's what I want. It's what you want'"), *The Satanic Verses* begins, impelling its plot into a highly overdetermined refiguration of the centrality of male desire in the confluence between colonial and postcolonial stories. Opening in the urgency of such an embrace, the novel uncannily manipulates the relation of betrayal and loss that subsists between its two central male characters further to allegorize the old complicities between colonizer and colonized, and the even more archaic novelty that bespeaks the secular Muslim's continued love for the body of the prophet of Islam. Both Gibreel Farishta and Saladin Chamcha must perforce be read, therefore, as synechdochical reminders of

the intimacy between the idea of culture and the course of history, with neither category ever assuming the epistemological surety that could declare
"the moment at which the processes of their transmutation began."

On a simplistic level, such transmutation can be easily transcribed into
a "what happened?" interpretation that can further reduce the text into life
histories: what happened is that Gibreel, the famous Indian film star, went
mad on his escape to England; what happened is that Saladin could not for-
give his embracing cosurvivor for refusing to acknowledge his human
presence when Saladin transmutes into the literal satanism of a goat; what
happened is that Gibreel's delusions drive him to suicide, whereas Saladin's
newly discovered racination leads him to new possibilities of an integrated
cultural life. But that is not what happens. Both Farishta and Chamcha—the
iconology of their names, of course, requires careful reading[13]—represent
aspects of colonial Muslim India that are most involved in both the prospect
of infiltration and, next, what it means to infiltrate. The two of them are accorded a unique status in relation to the former colonizer: for Chamcha,
"England was a peculiar-tasting smoked fish full of spikes and bones, and
nobody would ever tell him how to eat it" (*SV*, p. 44), while for Farishta, "the
trouble with the English was. . . . *their weather*. . . . 'City,' he cried, and
his voice rolled over the metropolis like thunder, 'I am going to tropicalize
you' " (*SV*, p. 354). Such acts of inverse racination, however, remain only the
ostensible point of a narrative far more interested in pursuing the idea of a
contraband historical betrayal operative on a keenly localized level, so that
the very tropology of cultural escape becomes the central fiction that *The
Satanic Verses* must dismantle. "What happens" translates back into the
conflictual model of homoerotic desire in Anglo-Indian narrative, which licenses Chamcha's and Farishta's utter complicity in the embodiment of each
other's stories.

Much as the happening of *A Passage to India* turns upon what fails to
happen to Adela Quested, making of her body the symbolic arena upon
which two men can articulate the cross-cultural idioms of loyalty and betrayal, so too *The Satanic Verses* manipulates heterosexual transgression as
merely a moment in the exchange between Gibreel and Saladin. Both must
see their stories through to the limit of retribution, which moves them beyond their literal transmogrifications into crazed angel and goatish devil:
their idioms meld in order to illustrate the radical obsolescence of prophesy.
In Saladin's vengeance on Gibreel, religious doubt is translated into sexual
doubt, causing the trope of the satanic verses to return in its postmodern ap-
parition as the anonymous telephone call. Drawing on the amatory confi-

dences that Gibreel has made to him, Saladin predicates his revenge on the banality of sexual jealousy by making the body of Gibreel's female lover the site for his trivializing of prophesy:

> Gibreel also got his share of voices . . . sneering gut-
> tersnipes, unctuous best-friend voices mingling warning and
> mock-commiseration, *a word to the wise, how stupid can you,*
> *don't you know yet what she's, anything in trousers.* . . . But one
> voice stood out from the rest . . . a voice that spoke exclusively
> in rhyme, reciting doggerel verses of an understated naïvety,
> even innocence, which contrasted so greatly with the mastur-
> batory coarseness of most of the other [calls] that Gibreel soon
> came to think of it as the most insidiously menacing of them all.
> > *I like coffee, I like tea,*
> > *I like things you do with me.*
> *Tell her that,* the voice swooned, and rang off. (*SV,* p. 444)

By blaspheming against sexual privacy, Saladin uses the female body as a conduit for his possession of the other's male imagination, thereby reinforc-ing the apocalyptic embrace of the narrative's opening. For both of these subcontinental men, to possess a European female body is an insufficient act of postcolonial self-definition: instead, they must understand the mutuality of their status as male voices and their relation to the verses in which they collaborate to construct.

In articulating such a collaboration, Rushdie moves curiously away from the language of cultural resolution into the more implicitly religious tropology of forgiveness. As London burns in racial hatred, Saladin and Gibreel once again jointly face a violent death; rather than punish his tor-mentor, however, Gibreel chooses to save him. Here, the narrative exudes a somewhat quaint nostalgia for a less complicated rhetoric of moralism, querying, "Is it possible that evil is never total, that its victory, no matter how overwhelming, is never absolute?" (*SV,* p. 467) In a text so interested in the course of cultural cataclysm, such a question seems misplaced, but its new logic nevertheless dictates the continuing confrontation between Saladin and Gibreel. Again, their transmutation must lead into an urgently deathly embrace: "Gibreel lets fall his trumpet; stoops; frees Saladin . . . and lifts him in his arms . . . whereupon Gibreel Farishta steps quickly for-ward, bearing Saladin along the path of forgiveness into the hot night air; so that on a night when the city is at war, a night heavy with enmity and rage, there is this small redeeming victory for love" (*SV,* p. 468). As the postsatanism of their collusion dissolves into a gesture of strikingly familial tenderness, Rushdie's utopian need for such regeneration disrupts its own closure by emblematizing what remains the central question of the text: what narratives of male desire are being enacted when the homoeroticism of the colonial paradigm is conflated with the body of the prophet of Islam?[14]

IF THE "MAHOUND" AND THE "RETURN TO JAHILIA" SECTIONS ARE TAKEN TO BE Rushdie's most literalized embodiments of blasphemy, then their elaborately surrealist narrative needs to be contextualized in two crucial ways. In the first place, their tonal peculiarities ask to be read as a continuation of Rushdie's obsession with cultural trespass, figured in *Shame* as those disruptive voices that reject the narrator's authority: *"Outsider! Trespasser! You have no right to this subject!* I know: nobody ever arrested me. Nor are they ever likely to. *Poacher! Pirate! We reject your authority. We know you, with your foreign language wrapped around you like a flag: speaking about us in your forked tongue, what can you tell but lies?* I reply with more questions: Is history to be considered the property of the participants solely?" (*Shame,* p. 28). Religion is similarly to be regarded as the provenance of more than mere believers, even though its cultural territory inevitably engenders a discourse of transgression and self-doubt. Furthermore, the two sections that constitute the satanic verses episode require a reading that takes into account the dialogical supplement of the Ayesha episode, which, in keeping with the tautological structure of the entire text, retells the tale of the satanic verses in a contemporary cultural context. These parallel crises underscore Rushdie's desire—albeit a dangerous one—to turn to Islam as a tropology, to use its history as a reformulation of nationalism as a disbanding fiction that bespeaks the productive absence of cultural cohesion. Blasphemy is therefore an enabling conceit, allowing the narrative to assume the highly ambitious task of rewriting the fiction of Muslim nationhood in India, and in so doing, attempting to locate an idiom for the feminization of Islam.

While the gendering of religion remains the burden of the Ayesha episode, the idea of nation is embodied in *The Satanic Verses'* representation of the prophet Muhammad, a representation far more deferential than its more hasty readership is prepared to discern. In Gibreel's dream version of Islam, "Here he is neither Mahomet nor MoeHammered; has adopted, instead, the demon-tag the farangis [foreigners] hung around his neck. *To turn insults into strengths, whigs, tories, Blacks all chose to wear with pride the names they were given in scorn:* likewise, our mountain-climbing, prophet-motivated solitary is to be the medieval baby-frightener, the Devil's synonym: Mahound" (*SV,* p. 93, emphasis added). In complete accordance with a multiplicity of Islamic literary traditions, Rushdie's solitary prophet is an embodiment of a unitary narrative and its concomitant elegance. The dignity accorded to this figure never degenerates into parody, producing instead a tonal gravity that lends a new equilibrium to the text, particularly in contrast to the hectic schizophrenia of the preceding chapter. Rather than read as a revisionary allegory of heresy, "Mahound" supplies a counterbalance to the narrative, or a somewhat devotional attention to the seductions of a unitary discourse. Thus the Grandee of the mythical pre-Islamic Mecca learns to fear Mahound precisely because of his capacity to embody oneness:

> He remembers the big one, the slave, Bilal: how his master asked him, outside the Lat temple, to enumerate the gods. "One," he answered in that huge musical voice. Blasphemy, punishable by death. They stretched him out in the fairground with a boulder on his chest. *How many did you say?* One, he repeated, one. . . . Why do I fear Mahound? For that: one one one, his terrifying singularity. Whereas I am always divided, always two or three or fifteen. . . . He always was an ambitious fellow. Ambitious, but also solitary. You don't rise to the top by climbing up a hill all by yourself. Unless, maybe, you meet an angel there . . . yes, that's it. I see what he's up to. He wouldn't understand me, though. *What kind of idea am I?* (*SV*, p. 102)

The "one" in question is hardly equated with aridity, but instead with a more supple, if obsessive, command of a novel historiography: history happens with less fuss when it is impelled by the modernity of a unitary narrative.

In her magisterial study of the veneration of the prophet in Islamic literary traditions, *And Muhammad Is His Messenger*, AnneMarie Schimmel outlines the striking intimacy with which Islamic literatures have represented their relation to Muhammad's humanity. In the sustained covenant of nonfigural representation that informs Islamic culture, this humanity is sustained by a communal refusal to produce a literal image of one whose representation would surely engender worship, even though such a body may be figuratively cited as a repository of both spiritual and physical beauty.[15] The "Mahound" chapter locates itself on the cusp of such a covenant, both supplying lineaments to a figure of crucial unrepresentability, and further aligning such representation with a literalization of such traditions as the Sufist celebration of its prophet's mortality. While Sufism is not an overt point of reference in *The Satanic Verses*, its segregation between the idioms of mysticism and prophecy implicitly inform Rushdie's reading of the collisions between a cultural schizophrenia and the plot of postcolonial history. In such a reading, the mystic is transcribed into the bitter hallucinations that send Gibreel Farishta to his death, while the prophet figures as the one body cognizant of the intransigent idea of nation. Here, it is important to keep in mind that to *The Satanic Verses*, Mahound represents a minority discourse, a solitary voice empowered by a single-minded commitment to the pragmatics of prophecy. Again, Rushdie is hardly unique in such a depiction of prophecy, which alludes instead to both Muslim and specifically subcontinental formulations of the social function of the prophet, or the metaphoric value of a "messenger" who chooses to uphold the vital mortality of messages. In his seminal work, *Reconstruction of Religious Thought in Islam*, the poet Iqbal opens his fifth chapter to delineate the significance of this choice:

> "Muhammad of Arabia ascended the highest heaven and re-turned. I swear by God that if I had reached that point, I should never have returned." These are the words of a great Muslim saint, Abdul Quddus of Gangoh. In the whole range of Sufi liter-ature it will probably be difficult to find words which, in a single sentence, disclose such an acute perception of the psychological difference between the prophetic and mystic types of con-sciousness. The mystic does not wish to return from the repose of "unitarian experience" [but] the prophet's return is creative. He returns to insert himself into the sweep of time with a view to control the forces of history, and thereby to create a fresh world of ideals. . . . Thus his return amounts to a kind of pragmatic test of religious experience.[16]

If the "Mahound" chapter is equally a "pragmatic test of the value of re-ligious experience," its readership is forced to repeat the text's own obsessive question, *"What kind of idea is he? What kind am I?"*

The Satanic Verses turns to the idea of doubt as the temporal condition, or the very historicity of belief: the episode itself unfolds as a complex his-torical metaphor that is less concerned with temptation than it is with the representation of the specificities of Rushdie's cultural context, which is of course the paradoxical grafting of Islam onto the Indian subcontinent, and the minority of this religion in relation to Hinduism. In rereading the mythic confrontation between the desires for Allah and Al-Lat, Rushdie constructs an elaborate figure for the uneasy intimacies that proliferate among subcon-tinental Muslim and Hindu epistemologies. While the highly politicized nature of such intimacies engenders competing nationalisms under colonial rule, Rushdie further attempts to return their mutual antagonism and allure into a formulation of archaic urgency: a polytheistic culture regards the monotheistic, both aware that they are historically doomed to test to the limits the other's apprehension of alterity. The episode of the satanic verses, therefore, serves as a proleptic figure for the seductions of cultural difference that obtain in the Indian subcontinent, and cannot be simply read as a somewhat naive questioning of the integrity of the Islamic ideas. The narrative of *The Satanic Verses* engages instead in a more precarious story, meditating on the intransigence that is lent to history when two exclusive religious integrities are by accident made bedfellows. Here, the satanic verses serve as a complex frame for the brilliant synecdoche of religious warfare that Rushdie locates in Gibreel Farishta. When Gibreel disappears in the opening chapter of the novel, the subcontinent mourns his loss as an obliteration of both religions:

> It was the death of God. Or something very much like it; for had not that outsize face, suspended over its devotees in the artificial cinematic night, shone like that on some supernal Entity that had its being at least halfway between the mortal and the divine? More than halfway, many would have argued, for Gibreel had spent the greater part of his unique career incarnating, with absolute conviction, the countless deities of the subcontinent in the popular genre movies known as "theologicals." It was part of the magic of his persona that he succeeded in crossing religious boundaries without giving offense. . . . For over a decade and a half he had represented, to hundreds of millions of believers in that country in which, to this day, the human population outnumbers the divine by less than three to one, the most acceptable, and instantly recognizable, face of the Supreme. (*SV*, pp. 16–17)

When *The Satanic Verses* turns in its second chapter to the mortal struggle that Allah and Al-Lat conduct within Mahound's head, its secret context is the cinematic crossings between delusion and desire that the theologicals represent to the Indian subcontinent.

Once the Allah/Al-Lat paradigm has been translated into the context of Indian cultural self-definition, it loses some, but not all, of its impact as gratuitous blasphemy. Here, of course, blasphemy must be apprehended as a narrative device rather than as a statement of religious conviction, as an aesthetic form that is indeed aligned to the structure of magic realism, or the favored shape of Rushdie's earlier novels. If the self-mocking secularism of the "miracle" of postcolonial nationhood enabled the narrative of *Midnight's Children*, then blasphemy performs a similarly disruptive psychic function in the stories of *The Satanic Verses*. As a language, it generates the infernal sadness with which Rushdie embodies his prophet, bringing the narrative dangerously close to its final articulation of male desire. "You can deny God," writes Iqbal, "but you cannot deny the Prophet."[17] The wrenching irony of Rushdie's text is that it predicates its narrative on such an absence of denial, allowing a rhetorical tenderness to shape its obsession with embodiment: "The businessman: looks like he should, high forehead, eaglenose, broad in the shoulders, narrow in the hip. Average height, brooding, dressed in two pieces of plain cloth, each four ells in length, one draped about his body, the other over his shoulder. Large eyes; long lashes like a girl's. His strides can seem too long for his legs, but he's a light-footed man" (*SV*, p. 93). Such a representation embodies the excess rather than the denial of devotion, exuding an intimacy that is almost too literal to inhabit safely its framing fiction. The density of *The Satanic Verses*, however, understands that to be too literal is to occupy the most tropological realm of all, that the unitary tale of Mahound must be retold and reshaped into the body of a woman, suggesting in its conclusion that the eros of religion can be most keenly apprehended from its periphery rather than from its center.

THE AYESHA EPISODE OF *THE SATANIC VERSES* IS BASED ON AN ACTUAL HISTOR-ical event that occurred in Pakistan. The Hawkes Bay case took place in February 1983, when thirty-eight Shia Muslims walked into the Arabian Sea in the expectation that the waters would part, allowing the pilgrims to walk on to Basra, and finally, to the sacred site of Karbala. They were inspired by a young woman, Naseem Fatima, who claimed to be in direct visionary contact with the twelfth Imam. By the time the Karachi police reached Hawkes Bay, most of the pilgrims had drowned; the police proceeded to arrest the survivors, on the grounds that they had attempted to leave Pakistan illegally without visas. In the notoriety that followed the Hawkes Bay case, "rich Shias, impressed by the devotion of the survivors, paid for their journey by air for a week to and from Karbala. In Iraq, influential Shias, equally impressed, presented them with gifts, including rare copies of the Holy Quran. Naseem's promise that they would visit Karbala without worldly means was fulfilled."[18]

Such fictive material renders magic realism obsolete, illustrating instead the radical instability of its status as allegory. Does it call to be read as a postcolonial parody of the idea of miracle, or is the gravity of its derangement too impervious to any interpretation at all? In *The Satanic Verses*, the tale is retold with both bemusement and affection, allowing the prophet as woman to rearticulate the powerful erotics of faith. That Rushdie sets the tale in India rather than in Pakistan, representing the pilgrims as generic Muslims rather than as Shias, emphasizes his narrative desire for the depiction of dislocation: the pilgrimage must end in the cinematic city of Bombay, in a tautological abundance of conflicting delusions. At the same time, however, the Ayesha pilgrimage reenacts the high seriousness of the Mahound story by providing a unitary narrative to the multiplicity of skepticisms that frame the peculiarities of its tale.

Ayesha, a young woman in the village of Titlipur ("Butterfly Abode"), is an oddity. Her extraordinary desirability is matched by her chastity, and by her insistence on feeding herself only on butterflies. While her language teeters between the discourses of imbecility and prophecy, its very uncertainty enhances her powers of seduction. To Ayesha, the Angel Gabriel will speak only in the idiom of popular film songs, so that the idea of miracle is both secularized and eroticized, lending the pilgrimage the phantasmagoric structure of a "theological." While the event culminates in an ambivalent disaster, the episode remains one of the more charming tales in *The Satanic Verses'* proliferation of stories: the narrative nostalgically recreates a desire for the tropology of miracle, allowing for miraculous accoutrement rather than for miracle itself. The angel enjoins Ayesha to lead the villagers on a pilgrimage to Mecca; she in turn understands the literalism of her desire as an expression of tautology. "Everything will be desired of us," she claims, "and everything will be given to us also" (*SV,* p. 225). To the skeptics of both the village and the subcontinent, such literalism translates into blasphemy itself, converting religious desire into a most dangerous transgression of social stability:

> The story of the village that was walking to the sea had spread all over the country, and in the ninth week the pilgrims were being pestered by journalists, local politicos in search of votes . . . foreign tourists looking for the mysteries of the East, nostalgic Gandhians. . . . When they saw the host of chameleon butterflies and the way they both clothed the girl Ayesha and provided her with her only solid food, these visitors were amazed, and retreated with confounded expectations . . . certain religious extremist groupings had issued statements denouncing the "Ayesha Haj" as an attempt to "hijack" public attention and to "incite communal sentiment." (*SV,* p. 488)

The pilgrimage thus extraordinarily embodies Rushdie's reading of the story of nationalism in the Indian subcontinent as a tale of perpetual partition, a parting of the waters that both cannot, and can always, occur.

If Ayesha embodies the inextricability of the idioms of blasphemy and faith, then she must further illustrate—as does the Mahound story—the centrality of dubiety in such a union. Her temptation comes in the form of a skeptic landlord who wishes to render more literal an already excessively literal journey by buying her an air ticket to Mecca: "'Partition was quite a disaster here on land,' he taunted her. 'Quite a few guys died, you might remember. You think it will be different in the water?'" (SV, p. 501). It is only through the course of Ayesha's temptation, however, that the question of the "Mahound" chapter ("What kind of idea are you? What kind am I?") can both be reformulated and receive its final reply: "His offer had contained an old question: *what kind of idea are you*? And she, in turn, had offered him an old answer: *I was tempted, but am renewed; am uncompromising; absolute; pure*" (SV, p. 500). In this reimagining of prophecy into the body of a young girl, clad in butterflies, *The Satanic Verses* locates its most compelling figure for the unitary intimacy between blasphemy and devotion. Even as the literalism of the pilgrimage ends in death by drowning for most of Ayesha's devotees, Rushdie turns the climactic moment of miracle inward, allowing the literal its final enfolding into the figurative. According to the testimony of the skeptical survivors, a parting of the waters did miraculously occur: "Just when my strength failed and I thought I would surely die there in the water, I saw it with my own eyes; I saw the sea divide, like hair being combed; and they were all there, far away, walking away from me" (SV, p. 504).

The Ayesha episode thus takes up the eros both to supply it with a female body and to alter vitally the enabling terms of its unitary narrative: Mahound's old idea of submission is now substituted by the idea of opening, which signifies that partings can be historically productive, even in their embodiments of loss. Finally, *The Satanic Verses'* rereading of "opening" is essentialized into the urgent sexuality with which the Ayesha episode ends, a scene that posits death as the site of the union between eros and miracle. When the last skeptic, Ayesha's tempter and old antagonist, is literally dying, he undergoes a figurative drowning that changes his equation with prophecy:

> Then the sea poured over him, and he was in the water beside Ayesha. . . . "Open," she was crying . . . "Open," she said. He closed.

He was a fortress with clanging gates.—He was drowning.—She was drowning, too. He saw the water fill her mouth,
heard it begin to gurgle into her lungs. Then something within
him refused that, made a different choice, and at the instant that
his heart broke, he opened.

His body split apart from his adam's-apple to his groin, so
that she could reach deep within him, and now she was open,
they all were, and at the moment of their opening the waters
parted, and they walked to Mecca across the bed of the Arabian
Sea. (*SV*, pp. 506–7)

In this extraordinary moment of a limpid and free-floating devotion, the
feminized prophet enters the body of dubiety, and the figurative miracle of
their union points less to Mecca than to Rushdie's need to articulate openings
in the structure of male desire.

If the feminization of prophecy generates an idiom of a certain revolutionary sweetness in the latter sections of *The Satanic Verses*, it is further
preparatory to the serene utopianism with which the novel somewhat sur-
prisingly ends. The Ayesha episode attempts to transcribe the dubiousness of
miracle into a framework of secular history, thereby providing postcolonial
narrative with a highly novel language of reconciliation and forgiveness.
Much as the course of the story melds the categories of blasphemy and devotion, so too its conclusion proffers the archaism of reconciliation as a newly
radical discourse, making "The Parting of the Arabian Sea" less a recuperation of Islam than a vital narrative bridge into Rushdie's problematizing
tropes of forgiveness. The contraband of the miraculous, in other words, has
been historicized in order that the text itself can anticipate its own pardon. In
the context of the writing of *The Satanic Verses*, however, pardoning is an act
of dense cultural complexity, closely aligned to the possibility of continual
postcolonial betrayal. In the final chapter of the novel, Rushdie turns with
meticulous naturalism to scenes of deathbed reconciliation between father
and son more in keeping with nineteenth-century narrative conventions and
with the most popular endings of Bombay's cinematic productions than with
the postmodernity of the text's opening. The Anglicized Saladin Chamcha
returns to Bombay to watch over his previously estranged and now dying
father; his union further signifies a recovery of his hitherto repressed Indian
past. As a crucial allegorizing of leave-taking, however, this familial act of
reconciliation allows the narrative to confront the paternity of religion in
order to claim, with an anachronistic lyricism, "To fall in love with one's father after the long angry decades was a serene and beautiful feeling; a

renewing, life-giving thing" (*SV*, p. 523). Yet the death of the father cannot constitute completion without such closure reconfiguring into another opening, or an acknowledgment of the planned obsolescence of such a desire for a simultaneous recovery and parting.

To embody opening is sufficient work for a single narrative. As Rushdie unravels the homoerotic desire of the colonial paradigm into postcolonial complications that gesture toward the aching comedy of its historiography, he opens narrative possibilities that threaten to be sealed by the furies attendant on the reception of *The Satanic Verses.* If a bewildered popular opinion seeks to magnify the text into the sensational proportions of a "theological," it is the duty of the academy to ensure that such closure be arrested, that the delicate and brave parameters of this piece of fiction are preserved for what they are. Cultural ignorance can also yield to openings: the academic model perhaps best suited to this intellectual crisis is the originary myth of Islam, where Gabriel's injunction to the potential prophet is simply, "Read." "I cannot read," replied Muhammad, at which point Gabriel—with a pedagogical patience that would certainly benefit the academy at the present time—repeated, "Read," until the prophet did.[19]

Notes

CHAPTER ONE

1. Rudyard Kipling, "Naboth," in *Life's Handicap: Being Stories of Mine Own People* (New York: Doubleday and McClure Co., 1899), p. 71.

2. See Homi K. Bhabha, "The Other Question," *Screen* 24, no. 6 (December 1983); and Gayatri C. Spivak, *In Other Worlds: Essays in Cultural Politics* (New York: Methuen, 1987). A text paradigmatic of the binarism I question, however, is Abdul R. JanMohamed's reading of alterity in *Manichean Aesthetics: The Politics of Literature in Colonial Africa* (Amherst: University of Massachusetts Press, 1983).

3. My reference is to Benedict Anderson's *Imagined Communities: Reflections on the Origin and Spread of Nationalism* (London: Verso, 1983).

4. Anderson, *Imagined Communities*, p. 129.

5. For an engaged reading of cultural terror, see Michael Taussig, *Shamanism, Colonialism and the Wild Man: A Study in Terror and Healing* (Chicago: University of Chicago Press, 1987).

6. Edward Thompson, *The Other Side of the Medal* (New York: Harcourt, Brace and Co., 1926; reprint, Westport, Conn.: Greenwood Press, 1974), pp. 26–27.

7. Gayatri C. Spivak, "Reading *The Satanic Verses*," *Public Culture* 2, no. 1 (Fall 1989): 85.

8. Anderson, *Imagined Communities*, p. 19.

9. Homi K. Bhabha, ed., *Nation and Narration* (New York: Routledge, 1990), p. 3.

10. Edward Said, "Orientalism Reconsidered," in *Literature, Politics and Theory*, ed. Francis Barker et al. (London: Methuen, 1986), p. 229.

11. S. P. Mohanty, "Us and Them: On the Philosophical Bases of Political Criticism," *Yale Journal of Criticism* 2, no. 2 (Spring 1989): 5.

12. Gauri Viswanathan, "Raymond Williams and British Colonialism," *Yale Journal of Criticism* 4, no. 2 (Spring 1991): 47–67.

13. Robert Sencourt, *India in English Literature* (London: Simpkin, Marshall, Hamilton and Kent, [1923]), pp. 456–57.

14. Spivak, *In Other Worlds*, p. 254.

15. Fredric Jameson, "Third World Literature in the Era of Multinational Corporations," *Social Text* 15 (Fall 1986): 69.

16. Aijaz Ahmad, "Jameson's Rhetoric of Otherness and the 'National Allegory,'" *Social Text* 17 (Fall 1987): 8–9.

17. Mohanty, "Us and Them," p. 13.

18. Edward Said, *Orientalism* (New York: Vintage, 1978), p. 222.

19. Robert Orme, *Historical Fragments of the Mogol Empire: Of the Morattoes, and the English Concerns, in Indostan, from the Year M,DC,LIX* (London: Printed for C. Nourse, 1782), p. 472.

20. Jawaharlal Nehru, *Towards Freedom: The Autobiography of Jawaharlal Nehru* (Boston: Beacon Press, 1967), p. 272.

21. Said, *Orientalism*, p. 207.

22. John Forbes Watson and John Wilson Kaye, eds., *The people of India: A Series of Photographic Illustrations, with Descriptive Letterpress, of the Races and Tribes of Hindustan* 8 vols. (London: India Museum, 1868–75).

23. James Mill, *The History of British India*, ed. John Clive (Chicago: University of Chicago Press, 1975). (Orig. pub. 1817)

24. Herbert Risley, *The People of India* (Calcutta: Thacker Spink and Co., 1908), p. 265.

25. Forbes Watson and Kaye, eds., *The people of India*, vol. 3, no. 139.

26. Sir Sayyid Ahmad Khan, Letter from London, 15 October 1869, in G. F. I. Graham, *The Life and Work of Sayed Ahmad Khan, C.S.I.* (London: Blackwood, 1885), pp. 188–89. I am grateful to David Lelyveld for drawing my attention to this passage.

27. Gayatri Spivak, *The Post-Colonial Critic*, ed. Sarah Harasym (New York: Routledge, 1990), p. 69.

28. Gauri Viswanathan, *Masks of Conquest: Literary Study and British Rule in India* (New York: Columbia University Press, 1989), pp. 8–9.

29. Salman Rushdie, *Midnight's Children* (New York: Knopf, 1980), p. 552.

CHAPTER TWO

1. Peter J. Stanlis, *Edmund Burke: Selected Writings and Speeches* (Gloucester, Mass.: Peter Smith, 1968), p. 387.

2. I refer to the consequences of the Regulating Act of 1773, which first brought the government directly into Company affairs in India and in England. This era should not be confused with the New Imperialism of the later nineteenth century. See Percival Spear, *The Oxford History of India*, 4th ed. (Delhi: Oxford University Press, 1968), pp. 518–28.

3. See Mill, *History of British India*, p. 379.

4. For a comprehensive overview of these proceedings, see P. J. Marshall, *The Impeachment of Warren Hastings* (London: Oxford University Press, 1965), p. 20.

5. P. J. Marshall and Glyndwr Williams, *The Great Map of Mankind* (London: Dent, 1982), p. 78

6. Recent critical studies have demonstrated "sympathy's" overdetermination in the eighteenth century's imagination at large. See, for example, David Marshall, *The Surprising Effects of Sympathy: Marivaux, Diderot, Rousseau, and Mary Shelley* (Chicago: University of Chicago Press, 1988).

7. See Mill, *History of British India*; Thomas Babington Macaulay, "Essay on Clive," *Edinburgh Review*, January 1840; Geoffrey Moorhouse, *India Britannica* (London: Harril Press, 1983), pp. 38–41.

8. Edmund Burke, "Speech on Mr. Fox's East India Bill," *The Complete Works of the Right Honourable Edmund Burke*, rev. ed. (Boston: Little, Brown and Co., 1866), vol. 2, p. 446. (Henceforth cited as *CW* in the text)

9. Hayden White, "The Politics of Historical Interpretation: Discipline and De-Sublimation," *Critical Inquiry* 9 (September 1982): 113–37; Donald E. Pease, "Sublime Politics," *Boundary* 2 (Spring/Fall 1984): 259–79.

10. Pease, "Sublime Politics," p. 275.

11. Bernard Cohn, "The Transformation of Objects into Artifacts," p. 7. I am grateful to Professor Cohn for allowing me to consult this manuscript.

12. Risley, *People of India.*

13. See Martin Green, *Dreams of Adventure, Deeds of Empire* (New York: Basic Books, 1979). The impulse to record and catalog is also evidenced by the proliferation of journals and diaries written during the colonial period. See Ketaki Kushari Dyson, *A Various Universe: A Study of the Journals and Memoirs of British Men and Women in the Indian Subcontinent 1765–1865* (Delhi: Oxford University Press, 1978).

14. Harriet Tytler, *An Englishwoman in India: The Memoirs of Harriet Tytler 1828–1858*, ed. Anthony Sattin (New York: Oxford University Press, 1986). Fanny Parks, *Wanderings of a Pilgrim in Search of the Picturesque*, 2 vols. (London: Pelham Richardson, 1850).

15. See Spear, *Oxford History of India*, pp. 450–51.

16. For an overview of the transformation of attitude toward India in the transition from Burke and Hastings to Mill and Macaulay, see Spear, *Oxford History of India*, p. 481.

17. Mill, *History of British India*, p. 27.

18. Thomas Babington Macaulay, "Minute on Indian Education," *Selected Writings*, ed. John Clive (Chicago: University of Chicago Press, 1972), p. 241.

19. Edmund Candler, *The Mantle of the East* (London: Blackwood, 1910), pp. 28–9.

20. See Spear, *Oxford History of India*, p. 446.

21. See James Boulton's introduction to Edmund Burke, *A Philosophical Enquiry into the Origin of Our Ideas of the Sublime and Beautiful* (Notre Dame: University of Notre Dame Press, 1968), pp. xv–cxxvii (orig. pub. 1958); Burke, *CW*, vol. 2, p. 434; and David Marshall, *The Figure of Theater: Shaftesbury, Defoe, Adam Smith, and George Eliot* (Baltimore: Johns Hopkins University Press, 1986).

22. Neil Hertz, *The End of the Line* (New York: Columbia University Press, 1985), pp. 40–60; Marshall, *Surprising Effects of Sympathy;* and also see Thomas Weiskel's reading of the negative sublime in *The Romantic Sublime: Studies in the Structure and Psychology of Transcendence* (Baltimore: Johns Hopkins University Press, 1976).

23. Angus Fletcher, *Allegory: The Theory of a Symbolic Mode* (Ithaca: Cornell University Press, 1964), pp. 234–35. See also Neil Hertz's reading of this passage in *The End of the Line*, pp. 47–48.

24. Hayden White, *The Content of the Form: Narrative discourse and Historical Representation* (Baltimore: Johns Hopkins University Press, 1987), p. 75.

25. White, *Content of the Form*, p. 68.

26. Weiskel, *Romantic Sublime*, p. 19.

27. See David Musselwhite, "The Trial of Warren Hastings," in *Literature, Politics and Theory* ed. Francis Barker et al. (London: Methuen, 1986); and for a more considered reading, see Marshall, *Impeachment of Warren Hastings*, pp. 1–21.

28. Bryan S. Turner, "Orientalism and the Problem of Civil Society in Islam," in *Orientalism, Islam and Islamists*, ed. Asaf Hussain et al. (Vermont: Amana Books, 1984), p. 39.

CHAPTER THREE

1. *History of the Trial of Warren Hastings: Containing the Whole of the Proceedings and Debates in Both Houses of Parliament* (London, 1796), p. 17. (Henceforth cited in the text as *HTH*.)

2. P. J. Marshall, *Impeachment of Warren Hastings*, p. 189.

3. H. Furber et al., eds., *The Correspondence of Edmund Burke* (Cambridge: Cambridge University Press, 1958–65, 23 December 1785, vol. 5, p. 245.

4. Of the twenty-two charges, the major four can be summarized as follows: (1) The Benares Charge rested on the events whereby the Company had reached a settlement after having gained control of Benares and its leader, Chait Singh, in 1775. Not content with the negotiated dues, the Company forced Chait Singh to make additional military contributions, leading him eventually to rebel in 1781. The suppression of this "rebellion" greatly facilitated the Company's absorption of the whole area into its provinces. 2) The Begums Charge was over an agreement between the Company and the mother and grandmother of the underage Nawab of Oudh. In 1781 Hastings broke the agreement, claiming that the Begums had assisted Chait Singh's rebellion, and he confiscated both lands and treasure as punishment. (3) The Presents Charge arose out of the Company's restrictions, in force since the 1760s, against the acceptance of presents and misuse of private trade privileges to supplement employees' incomes. the Regulating Act of 1773 strengthened this stricture, and the Company denied the employees' distinction between accepting presents and taking bribes. Hastings was charged with both accepting and demanding presents, as well as forcing bribes and offering political and military favors in exchange. (4) Contracts. Here, Hastings was accused of misusing, for the benefit of the Company and other English agents, the granting of contracts for opium, military supplies, and emergency shipments of grain. He was further accused of abusing his patronage in increasing salaries and influencing appointments.

5. *Bhagavad Gita*, trans. Charles Wilkins (London: C. Nourse, 1785).

6. See Ramkrishna Mukherjee, *The Rise and Fall of the East India Company: A Sociological Appraisal* (New York: Monthly Review Press, 1974). See in particular chapter 5, "Company as Ruler." Also worthy of note is the Nanda Kumar incident, which never became a part of the impeachment but nevertheless hung over the proceedings. In 1775 Nanda Kumar had accused Hastings of accepting a large bribe from one of the Begums, but Kumar was arrested soon afterward for an unrelated alleged infraction of his own. The newly formed supreme Court in Calcutta, under Chief Justice Ilijah Impey, tried and executed him for the crime of forgery. In addition to removing Hastings's accuser, this case also exposed the aggressive imposition of

English law over those of the land. For more detailed discussions of this case see Spear, *Oxford History of India*, pp. 504−7; and Mukherjee, *Rise and Fall of the East India Company*, pp. 318−19.

7. I refer to David Musselwhite's reading in "The Trial of Warren Hastings," in *Literature, Politics and Theory*, pp. 77−103.

8. Leslie A. Marchand, ed., *Byron's Letters and Journals* (Cambridge, Mass.: Belknap Press, 1974), vol. 3 (1813−14), p. 239.

9. Fanny Burney, *Diary and Letters of Madame D'Arblay* (London: Henry Colburn, Publisher, 1842), pp. 58−129.

10. Gilbert Elliot, *Memoir,* quoted in Keith Feiling, *Warren Hastings,* (London: Macmillan, 1954), p. 347.

11. Ibid., p. 353.

12. A significant example is the Ilijah Impey judgment on Raja Nundkumar.

13. P. J. Marshall, *Impeachment of Warren Hastings,* p. 78.

14. Burney, *Diaries and Letters,* p. 63.

15. Ibid., p. 105.

16. Thomas Babington Macaulay, *The Works of Lord Macaulay,* ed. Lady Trevelyan (London: Longmans, Green and Co., 1866), vol. 6, pp. 633−34.

17. Ibid., p. 620.

18. Ibid., p. 619.

19. Ibid., p. 620.

20. Musselwhite, "Trial of Warren Hastings," in *Literature, Politics and Theory,* pp. 95−96.

21. Ibid., p. 98.

22. Mill, *History of British India,* vol. 5, pp. 231−32.

23. Ibid., p. 232.

24. Duchess of Devonshire's Diary, 20 November 1788; Marshall, *Impeachment of Warren Hastings,* p. 78.

25. Quoted in the introduction to *Plays and Poems of Richard Brinsley Sheridan,* ed. R. Crompton Rhodes (New York: Macmillan, 1929), vol. 3, p. 11. (Henceforth cited in the text)

26. For figures of receipts and a sample of contemporary reviews, see *The London Stage,* ed. Charles Beecher Hogan (Carbondale, Ill.: Southern Illinois University Press, 1978), pp. 2095, 2177−90, 2202. For an account of the play's continuing popularity in the nineteenth century, see John Loftis, *Sheridan and the Drama of Georgian England* (Oxford: Basil Blackwell, 1976).

27. I refer of course to the increasing literalization of theatricality on the nineteenth-century stage, where the ever-growing machinery created larger and more extravagant spectacles. See *The London Stage,* vols. 3 and 4 for the evolution of theaters' capability to house elaborate mechanisms.

28. The plot of the play is simple: bad Pizarro returns to Peru with his good mistress, Elvira, who has suffered shame and familial excommunication for her union with the leader of the Spaniards, and whose goodness has further elicited the love of Pizarro's secretary, Valverde. Pizarro himself is angry with Alonzo, a surrogate son who through the preachings of Las-Casas has renounced the Spanish cause and become along with Rolla one of the generals of the Peruvian forces. Once among the

Incas, Alonzo wins the love of Cora, formerly Rolla's beloved, but his marriage to her does not one jot deter the brotherhood between the two men. *Pizzaro* opens with the promise of colonial retribution, and in the ensuing battle Alonzo falls prisoner to the Spanish troops. He had earlier made Rolla swear that in the event of his death, Rolla would take on the sacred charge of being husband to Cora and father to their beloved son. Act 3 sees Rolla in Alonzo's continuing absence proposing such a substitution to Cora, whose indignant rejection implies that Rolla has basely let Alonzo die in order to make such a proposition. A spiritually injured and disguised Rolla slips into the Spanish camp and convinces Alonzo to assume his disguise and flee to freedom and Cora. Good Elvira, disgusted with Pizarro's excesses, comes to Alonzo's prison with the plea that he stab Pizarro in his sleep; she is perturbed to find Rolla in his stead. The nobility of Rolla of course prevents him from slaying a sleeping man and the two instead discourse on their alternative political positions, while Elvira—much to Rolla's distress—is condemned to death.

Pizzaro's admiration of Rolla's bravery causes him to release his enemy, but before he quits the stage two Spanish soldiers enter with a babe that Rolla instantly recognizes as none other than Alonzo's son. He seizes the child, and makes an intrepid escape by uprooting a tree that holds the bridge over which the Spaniards could have followed him. Wounded Rolla reaches the Peruvian camp to hand over the infant to Alonzo and Cora; when Cora exclaims over the bloodiness of the babe, Rolla tells her, "It is my blood, Cora," and then proceeds to die. Pizarro meanwhile has ordered an attack on the stronghold where the Peruvian women and treasure are concealed, and even as he is committing such a violation, Alonzo arrives to challenge the Spaniard to mortal combat in act 5. They fight; Alonzo is on the verge of defeat when good Elvira—saved by the secretary's love—enters in a nun's habit, causing Pizarro to start and be slain. His death summons Rolla's funeral, a solemn march, during which "*Alonzo* and *Cora* kneel on either side of [the bier], and kiss *Rolla's* hands in silent agony—In the looks of a King, and of all present, the Triumph of the Day is lost, in mourning for their Hero."

29. James Morwood, *The Life and Works of Richard Brinsley Sheridan* (Edinburgh: Scottish Academic Press, 1985), p. 161.

30. Thomas Moore, *Memoirs of the Life of the Right Honourable Richard Brinsley Sheridan* (London, 1825), p. 366.

CHAPTER FOUR

1. Lady Lawrence, *Indian Embers* (London: George Ronald, n.d.), p. 26.

2. Francis Hutchins, *The Illusion of Permanence: British Imperialism in India* (Princeton: Princeton University Press, 1967), pp. 101–19.

3. Kenneth Ballhatchet, *Race, Sex and Class under the Raj: Imperial Attitudes and Policies and Their Critics, 1793–1905* (London: Weidenfeld and Nicolson, 1980).

4. V. S. Naipaul, *An Area of Darkness* (London: Andre Deutch, 1964), p. 222.

5. Lata Mani, "Contentious Traditions: The Debate on *Sati* in Colonial India," *Cultural Critique* 7 (Fall 1987): 152–53.

6. Margaret MacMillan, *Women of the Raj* (New York: Thames and Hudson,

1988), p. 7; Pat Barr, *The Memsahibs: The Women of Victorian India* (London: Secker and Warburg, 1976).

7. John McBratney, "Images of Women in Rudyard Kipling: A Case of Doubling Discourse," *Inscriptions*, 1988, nos. 3/4: 54.

8. Ballhatchet, *Race, Sex and Class under the Raj*, p. 5.

9. See Bernard S. Cohn's admirable reading of such displays in "Representing Authority in Victorian India," in *The Invention of Tradition*, ed. Eric Hobsbawm and Terence Ranger (Cambridge: Cambridge University Press, 1983), pp. 165–209.

10. Mary Martha Sherwood, *The Life of Mrs. Sherwood* (London, 1854), p. 365.

11. Major Edward Caulfield Archer, *Tours in Upper India, and in Parts of the Himalaya Mountains; with Accounts of the Courts of Native Princes, Etc.*, 2 vols. (London, 1833).

12. Archer, *Tours*, vol. 1, p. 155.

13. Parks, *Wanderings* (Henceforth cited as *WP*.)

14. For Coleridge's interest in Indian mythology and correspondence with Sir William Jones, see John Drew, *India in the Romantic Imagination* (Delhi: Oxford University Press, 1987), pp. 185–94.

15. MacMillan, *Women of the Raj*, p. 8.

16. Captain Thomas Skinner, *Excursions in India; Including a Walk over the Himalaya Mountains, to the Sources of the Jumna and the Ganges*, 2 vols. (London, 1832), vol. 2, pp. 212–13.

17. Quoted in Dyson, *A Various Universe*, p. 81.

18. Ibid., p. 147.

19. Partha Mitter, *Much Maligned Monsters*, p. 207; See especially his succinct survey, "The Sublime, the Picturesque, and Indian Architecture," pp. 120–39.

20. Tytler, *English Woman in India*, p. 109. (Henceforth cited as HT)

21. In the popular imagination the inception of the mutiny has traditionally been traced from the issue of the animal fats used to grease the cartridges used by the Indian troops. Even contemporary studies, such as Patrick Brantlinger's *Rule of Darkness*, comply with the originary myth: "The immediate cause of the rebellion was ammunition for the new Enfield rifles; the sepoys of the Bengal Army suspected that the cartridges had been greased with cow and pig fat. The paper ends had to be bitten off before use, and because cow fat was taboo for Hindus and pork fat for Muslims, the British seemed to be forcing both groups of sepoys to commit sacrilege. Of course there were more important causes—Disraeli said in Parliament that 'the rise and fall of empires are not affairs of greased cartridges'—but most British analysts found discontent only within the native regiments, which saved them from acknowledging widespread unrest" (p. 200).

22. See Cohn, "Representing Authority," in *Invention of Tradition*, pp. 199–200.

23. Ibid., p. 179.

24. Ray Desmond, *The India Museum, 1801–1879* (London: Her Majesty's India Office Library and Records Stationery Office, 1982), p. 122.

25. Macaulay, "Minute on Indian Education," p. 249.

26. Robert Knox, *The Races of Men: A Fragment* (Philadelphia: Lea & Blanchard, 1850), pp. 246–47.

27. Khan, Letter from London, 15 October 1869, in Graham, *Life and Work*, pp. 188–89.

28. Forbes Watson and Kay, eds., *The people of India*, vol. 5, plate 232. (Henceforth cited in the text as *PI*.)

CHAPTER FIVE

1. Oscar Wilde, "The True Function and Nature of Criticism," reprinted in *Kipling: The Critical Heritage*, ed. Roger Lancelyn Green (London: Routledge and Kegan Paul, 1971), p. 104.

2. Edward Said, "Kim: The Pleasures of Imperialism," *Raritan* 2 (Fall 1987): 29.

3. Edmund Wilson, "The Kipling That Nobody Read," in *Kipling's Mind and Art: Selected Critical Essays*, ed. Andrew Rutherford (Stanford: Stanford University Press, 1964), p. 30. Wilson's essay was originally published in *Atlantic Monthly* 167 (1941), and was reprinted in Edmund Wilson, *The Wound and the Bow* (London, 1952).

4. Said, *"Kim,"* p. 43.

5. Rudyard Kipling, "The Conversion of Aurelian McGoggin," in *Plain Tales from the Hills* (London: Penguin, 1987), p. 118. (Orig. pub. 1888)

6. Ibid., p. 121.

7. Rudyard Kipling, *Kim* (London, 1901), p. 8. (Henceforth cited in the text.)

8. Mark Kinkead-Weekes, "Vision in Kipling's Novels," in *Kipling's Mind and Art*, ed. Andrew Rutherford (London: Oliver and Boyd, 1964), p. 217.

9. Said, *"Kim,"* p. 41.

10. Hutchins, *Illusion of Permanence*.

11. S. P. Mohanty, "Kipling's Children and the Colour Line," *Race and Class* 31, no. 1 (July/Sept. 1989): 21.

12. Ibid., p. 31.

13. Macaulay, "Minute on Indian Education," p. 249.

14. David Bromwich, "Kipling's Jest," *Grand Street* (Winter 1985): 175.

15. Rudyard Kipling, "A Free Hand," *Pioneer* 10 (November 1888). Quoted in Lewis D. Wurgaft, *The Imperial Imagination: Magic and Myth in Kipling's India* (Middletown, Conn.: Wesleyan University Press, 1983), p. 129.

16. Bromwich, "Kipling's Jest," p. 175.

17. Viswanathan, *Masks of Conquest*, p. 11.

18. Said, *"Kim,"* p. 53.

CHAPTER SIX

1. Letter to Syed Ross Masood, 27 September 1922, quoted in P. N. Furbank, *E. M. Forster: A Life* (Oxford: Oxford University Press, 1979), p. 106.

2. E. M. Forster, *A Passage to India* (London: Harcourt Brace and World, 1924), pp. 10–11. (Subsequent page references included in the text)

3. Rustom Bharucha, "Forster's Friends," in *Modern Critical Interpretations: E. M. Forster's* A Passage to India, ed. Harold Bloom (New York: Chelsea House, 1987), p. 95.

4. Furbank, *E. M. Forster*, p. 114.

5. Ibid., p. 114.

6. Ibid., p. 106.

7. Benita Parry, *Delusions and Discoveries:* Studies on India in the British Imagination (Berkeley: University of California Press, 1972), p. 270.

8. Ibid., p. 284.

9. Kaja Silverman, "White Skin, Brown Masks: The Double Mimesis, or With Lawrence in Arabia," *differences: A Journal of Feminist Cultural Studies* 1, no. 3 (1989): 48.

10. Sencourt, *India in English Literature*, pp. 24–25.

11. Ibid., p. viii.

12. Furbank, *E. M. Forster*, pp. 134–35.

CHAPTER SEVEN

1. V. S. Naipaul, "Conrad's Darkness," reprinted in *The Return of Eva Peron with the Killings in Trinidad* (New York: Vintage, 1981), pp. 221–45. (Henceforth cited as *REP*)

2. V. S. Naipaul, *The Enigma of Arrival: A Novel* (New York: Knopf, 1987). (Henceforth cited as *E.*)

3. V. S. Naipaul, *A House for Mr. Biswas* (London: Andre Deutch, 1961). Naipaul had already embarked on a series of autobiographical, journalistic, and travel-related writings for major British magazines and journals from as early as 1958. Many of these pieces have since been collected as *The Overcrowded Barracoon* (London: Andre Deutch, 1972). *The Middle Passage: Impressions of Five Societies—British, French and Dutch—in the West Indies and South America* (London: Andre Deutch, 1962) he acknowledges as "my first travel book," "Forward to the Vintage Edition" (New York: Vintage, 1981). This is the volume referred to by *Enigma's* narrator (*E*, p. 153) when he documents the ambivalence that developed between the book's commission and its execution. Naipaul had already ridden the tide of early visceral reactions to his works, the most famous of which is George Lamming's in his *The Pleasures of Exile* (London: Michael Joseph, 1960). Views about Naipaul's ideological ambivalence, or lack thereof, became the target of a far more widespread debate with the publication of *An Area of Darkness* (London: Andre Deutch, 1964), where his artistry, already characterized as "a mastery of the English language," was matched against catalogs of his shoddy choices in the ways he characterized India. See in particular Nissam Ezekiel, "Naipaul's India and Mine" 1965), reprinted in *New Writing in India*, ed. Adil Jussawalla (London: Penguin, 1974), pp. 77–90.

4. Joseph Conrad, *Heart of Darkness* (London: Penguin, 1984), p. 93. Homi K. Bhabha in his "Signs Taken for Wonders: Questions of Ambivalence and Authority under a Tree outside Delhi, May, 1817," *Critical Inquiry* 12, no. 1 (Autumn 1985): 144–65 reads this moment as a classic example of the Word transmogrified as Book (p. 148).

5. Chinua Achebe, "An Image of Africa," *Massachusetts Review* 18, no. 4 (1977): 782–94. Also see JanMohamed, *Manichean Aesthetics*, p. 153, for an excerpt from his interview with Achebe on the subject.

6. For a recent example of this kind of criticism see Edward Said's positioning of Naipaul in "The Intellectual in the Post-Colonial World" and the following debate on Naipaul in "The Post-Colonial Intellectual: A Discussion with Conor Cruise O'Brien, Edward Said and John Lukacs," *Salmagundi*, no. 70–71 (Spring/Summer 1986): 44–81; and Rob Nixon, "London Calling: V. S. Naipaul and the License of Exile," Paper delivered at "The Challenge of Third World Culture," Duke University, September 1986. It is also interesting to contrast Fergus Bordowich, "Anti-Political Man: V. S. Naipaul Reconsidered," *Working Papers* 9, no. 5 September/October 1982): 36–41, with two *Newsweek* cover stories, 18 August 1980 and 16 November 1981.

7. Again, see Edward Said's "Intellectuals in the Post-Colonial World" for its sensitive study of the dictatorial demands made on postcolonial writers and the difficult options such writers often have before them. A latter-day example of the imperial making and unmaking of careers and reputations in the academy is perhaps the deeply internalized referential status Naipaul achieves in the emergence of what is called the "Naipaul fallacy." For the birth of this phrase see Henry Louis Gates, Jr., "Editor's Introduction: Writing 'Race' and the Difference It Makes," *Critical Inquiry*, Autumn 1985: 1–20. In the same issue, however, also see Abdul R. JanMohamed, "The Economy of Manichean Allegory: The Function of Racial Difference in Colonialist Literature," pp. 59–87; and Bhabha, "Signs Taken for Wonders," for their allusions to Naipaul, which together with Gates's application of Anthony Appiah's coinage, unwittingly present a curious collusion of attitude toward Naipaul. His "presence" is submerged but vital. For a more extended discussion of this postcolonial collusion, see Fawzia Mustafa, "Africa Unbound: Works of V. S. Naipaul and Athol Fugard" (Ph. D. diss., Indiana University, 1986).

8. There are isolated exceptions to the polarity of views that characterize reactions to Naipaul's works. See Christopher L. Miller, *Blank Darkness* (Chicago: University of Chicago Press, 1985), p. 172, who sees the crucial disjunction between *Heart of Darkness* and *A Bend in the River*. Also see Vijay Seshadri, "Naipaul from the Other Side," *Threepenny Review* 22 (Summer 1985): 5–6 for a general review that recognizes "that Naipaul's writing can so effortlessly revise a longstanding interpretation of a distinguished text is only one of its many virtues, but it's one for which he hasn't been given sufficient credit."

9. Said, "The Intellectual in the Post-Colonial World," p. 53. What must be added, however, is that Said's subsequent critique of Naipaul's *Among the Believers* (New York: Knopf, 1981) cannot be faulted. Furthermore, prior to the publication of *Among the Believers*, Said had already singled out Naipaul's antipathy to Islam in Said's *Covering Islam* (New York: Pantheon, 1981), p. 6, though he, too, lumps *A Bend in the River* into the general pool of indictments against Islam. Seshadri is also dismissive: "*Among the Believers*, his book on Islamic societies, doesn't even have the customary virtue of being well written to compensate for its literary and historiographic vices" ("Naipaul from the Other Side," p. 6).

10. Anthony Appiah, "Strictures on Structures: The Prospects for a Struc-

turalist Poetics of African Fiction," in *Black Literature and Literary Theory*, ed. Henry Louis Gates, Jr. (New York: Methuen, 1984). Also quoted in Gates's "Editor's Introduction," cited above.

11. See Ezekiel cited above, and my "Amorphous India: Questions of Geography," *Southwest Review* 71, no. 3 (Summer 1986): pp. 389–400.

12. Said, "Intellectuals in the Post-Colonial World," p. 53.

13. Bhabha, "Signs Taken for Wonders," p. 154.

14. Ibid., p. 149.

15. References to Prospero and Caliban have been obsessive figures in much writing about colonial and postcolonial texts. For a recent survey, see Rob Nixon, "African and Caribbean Appropriations of *The Tempest*," *Critical Inquiry* 13 (Spring 1987): 557–78.

16. I am aware that this is a simplification of a complex mode of narration. See Asaf Hussain et al. eds., *Orientalism, Islam, and Islamists* (Vermont: Amana Books, 1984); and Said, "Orientalism Reconsidered," pp. 210–29.

17. Conrad, *Heart of Darkness*, p. 83.

18. Frantz Fanon, *Black Skin, White Masks* (New York: Grove Press, 1967), p. 112.

19. The body of literature on the theme of exile in the colonial and postcolonial situations is vast and predominantly preoccupied with the existentialist anguish that it seems to give rise to. For a range see Gareth Griffiths, *A Double Exile* (London: Marian Boyers, 1978); Andrew Gurr, *Writers in Exile: The Creative Use of Home in Modern Literature* (New Jersey: Humanities, 1981); and Alastair Niven, ed., *The Commonwealth Writer Overseas: Themes of Exile and Expatriation* (Brussels: Didier, 1976).

20. For early responses to *An Area of Darkness*, see Raja Rao, "Out of Step with Shiva," *Book Week*, 29 August 1965, pp. 4, 14; Austen Delancy, "Mother India as Bitch," *Transition* 26 (1966): 50; and "Mr. Naipaul's Passage to India," *Times Literary Supplement* 24 September 1964, p. 881.

21. Frank Kermode, "In the Garden of the Oppressor," *New York Times Book Review*, 22 March 1987, pp. 11–12.

22. V. S. Naipaul, *Finding the Centre* (New York: Knopf, 1984), pp. 1–72. While Naipaul's father served as the model for Mr. Biswas, "Prologue to an Autobiography" is one of the few narratives that deals with the father's relation to the son.

CHAPTER EIGHT

1. Salman Rushdie, *Shame*, (London: Picador, 1983). The novel's engagement in both the execution of Pakistan's former president and the familial problems of the late President Zia ul Haq rendered it far too inflammatory for the censors of that third-world nation. It is therefore written in a calm assumption that its audience will not have lived through the historical poignancies it caricatures.

2. Salman Rushdie, live interview for *Paris Review*, given at YHMA, New York, 23 March 1987.

3. JanMohamed, "The Economy of Manichean Allegory," p. 59.

4. Bhabha, "The Other Question," p. 19.

5. Rushdie, *Paris Review* interview, 23 March 1987.

6. David Rubin, *After the Raj* (Hanover: University Press of New England, 1986), pp. 57–63.

7. Stanley Wolpert, *Jinnah of Pakistan* (New York: Oxford University Press, 1984).

8. KumKum Sangari, "Salman Rushdie: A Literary Conversation," *Book Review* 8, no. 5, (April 1984): 248.

9. David Lelyveld, *Aligarh's First Generation* (Princeton, N.J.: Princeton, 1978), pp. 35–92.

10. Salman Rushdie, *The Satanic Verses* (London: Viking, 1988), p. 111. (Henceforth cited in the text as *SV*.)

11. This hasty list pays mere lip service to a poetic tradition as yet unread in the Anglo-American academy at large. My reference is less to a traditional canon than to specific verses that assume the rhetorical burden of devotional blasphemy, as in Ghalib's fastidious assertion: "Where irreligion compels, faith retards: / Ka'aba is behind me; a church, before" (my translation).

12. See A. G. Mojtabai's review of *The Satanic Verses* in *New York Times Book Review*, 29 January 1989, p. 3; and Bharati Mukherjee's "Prophet and Loss: Salman Rushdie's Migration of Souls," *Voice Literary Supplement*, March 1989, pp. 9–12.

13. "Gibreel Farishta" signifies an elaborate Islamic tautology, translating as it does into "Gabriel Angel," hardly the most appropriate name for an actor renowned for his representation of cinematic versions of Hindu deities. "Saladin Chamcha" evokes both the only recuperable Muslim name that the Western rhetoric of the Crusades licensed, and furthermore, plays upon the idiomatic connotations of Chamcha. Chamcha, or "spoon," is in colloquial parlance a sycophant.

14. God of Islam, prevent in your beneficence and mercy any true believer from reading this sentence.

15. AnneMarie Schimmel, *And Muhammad Is His Messenger: The Veneration of the Prophet in Islamic Piety* (Chapel Hill: University of North Carolina Press, 1985). See in particular chapter 1, "Muhammad the Beautiful Model," pp. 24–55.

16. Muhammad Iqbal, *Six Lectures on the Reconstruction of Religious Thought in Islam* (Lahore: Ashraf, 1930), p. 124.

17. Muhammad Iqbal, *Javidnama*, quoted in Schimmel, p. 239.

18. Akbar S. Ahmad, *Pakistan Society: Islam, Ethnicity, and Leadership in South Asia* (Karachi: Oxford University Press, 1986), p. 56. See in particular chapter 4, "Death in Islam: The Hawkes Bay Case," pp. 46–67.

19. Afterword:

Dear Mr. Rushdie,

While your recent embrace of Islam does little to change the arguments or opinions expressed in the preceding essay, the rhetoric of your erotic engagement with religion certainly demands some additional attention. Ever since the *Verses* was published, I have argued for the devotional thrust of your narrative: blasphemy, as many of us have claimed, can only be articulated within the context of belief. The Islam to which I read you as paying homage, however, was a specifically cultural phenomenon. Your love was for the cultural artifacts and atmosphere that Islam generated in the Indian subcontinent, causing your engagement in the Allah/Al-Lat allegory to reflect the attraction and repulsion that obtains between Islam and Hinduism in that area of the world. Your concern in such stories, I could have sworn, was cultural and historical, and allowed you to reread religion as a crucial issue of postcolonial migrancy.

The New York Times of December 28, 1990, informs me that I was wrong. You apparently do accept religion less as a cultural system than as a series of immutable beliefs that can be universal and transhistorical. Even though such claims surprise me, your safety is of sufficient importance to your readers that we will accept your newly found faith just as we welcomed the invigorating cultural skepticism of your narrative. We also know that you are a very naïve reader of your own texts, and were equally impatient with your earlier claims that you were *not* a Muslim as with your current declaration that you *are*. Is cultural history really a matter of choice, we seek to ask? Nevertheless, your safety is important to us.

On that score alone, let me caution you against the rhetoric of "love" and "family" that your latest statement deploys. What idealism allows you to use those terms as though they were unproblematically "good"? You claim that the Rushdie crisis was a "family quarrel" and that you are now "inside the family." Is it any comfort to know that most murderous crimes of passion are committed precisely within familial boundaries? Similarly, your utopian hope that "the language of enmity will be replaced by the language of love" drearily reiterates a dichotomy that your text sought to break down in its moving representation of the multiple hatreds and tyrannies of affection.

Let us remind you that your novel engenders love on a deathbed: "To fall in love with one's father after the long angry decades was a serene and beautiful feeling; a renewing, life-giving thing." Is your conversion somehow willing the death of fundamentalist Islam, an eventuality that the more pragmatic readers of postcolonialism can never imagine? Still, we desire your safety.

Perhaps you have not realized that the Rushdie crisis forced many cultural migrants like yourself finally to claim that they were Muslim. I know I speak for both Akeel Bilgrami and myself when I assert that our new adoption of Islam had nothing to do with notions of family and love. As secular Muslims, we remain resolutely outside such conciliatory boundaries.

A final anecdote: in the hill-station of Nathia Gali, which you may know, there is a rather charming little church perched on one mountainous verge. The last time I glanced at its visitor's book, I was struck by an entry that declared, "Thank God I am a Muslim!" The chill it gave me was somewhat similar to the depression induced by your "I am a Muslim" piece in the *Times*. I nonetheless hope for your safety.

I remain, with all good wishes,

Your reader

Index